THE ARMY AND
LOW INTENSITY CONFLICT

Rick Waddell

I0156653

FORTIS

A NONFICTION IMPRINT FROM ADDUCENT

www.Adducent.co

Titles Distributed In
North America
United Kingdom
Western Europe
South America
Australia

THE ARMY AND
LOW INTENSITY CONFLICT

Rick Waddell

The Army and Low Intensity Conflict

By Rick Waddell

ISBN 978-1-937592-32-5

Published by Adducent (under its *Fortis* nonfiction imprint)
Jacksonville, Florida
www.Adducent.Co

Published in the United States of America

TABLE OF CONTENTS

FOREWORD

This book began as my dissertation at Columbia. The research was conducted from 1991 until 1993. The genesis began with the collapse of the Berlin Wall in November 1989 while I was an Army officer completing graduate studies in-residence at Columbia. The sudden separation of the Eastern European nations of the Warsaw Pact from their Soviet overlords indicated the de facto end of the Cold War. Less than a year later, on 2 August 1990, President George H.W. Bush gave a major foreign policy speech in Aspen, Colorado, addressing the challenges of the new post-Cold War world. The new U.S. policy would be "peacetime engagement," a policy designed to keep the United States from lapsing back into isolationism absent a clear threat from a peer competitor.

But what did "engagement" mean – what sort of foreign involvement was intended, particularly military involvement? To be engaged with the world, while the American military slipped into almost ridiculous weakness as it had in the years between the First and Second World Wars, would seem to invite adventurism by rogue nations and increasingly powerful non-state actors. Despite hopes to the contrary, the United Nations, widely decried by its American critics as little more than "a debating society," was unlikely to have the institutional capability or the credibility and legitimacy among its members to lead efforts against such adventurism; the most that might be expected was for the UN to provide a forum for the formation of "coalitions of the willing." So, as the sole remaining superpower, much of what was previously known as policing the world fell to the U.S.

The journey from presidential speech to clear policy to coherent actions is always difficult in a pluralistic democracy.

Ironically, on the same day as the Aspen speech, Saddam Hussein invaded Kuwait, ushering in the first war of the new era, and providing an immediate test of the new policy. The State Department had been wrong about Saddam's intentions and the U.S. intelligence community missed the warning signs of impending attack, but the U.S. marshaled a coalition of nations and passed the test posed by the Gulf War. Afterwards, "peacetime engagement" returned to being a policy in search of activities. In the waning days of the Bush administration in late 1992, the administration sent thousands of troops into Somalia to perform armed humanitarian intervention to relieve a grievous famine. The incoming Clinton Administration then changed the Somalia mission to coercive nation-building as an example of its intended policy of "assertive multilateralism" which was later changed to "engagement and enlargement" – that is, engagement with the world and enlargement of the spheres of democracy and free markets.

Since the major focus of American foreign policy since the early 1940s – industrialized warfare in the heart of Europe – had just disappeared, and with it the organizing principle for so much of the defense establishment, how would the armed services cope with change, particularly the Army since it was the main service tasked with deploying and undertaking these often unclear missions in the midst of potentially hostile populations? The first intellectual hurdle to overcome in this study was the perceived lack of importance that such missions would have in the post-Cold War world, given the absence of a paramount threat. As one senior professor at Columbia made clear to me – nobody of importance was studying low intensity missions, and besides, America had just engaged in a heavy-armored modern interstate war against the world's fourth largest military. Hence, these "major regional contingencies" like the Gulf War were likely to be the new focus of military effort.

The second intellectual hurdle in the early 1990s was Vietnam, which was still the conceptual and political burden overhanging much of academia and much of the military, even 20 years after most American ground forces had departed Southeast Asia. Any Army topic dealing with "peripheral missions" had to deal with the Vietnam era, when such missions had led to strategic and institutional failures that generated enormous political upheaval at home. However, one could fairly argue that understanding the Army's institutional response to these sorts of conflicts was fundamental to avoiding such failure and upheavals in the future. This was the underlying premise of the study that led to this book.

My dissertation was finished just as the famous "Blackhawk Down" incident provided a substantial brake to the incipient policy of "assertive multilateralism." The security concerns of the rest of the 1990s included finding some return on the investment in the military, often termed the "peace dividend," as the World War II generation of President George H.W. Bush gave way to the Vietnam generation of President Bill Clinton. This dividend included such diverse missions as humanitarian interventions, peacekeeping, and peace enforcement. Some politicians and defense pundits even suggested that military assets could and should be used to track whales, teach American school children, vaccinate inner city residents, and fight forest fires. After the Somali debacle, most interventions were termed "peace operations" since the word "peace" polled so much better than "military intervention." This period from early 1993 until the 9-11 attacks merits its own in-depth study beyond the scope of this book. Likewise, the period after 11 September 2001 is also beyond the scope of this book; however, this study should provide a basis for understanding some of the changes that the Army experienced in the later 1990s and in the new "counterinsurgency era." The concluding chapter will provide a brief glimpse about the applicability of the arguments herein to the Surge in Iraq.

One final introductory comment: being critical of the officers described in this study as "traditionalists" is not to denigrate them or their service. In the tough times following the self-imposed defeat in Southeast Asia, and in the face of a Soviet-bloc threat in the 1970s and 1980s that made deep inroads in Central America, large swaths of Africa, and in Central Asia, these officers remade the American Army. They did so in such a way as to secure the key armed frontiers in Europe and Korea, and to produce the stupendous result in the Gulf War, an outcome largely unexpected by the many critics involved in the Defense Reform movement of the 1980s. Under their leadership, the Army became more professional than at any other time in its history. This study is one of contrasting visions – "traditionalist" versus "visionary" - and the resulting impact on the Army as it faced uncertain threats abroad and political contention at home.

Much of the necessary evidence would not have been available had it not been for a remarkable group of retired officers from this era. These officers, an extraordinary mixture of intellectuals and implementers, not only refashioned the force structure and acquired new equipment - the most obvious and perhaps most superficial aspects of any army - they also reinvigorated the all-important intangibles that undergird the service: duty, loyalty, sacrifice, leadership. My heartfelt thanks to Generals Donn A. Starry, E. C. Meyer, John A. Wickham, Wallace H. Nutting, Paul F. Gorman, John R. Galvin, John W. Foss, William R. Richardson, Samuel V. Wilson, and William P. Yarborough who shared their precious time and their important insights with the young officer that I was.

As Graham Allison once said, organizational studies really amount to "loosely formulated propositions" about tendencies that "hold – more or less."[1]   In the period 1961-1993, some officers tended to be more traditionalist in their view of threats and the required Army response to the threats; others tended, more or less, to be reformers willing to change the Army to take on other, but lesser, threats and missions. While they differed with each other over how much emphasis to place on armored or light   forces,   or on firepower versus maneuver,   and certainly over the amount of attention that the Army should focus on low intensity conflict, they remained steadfast in their dedication to the security of the nation.

When I began this project as a dissertation I was a member of an incomparable group - the Department of Social Sciences at the U.S. Military Academy. The Department was rich in the amount of expertise and tutelage available. In particular, my thanks go to James Golden and Daniel Kaufman for their leadership and understanding as the Department Head and Deputy respectively in the era of change in the early 1990s. Ace Clark and Joe Collins were my direct supervisors. As such, they suffered through many draft ideas, proposals, and chapters with good cheer, encouragement, and healthy skepticism.

Aside from superb leadership in the Department of Social Sciences, my peers there were another stroke of good fortune. All were highly motivated, energetic, and well-educated.   Tom Lynch, Rich Hooker, Mike Meese, and Curt Masiello proved to be first-rate academic foils that were quite ready to shoot down flimsy ideas and shallow arguments.   They also shared readily of their source materials, expertise, and experiences. Others such as Ron McMullen, Jay Parker, and Wally Walters could be counted on to provide any missing sparks of inspiration. Most have passed on from long, honorable service into their next careers. But Mike Meese now heads the Department of Social Sciences; Rich Hooker is the Dean of the NATO Defence College in Rome; Tom Lynch is the Distinguished Research Fellow for the Near East and South Asia at the National Defense University; and Ron McMullen is a member of the Senior Foreign Service, having served as the Ambassador to Eritrea. I was fortunate indeed in the quality of my peers and friends.

---

[1] Graham T. Allison, "Conceptual Models and the Cuban Missile Crisis," *Understanding International Relations: The Value of Alternative Lenses*, ed. Asa A Clark IV, Thomas F. Lynch III, and Rick Waddell (New York: McGraw-Hill, 1993) 403.

CHAPTER 1
INTRODUCTION

ARGUMENT

Instability is a constant and significant fact in international politics. Often this instability takes some form of "low intensity conflict." The patterns of low intensity conflict have remained remarkably constant since World War II. Within the national security establishment in the 1980s, and periodically before in U.S. history, the phenomenon referred to by many professionals as "LIC" became a hot, albeit problematic and confusing topic. This book will use hypotheses developed by Barry Posen and Stephen Rosen to explore the Army's response to the challenge of low intensity conflict in the period 1961-1993.[1] The findings indicate that neither Posen nor Rosen is entirely accurate, and that a synthesis of their views is possible and warranted.

Consequently, this book will argue that four possible causes prompt change in the behavior of the U.S. Army as measured in terms of its doctrinal concepts, force structure, and training programs. The first two causes require external civilian reformers to intervene in Army affairs to prompt changes in doctrine, forces, and training. If the civilians try to enact reform via the dominant group in the Army, the resulting change will be incremental and easily reversed. If the civilians find and use officers with mainstream credentials, but who share their vision of the needs of future warfare, then the Army will change or significantly modify what it views as its primary mission.

The other two possible causes require no civilian intervention. Rather, they focus on conflict within the Army between the dominant group, called traditionalists, and competing groups called visionaries. If the visionaries convert mainstream Army leaders to their views, and convince them to

7

create pathways for the promotion of younger adherents, fundamental change in the Army's preparation for future conflict will occur over time. The intergroup conflict may also be inconclusive, prompting incremental change which serves to indicate either 1) an attempt by the traditionalists to co-opt the visionaries, or 2) that the visionaries have achieved a partial success which may further indicate a renewal of intergroup conflict in the future.

DEFINITION

There remains confusion about exactly what low intensity conflict was in the period under study, since official definitions were extraordinarily broad, vague, and contentious. This confusion was itself a major problem that interfered with the clarity of policy issues and with analysis of those issues.

Low intensity conflict was easily dismissed as a residual category into which was dumped all manner of military operations that did not fit into accepted definitions of war or conflict. Yet, political science requires simplified categories of complex phenomena which permit the establishment of cause and effect relationships. In this chapter, I will offer a definition for low intensity conflict by creating simplified, but broad, categories of conflict. After the definition, I will discuss the reason for studying the Army as the primary service involved with low intensity conflict, and then lay out the organizing theoretical framework for this study by discussing the two most relevant, and competing, explanations for military change. The next chapter will explore the ambiguities of low intensity conflict in greater detail. It will also highlight enduring misconceptions about this phenomenon that proceed from the ambiguities, and detail some of the effects that these had on the politics surrounding U.S. national defense.

Low intensity conflict went by many names over the

decades: people's war, revolutionary war, small wars, operations short of war, guerrilla war, war in the shadows, and unconventional war were some of the more popular names. One military author catalogued over 50 such names.[2] In 1988, the U.S. government defined low intensity conflict as: "a politico-military confrontation between contending states or groups below conventional war and above the routine, peaceful competition among states."[3] Formal missions contained within the low intensity conflict doctrine of this era were insurgency and counterinsurgency, combating terrorism, peacekeeping operations, and peacetime contingency operations. The last category contained military operations which were characterized by constraints on the use of force, the rapidity of their execution, their extreme political sensitivity, and their short duration. Examples included raids, reprisals, rescues, and humanitarian assistance.

Why call this category of armed conflict "low intensity" as opposed to any of the other terms available? Often those terms were too restrictive, or too prone to confusion with types of tactical operations. A criticism often heard from within the military of this era was that "'LIC' may be many things, but what it is not is conflict that is low in intensity."[4] To the soldier in a firefight or in a minefield, war is war. For example, Eliot Cohen, Harry Summers, and others argued that "small wars" was a more accurate definition than "low intensity conflict," because "war" evoked the violence involved.[5] However, since many of the armed confrontations in low intensity conflict occurred between states and non-state entities, "war" is too restrictive as a term. Moreover, in some low intensity operations, violence is only a possibility. "Small wars" is, thus, descriptively accurate only for some of the conflicts that this book addresses.

The terms "unconventional warfare," "special operations," and "guerrilla war," on the other hand, are evocative of particular types or styles of tactical operations. The first two are generally synonymous and often refer to operations behind enemy lines, such as raids, deep reconnaissance, or support to partisans resisting an occupying force.[6] Militaries can use unconventional warfare or special operations at any level of conflict or war. "Guerrilla war" is often the choice of a weaker military force facing superior strength and firepower. As Donald M. Snow characterized it, guerrilla war is "war on the cheap," or "poor man's war," which employs "such tactics as ambush, hit-and-run, and avoidance of contact where superiority at the point of engagement does not guarantee victory."[7] The only name that offers true competition is "operations short of war," or "operations other than war."[8] Both capture the idea that this category of the use of force is different than war. However, I choose to use "low intensity conflict" because it was still the official interagency term used within the U.S. government, and the one most commonly used inside and outside the military, in the 1980s and early 1990s.[9]

A full understanding and definition of low intensity conflict requires an understanding of concepts like conflict, war, and combat. Webster defines conflict as, variously, "competitive or opposing action of incompatibles," or a "hostile encounter."[10] This definition is so broad as to admit anything from small children squabbling over toys to full-scale nuclear war. It is the use of force in conflict that most concerns students of international relations. Clausewitz defined war as "an act of force intended to compel our enemy to do our will."[11] But which "enemy"? Certainly an act of force to compel another human being to give up his wallet is not war. Similarly, an act of force by policemen to compel a band of criminals to cease their activities is not war, either. Nor is it war when two or more street gangs engage in armed struggle with each other. These acts of force are respectively crime, policing, and chaos. They are each domestic.

What about the use of force internationally? When U.S. planes bomb a terrorist camp, or U.S. Special Forces aid in the destruction of a drug laboratory in a Colombian jungle, is this war? Not as commonly understood. Clausewitz's definition makes sense only if applied to acts of force between sovereign nation-states. The condition of sovereignty - political control of a people and territory embodied in a government - permits the use of force by one such entity to compel another such entity. The force compels by threatening or damaging the people, the territory, the political control of the government, or their extensions in the form of national interests. Hence, war is best defined as the use of force between nation-states. But, is all war the same? Again we need simplified categories. J. David Singer and Melvin Small suggested that a starting point for defining war is an armed conflict between nation-states which produces at least 1000 battle-connected deaths per year.[12] While this establishes a starting point, further refinement is needed. I shall further divide war into high intensity and mid-intensity categories.

High intensity war is here defined as armed interstate conflict in which occurs the use of weapons of mass destruction - nuclear, biological, or chemical. Mid-intensity war can then be defined as all other armed conflicts that occur between nation-states that result in 1000 or more deaths in battle. As other scholars have pointed out, wars of annihilation or mass death do not require modern weapons of mass destruction - Rome utterly destroyed Carthage and made sure that it would never re-build - but it is the sudden, immediate nature of the modern weapons, and the attendant policies, that enable us to create two separate categories.[13] These simplified categories are not perfect. They would lead one to describe the murderous Thirty Years War or the Napoleonic Wars as mid-intensity, but World War II as high-intensity simply because of the two atomic bombs dropped on

Japan. However, like social scientific models, these definitions do not have to be perfect. The utility of simplified definitions and models lies in "the capturing of essential or important features in something simpler than the object."14

What's left? The residual category of low intensity conflict - a grab bag full of activities. If international conflict can be any "hostile encounter," then trade embargoes, threats to cut off aid, the beaming of propaganda through the electronic media, and a host of diplomatic endeavors could be defined as low intensity conflict.15 However, we should remain focused on armed conflict because the stakes involved are greater than the other forms of non-war conflict. I propose that low intensity conflict be defined as the use of armed force internationally between states that produces less than 1000 battle deaths per year, or the use of force internationally between a nation-state and non-state actor such as a terrorist group or an insurgent movement. Consequently, the U.S. operation against Grenada, a sovereign state, was a low intensity conflict because the operation caused less than a 1000 battle deaths. The U. S.-supported operations against a non-state actor, the Viet Cong, in South Vietnam in the period 1961-1964 also constituted a low intensity conflict, even though many thousands died. On the other hand, that conflict ceased to be low intensity and became mid-intensity war when the forces of North Vietnam and the United States engaged in combat in the Ia Drang valley in 1965 and subsequently.16

The "use of armed force" is a notion sufficiently expansive to allow also for the threat of force. Consequently the lower boundary of low intensity conflict requires that the threat of combat exist. This boundary then excludes uses of the military for a host of domestic or international activities that rely on the military's manpower or non-combat resources, such as fighting forest fires or sandbagging levees on the Mississippi. Under this definition, what do the military missions in low intensity conflicts have in common? Whether the mission is counterinsurgency, a reprisal in response to a terrorist act or peacekeeping, generally lightly armed forces carry them out. Lightly armed, that is, compared to the weapons and forces needed to wage mid- or high intensity war.

Another common characteristic is that the application of firepower and its consequent destruction is not the focus of the military effort in low intensity conflict as it is in war. Restraint and the judicious use of firepower - much like the restraint practiced by police forces - is required if military forces are not to do more harm than good in low intensity missions. Also, in the case of the U.S. Army, these low intensity missions all share another characteristic - they were not the primary mission for which the service existed in the period under investigation. The Army's primary mission was the defense of two borders - the Inter-German Border (IGB) and the Korean Demilitarized Zone (DMZ), with the former being by far the more important. Low intensity conflict was the Army's peripheral mission. The common characteristics of the low intensity missions make it possible to study them as a whole, despite the many differences.

Even though this category of conflict is called low intensity, many thousands may die, but, again, this is a simplification of a bloody, but necessary sort. What of possible terrorist acts, using weapons of mass destruction, that kill more than 1000 people, or the use of airliners to kill thousands as happened on 11 September 2001? This had been more the subject of fiction thrillers than reality, but such acts could muddy the simplified categories above, although as we have seen, the national response to such an act, as in Iraq and Afghanistan, falls more clearly into the categories above. Moreover, given the difficulty of compelling that which cannot be easily seen - the non-state actor as opposed to the easily found and targeted nation-state - we can still shoehorn this anomaly into our definition.

What of combat? Combat is merely fighting. It is focused on the individual soldier. Combat can take many forms based on a variety of situations and weapons.[17] A common error is to mistake fighting for war. Certainly not all combat occurs in war. As we have defined it, war is much more than just fighting - it is the context within which the fighting occurs. The context matters because it will determine the constraints on the fighting and the fighters in terms of weapons, tactics, and goals.

Combat often occurs in low intensity conflict, too, and is to be expected in such low intensity missions as counterinsurgency or reprisals. The context of these operations, though, generally constrains the combat much more than in war. In other low intensity missions, such as peacekeeping, nation-building, or humanitarian assistance, combat looms as a threat, a potentiality. That is why soldiers are sent - just in case. If they are sent, they should be ready.

As one who studied the challenge of low intensity conflict put it, "It is better that we halt the persistent controversy over what to call this kind of conflict... and move on to conceptual models and organizational structures..."[18] While I will return to the political and organizational impact of the controversy in the next chapter, I will now move on to explain why the Army is the appropriate organization to study. Then I will discuss the conceptual models that help explain the Army's behavior with respect to low intensity conflict.

WHY STUDY THE ARMY?

The U.S. Air Force and the U.S. Navy both maintain some special operations units that have low intensity missions, but since such conflict occurs almost entirely on the ground, neither of these services had staked much claim on a large share of the action in low intensity conflict in the period studied. They functioned in ancillary roles.[19]

Aside from the Army, within the military only the Marine Corps has a history of dealing on the ground with low intensity conflicts. In the late 1980s and early 1990s, the Marines took definite steps to enhance their low intensity capabilities.[20] However, for the Marines to adopt low intensity conflict as a primary mission would have been to return the organization to an earlier period of its history, and forego its current organizing principle of amphibious warfare.[21]

Interservice rivalry over low intensity missions, albeit rare, centered on "contingency operations" - military missions characterized by political sensitivity, rapidity of execution, and short term duration, such as a hostage rescue or a raid conducted as a counterterrorist reprisal. Even here the rivalry reflected the accepted missions and roles of the services. Thus, the U.S. Air Force saw its role as providing a strike capability similar to the one used against Libya in 1986, and as some policy makers advocated should have been used to punish Serbia for its actions in the Balkans in the early 1990s.[22] The use of the Navy to "show the flag" in the Gulf of Sidra in the 1980s was an example of a traditional use of the Navy for contingency purposes. With naval support, the Marines conducted operations in coastal areas such as peacekeeping in Beirut in 1982 and 1983, refugee evacuation in Liberia while Desert Shield progressed, and international relief as they did in Somalia in 1992-1993. The Marines also remained useful for low intensity ground warfare missions that had an amphibious character, such as their role in the Grenada contingency operation.[23] The Army, though, still had and has the tendency to dominate inland activities, especially if these missions last for some time.

In the period of study, some of the phenomena officially lumped under the category of low intensity conflict occurred frequently and involved the employment of U.S. military forces. Consequently, they were prominent in the public eye, and were considered important challenges to U.S. foreign policy in the views of many political leaders or other strategists, and were therefore important problems for the military to address. Among the military services, the Army received the bulk of the low intensity conflict responsibility.[24] One would expect, therefore, that the U.S. Army, the principal military force for engaging in low intensity conflict, would have invested seriously in thinking about, organizing for, and training for low intensity conflict. Surprisingly, given a fairly constant low intensity conflict environment facing the United States, there were apparent anomalies in the Army's institutional response to this officially designated security challenge, especially a greater degree of opposition to giving these various functions the high priority that many civilian leaders believed they deserved. Given Army performance in Vietnam, at Desert One in Iran, Grenada, and in Somalia, the failure of the Army to prepare for such missions was measured in lost lives and damage to national interests and prestige. Those costs make this topic worthy of study for the student of politics and military institutions.

Moreover, in the twenty years subsequent to this study, the Army engaged in multiple armed interventions in Haiti, Bosnia, and Kosovo that led to long-term occupation duty – dubbed "peace operations" - but always at the lower end of the spectrum of conflict. After the 9-11 attacks in 2001, the Army briefly conducted interstate regime-change warfare in Iraq and Afghanistan, but soon found itself embroiled directly or indirectly in counterinsurgencies against non-state actors in several countries. Understanding how the Army was structured and how changes in thinking about conflict and the resulting policy evolution underway by 1993 should help subsequent researchers trace the results through this new period of interventions and counterinsurgency up to the present.

This book proposes to investigate the oscillations in the

U.S. Army's response to the challenges of peacetime low intensity conflicts in the period 1961 to 1993. A significant portion of this investigation requires the accomplishment of two goals: 1) the charting of the Army's response in terms of doctrinal production, the establishment of training programs, and force structure changes. 2) The answering of the question: why did the Army respond to low intensity conflict at certain times, but ignore or play down low intensity conflict at other times? The former goal is historical while the latter is analytical.

SOURCES OF CHANGE IN MILITARY ORGANIZATIONS

Before we seek to explain it, we must first understand what organizational change entails. There are two varieties of organizational change: fundamental and peripheral.

FUNDAMENTAL AND PERIPHERAL CHANGE

Organizations, private or public, exist to accomplish some function. Around the functionally-oriented efforts of the organization grows up a "culture." As James Q. Wilson describes it, "Every organization has a culture, that is, a persistent, patterned way of thinking about the central tasks of and human relationships within an organization."[25] Halperin and Kanter call this same characteristic "organizational essence" - "the notion held by members of an organization as to what the main capabilities and primary mission of the organization should be."[26] With respect to military organizations, Carl Builder called this quality the "mask of war."[27] Culture, essence, or mask, is the organization's "personality."[28] The organization's culture is indelibly linked to the organization's primary function - its mission - and the routine tasks that the organization performs to accomplish the mission. For an organization to undergo a fundamental change, the primary mission must change, which would necessitate "the performance of new tasks or a significant alteration in the way in which existing tasks are performed."[29] For the U.S. Army, the primary function had been, from 1945 until 1992, the defense of Central Europe against an armored thrust by Soviet armies. Its secondary function was the defense of the Korean DMZ, a task similar enough to the European defense that the same forces, equipment, and training were sufficient.

Fundamental change is rare. The second category, peripheral change, is more likely (for reasons which will be discussed below). Peripheral change, also called incremental change, is what Wilson called an "add-on:" "a new program is added on to existing tasks without changing the cores tasks or altering the organizational culture."[30] Peripheral change results in peripheral missions. What makes the mission peripheral is that the organization sees it as inconsequential to its essence. Examples of peripheral missions for military organizations include sealift for the U.S. Navy, close air support for the U.S. Air Force, and the guarding of embassies for the U.S. Marines. Since the U.S. Army's primary mission was the defense of Western Europe, the several facets of low intensity conflict represented such peripheral missions for this organization. Hence, this book will study primarily the process and significance of peripheral change in military organizations.

Why is peripheral change so important? First, the adoption of a peripheral mission can herald further, perhaps revolutionary, change in the long term. This depends on the point of view of the observer. Fundamental change often requires many years. If an observer were plunked down in the middle of a fundamental change, the process might look like peripheral change. For example, the tank was adopted in the armies of the great powers during and after World War I primarily as an infantry support weapon. These militaries had changed at the margins in accepting the tank, but it took a revolution in tactics and logistical organization to make the tank a primary weapon of decision in World War II. The tank existed on the periphery for more than 20 years while a body of conceptual thought on its use slowly developed. Then, the revolution came quickly and dramatically. Understanding and investigating peripheral military change in this light provides policy makers with the opportunity to adjust to the potentialities of the changing military.[31]

Second, the adoption of a peripheral mission can signal an effort by the military organization to preserve and enhance its self-defined "organizational essence." This is a defensive strategy where the organization adopts a peripheral mission in lieu of having wider changes forced upon it.[32] The civilian leaders of the United States have the responsibility to ensure that the military services accurately respond to the strategic needs of the United States. The degree to which the Army's actions with respect to low intensity conflict reflect narrow institutional self-interest in defense of a different preferred mission indicates a potentially serious lack of responsiveness to civilian direction.

A variety of studies have attempted to explain military change. These studies, though, have often attempted to explain grand, sweeping military changes of the most noticeable kind: the mechanization of war for example. Rarely have these studies touched on peripheral change as a primary topic. The organizing theoretical framework for this book will be the competing hypotheses of two explanations for military change – Barry Posen's *The Sources of Military Doctrine* and Stephen Peter Rosen's *Winning the Next War*. The Posen and Rosen explanations are particularly useful because they subsume under their hypotheses many of the other popular explanations for change in military organizations. In Posen's model, change is wrought by civilian reformers external to the military. The reformers often employ individual "maverick" military officers as agents of change. In direct contrast to Posen, the Rosen model argues that forces internal to the military bring about organizational change. Neither civilian reformers nor military mavericks are seen as effective agents of change. True change is a product of conflict among groups of officers internal to the military, who seek to enshrine their own visions of future warfare. The change comes when a new group comes to power. While both Posen and Rosen used their models to explain fundamental change, the models also are useful to explore the process and significance of peripheral change.

EXTERNAL REFORMERS

Kurt Lang once argued that meaningful military change generally derives from the action of civilians who intervene from outside the military organization.[33] Barry Posen took that argument and made it more rigorous. For Posen, military innovations are likely to come when a given state is under external threat and civilians and military leaders take action to reorganize their forces to confront the threat.[34] That these reforms must await a heightened threat is explained by the view of organizations that Posen takes.

Posen's is a common view of organizations.[35] Because of the complexity of their environment, organizations must develop shorthand methods for accomplishing daily tasks.[36] Since organizations, especially public ones, are created for some specific purpose, those who run organizations are particularly interested in control and reliability of performance. The need for predictable, reliable behavior reinforces the use of shorthand methods, or standard operating procedures (SOPs).[37] The convenience and utility of SOPs create within organizations a preference for the status quo, for the known rather than the unknown. Hence, organizations change reluctantly. When they do change, they change incrementally, unless forced into dramatic change by some crisis.[38] Additionally, organizations are seen as parochial, not altruistic. Given a general tendency to stability, organizations do not seek to maximize their output, for maximization might require radical reforms. [39]

As a special subset of organizations, Posen sees military organizations as particularly set in their ways, because of the dangerous nature of their mission and the deadly consequences of experiments that go wrong. Posen calls militaries "the most 'organized' of organizations."[40] Certainly the effect of the organizational hierarchy's concern for control, predictability, and reliability should work the strongest in military organizations where the consequences of organizational defeat are extremely high. Militaries become extremely concerned with controlling the unpredictability of their suborganizations, individual members and the external environment. Militaries are also "endowed with all sorts of resources, and masters of a particularly arcane technology...."[41] Within this view, militaries are like all other organizations in that they develop a parochial bias toward the means they create to accomplish their mission. Militaries see themselves as expert in the special province of warfare. Parochialism - the natural autonomy derived from special resources and the arcana of the military subject - and concern for predictability, according to Posen, are the key factors that inhibit military innovation absent some external threat that civilian and/or military leaders recognize as compelling change. In fact, Posen argues that the concern for certainty in the external environment leads militaries to seek even greater autonomy from the civil state on one hand, and on the other, to apply standard scenarios to all situations - the imposing of order on the unknown outside the civil state.[42]

The roots of the above view of organizations can be traced to the neoclassical and modern structural view of organizations.[43] These schools of thought focus on the total organization, its purpose, and the vertical subdivisions within the organization which are designed to focus on the critical tasks necessary to accomplish the primary organizational mission.[44]

Scholars of these schools see organizational dysfunctions as deriving from poor design which creates constraints on rational or functional behavior.[45] If key organizational leaders do not receive adequate information from lower levels, then the design of the organization does not properly allow for integration of effort. Conversely, if organizational components do not respond quickly enough, or adequately, to assigned tasks, the design may not allow for the appropriate amount of delegation of authority.[46] Finding the right mix of integration and delegation is crucial to those who take the structural view of organizations.

Militaries are subordinate components of a larger entity - a national government. The problem that Posen addressed in his study of military innovation was precisely the nexus between integration and delegation. Military innovations, to be useful to the government, had to match the strategic needs as perceived by the non-military leadership of the state. Yet, Posen's research showed that civilians had to actively intervene in military affairs to prompt innovation. Given a lack of military expertise, this "civilian intervention [was] dependent on finding sources of military knowledge."[47] The most ready sources of military knowledge were general officers who agreed with the thrust of the civilian-induced reforms, or as Posen also calls them, "military mavericks" - officers willing to act against the commonly accepted interests of their service, as those interests were perceived by the bulk of the officer corps.[48] On the other hand, the civilian reformers had to be willing to support the military mavericks, to give them a certain amount of delegated freedom to act. Posen calls this "the 'knitting together' of political ends and military means...."[49]

According to the structural view, organizations have a

general tendency[50] to seek solutions to dysfunctional behavior through better design.[51] For example, if the functional subdivisions of an organization constrain the proper flow of feedback from lower levels, if criticism of process or product does not flow upwards as it should from the lowest levels, organizational redesign might include an ombudsman to which members can complain directly.[52] Similarly, if the structure of the organization constrains innovation, or integration, new subdivisions may be created to address these problems.

In Posen's study of successful military innovations, governments created special offices to provide for the control of new military capabilities. In Britain, it was the creation of Fighter Command under Air Chief Marshall Hugh Dowding.[53] In Hitler's Germany, it was the Oberkommando der Wehrmacht (OKW).[54] Even in France, where Posen found no innovation, the civilians elevated one officer, Marshall Henri Petain, to the special office of "Inspector General." The office was designed to provide tighter civilian control.[55] In this the French civilians were successful. However, control was so stringent that French innovation was hindered.

In the final analysis, Posen's explanation of change gives more explanatory power to the impact of the international system on state behavior than it does to organizational determinants.[56] However, this is an oversimplification. Posen actually traces a process that incorporates determinants external to the state, internal to the state but external to the military, and within the military itself. These determinants include the relative economic power of the state, the influence of geography, technological change, international threats, and both civilian and military leadership.[57] For the sake of simplicity, the determinants which affect both the civilian and military leaders will be referred to hereafter as the "security environment." Furthermore, for the Posen model, the security environment is a set of permissive, or necessary, conditions for change which is not sufficient in itself. The sufficient condition for change is the intervention into military affairs by civilian officials.

INTRAORGANIZATIONAL GROUP CONFLICT

Whereas Posen takes a structural view of organizational behavior, Rosen proceeds from the human resources view of organizational behavior. The differences between these two schools of thought derive from the different fundamental question each seeks to answer. The structural view seeks to explain "how and why organizations behave as they do" while the human resources approach seeks to answer "how and why do individuals in organizations behave as they do."[58] The structural view bases its explanations of organizational behavior on the benefits and constraints inherent in the rationalization of task accomplishment. The human resource view focuses on the motivation and capabilities of individual organizational members to accomplish assigned tasks. A human resources approach to explaining military innovation should be quite different from a structural approach. Surprisingly, there are also striking similarities as this analysis will show. Directly contrary to Posen, Rosen concluded that outside intervention by civilians is not necessary, and might even retard the process of change.

Rosen suggests that we should:

> "regard military organizations as complex political communities in which the central concerns are those of any political community: who should rule, and how should the "citizens" live. The fundamental political values that answer those questions are from time to time the subject of debate among the citizens of that community.

> Military organizations have this political character to a greater degree than other bureaucratic organizations because they govern almost every aspect of the lives of members of the community. They determine who will live, who will die, and how; who will be honored and who will sit on the sidelines when war occurs."[59]

This is a view of organizations that also approximates pluralistic views of domestic politics - a clash of competing groups. The group that wins, governs.[60]

Initiating the process for Rosen, much like Posen, is some change in the environment external to the military organization. To Rosen, the "international security environment is composed of those factors not under the control of either the United States military or the government of hostile powers but that constrain or create opportunities for the military."[61] Such factors include technological change and changes in the international distribution of power.[62] By extension, domestic economic and political factors are also generally outside the control of the U.S. military. As with the Posen model, these determinants external to the military can be labeled the "security environment." These determinants, too, function as necessary causes for Rosen. They provide the catalysts to start the change process, but are not sufficient in themselves.

After the catalyst, the change process in Rosen's model continues through four steps. The first step is intellectual creativity which brings forth a new concept about combat operations. The source of this creative leap is immaterial. In the U.S. Marine Corps, the idea for amphibious warfare came from a relatively low-ranking officer, Major Earl H. Ellis.[63] The spark of creativity leading to carrier aviation in the U.S. Navy sprang from conclusions reached through a series of simulated naval exercises and is not clearly identified with the thinking of any one person.[64] The officers who provide the intellectual leaps, and their adherents, we can call "visionaries."

The next three steps require the institutionalization of the change within the military organization. The institutionalization changes the face of the organization. According to Rosen, this process "has...shown a persistent regularity."[65] Rosen refers to this as a political process. The conflict between the old and the new ways of organizing for war amounts to an "'ideological' struggle" to define the military organization's "new theory of victory."[66] The second step occurs when the visionary officers who provided the intellectual conception for the new way of war translate that vision into combat tasks that would provide the basis for training soldiers and units. Third, this group must then convert one or more very senior officers with impeccable mainstream credentials to their views. Those senior officers adopt and propel the new thinking forward through the implementation of the new combat tasks, and by providing pathways for advancement of the adherents of the new thinking.[67] Fourth, once the younger adherents advance to higher rank, the military innovation is truly safe.[68] The actions of the visionary group are the sufficient cause of change in Rosen's model.

Rosen's view of organizations has much in common with the human resources school of organizational theory. According to Shafritz and Ott, this school arose from the U.S. military's requirement in World War II to "find and shape people to fit its needs."[69] Within this view, people are seen as more important to mission accomplishment than the organization or its structural subdivisions. The independent variables of organizational behavior within this view include individuals, groups, and the interaction between individuals, groups, and the formal organization.

Rosen's view of the organization as a pluralistic community of contending groups is also directly analogous to strands of the human resources view. Cyert and March's early work proposed viewing organizations as composed of coalitions and subcoalitions.[70] Pfeffer has argued that conflict among such groups is inevitable.[71] This literature also contains studies of the behavior of organizational "losers." Groups that lose the ideological competition often do not accept defeat, which can help explain why lasting change takes so long to implement and institutionalize.[72]

Finally, Rosen's change process is quite similar to the concepts of Rosabeth Moss Kanter.[73] For Kanter, the innovation process "consists of the ability to conceive, construct, and convert into behavior a new view of organizational reality."[74] Like Rosen, Kanter sees the most effective change as coming from internal political movements that operate under the guidance of strong leaders: "The skill of corporate leaders, the ultimate change masters, lies in their ability to envision a new reality and aid in its translation into concrete terms."[75] In a further direct parallel to Rosen, Kanter describes the outcome of the change process as being "concretized in actual procedures or structures or communications channels or appraisal measures or work methods or rewards."[76]

A variety of other studies have attempted to explain military change in terms of technology,[77] budgeting,[78] and interservice rivalry.[79] From the standpoint of simplicity, or parsimony as it is often called, Posen and Rosen have rolled into their approaches many of these previously used explanations. Rosen and Posen have made them subordinate to the processes they describe by including them, explicitly or implicitly, in the security environments of military organizations. As parts of the environment, if these factors have any influence on military change at all, it is as permissive, or necessary, causes.[80] For Posen, the primary, or sufficient, cause for change is the action of civilian reformers. For Rosen, the primary cause is the actions of a visionary group within the military.

METHODOLOGY

To appropriately address the analytical goal of this book, I will apply the positivist method.[81] The positivist method consists of five steps: 1) the formulation of causal generalizations between independent and dependent variables; 2) the operational definition of the variables; 3) the establishment of covariation between the variables; 4) the ruling out of alternatives; and 5) the application of the findings to deductive theory.

I will formulate causal generalizations and define the variables below. The establishment of covariation among independent and dependent variables, and the ruling out of alternatives becomes the more difficult task. The difficulty derives from the problem of "many variables, small number of cases."[82] Unlike laboratory experiments where causal relationships can be tested using control groups, most social and political phenomena do not lend themselves to such manipulation. Nor do many of these situations occur so frequently as to permit the gathering of sufficient data to make possible the use of statistical methods of measurement and comparison. Thus, a given occurrence might seem to stem from many possible causes, all worthy of some investigative effort. I propose to attack the problems of covariation and the elimination of alternatives through the application of methodological techniques found in the writings of Alexander George and Arend Lijphart. I will use "congruence procedure" and "process tracing" to establish covariation and causal direction. I will also use the techniques of combining of variables, comparable cases, and "key" variables to eliminate alternatives.

According to Alexander George, the "congruence procedure" proceeds deductively "to establish whether the outcome of the dependent variable is consistent with the...presumed causal implications of the independent variable."[83] The congruence procedure becomes useful, according to George, for "within case" explanations to establish covariation. However, to address causal direction between cause and effect more adequately, George suggests utilizing "process tracing" as a supplement. "The process-tracing procedure... attempts to assess the possibility of a causal relationship between independent and dependent variables by identifying intervening steps, or cause-and-effect links, between them."[84] The "process-tracing" technique requires detailed case investigations.

An illustration of the potential of these methods is provided in Stephen Rosen's critique of Barry Posen's explanation of the development of British Air Defense prior to the Second World War. Rosen focused his critique on the supposed relationship between reform-minded civilians and the uniformed maverick, Air Marshall Dowding. Rosen found no direct causal link between the civilians and the maverick. Furthermore, Rosen traced a causal path that proceeded entirely within the British Royal Air Force, independent of the efforts of civilians.[85]

In the cases used in this study to further test Rosen against Posen, both the congruence procedure and process tracing will be useful. The cases contain reform-minded civilians (in the early 1960s and in the mid-1980s) and conflict within the Army community between groups of the community's "citizens." Sometimes both variables operate simultaneously. Process tracing will be key to deciding in these particular instances which of the variables had a more decisive effect.

According to Lijphart, several techniques are available to eliminate alternative explanations despite a small number of cases. Most important for this study are the combining of variables, focusing only on the key variables, and the use of comparable cases.[86] Lijphart contends that "[if] the sample of cases cannot be increased, it may be possible to combine two or more variables that express an essentially similar underlying characteristic into a single variable"[87] In both the Rosen and Posen models, the impact of the external security environment, with its various domestic and international components, is an example of this technique. As noted above, subsumed under the security environment are such variables as technology, budgets, geography, international threats, and domestic political support for the military. By combining these variables into a set of permissive conditions, the Posen and Rosen models are able to focus on what Lijphart calls "the really key variables" - respectively, civilian-maverick interaction and group conflict.[88]

The use of "comparable cases" allows one to hold a variety of variables constant. This is so because the cases are "similar in a large number of important characteristics."[89] One handy way of maximizing similarity is to subdivide a case from a single country over time. We can look at a thirty year period as three ten year segments, especially if there are crucial differences between those segments. The crucial differences allow us to test changes in the variables under investigation. On the other hand, many other societal variables are held constant. Moreover, the use of the same institution within one nation, over a restricted period of time, eliminates the need to worry about cross-cultural, cross-national, or cross-organizational variables.[90]

Using Lijphart's guidance, in this book I will focus only on the U.S. Army from 1961 until 1993, and, thus, will not seek to compare my findings with the U.S. Army in earlier historical periods, with other U.S. militaries, or with foreign militaries. The Army of the 1960s is sufficiently similar to the Army that concluded the Cold War that we can treat it as the same organization.[91] This is also true of American society and the U.S. position in the bipolar international system. Consequently, many organizational, societal, and international variables can be held constant, allowing a more detailed focus on Posen's and Rosen's key variables.

Creating historically linked, focused cases also allows me to utilize Harry Eckstein's disciplined-configurative case study. Eckstein says such studies do "not just passively apply general laws or statements of probabilities to particular cases."[92] One can also use a case to "impugn established theories" where the theories should fit, but do not. Doing so is the first step in suggesting modifications to the theories studied. The outcome of this study will suggest modifications to the tested models where warranted, thus fulfilling the fifth step of the positivist method.

Since the Army response to the challenge of low intensity conflict, the dependent variable of this study, has oscillated over the periods considered, I will use John Stuart Mill's Second Canon of Logic, the Method of Difference, to provide the final test of the comparative explanatory strength of the two approaches. This method requires finding some cases where the dependent variable is present, and others where it is not. These cases should be as similar as possible. In this way the researcher can focus on the few differences in the cases as the possible causes of the variation in the dependent variable. In this manner, the researcher can establish covariation.[93]

While none of the techniques above is foolproof, by using them in combination, a more rigorous analysis results.

OPERATIONALIZING THE VARIABLES: INDEPENDENT VARIABLES

Posen and Rosen offer competing research propositions that can be generalized as follows:

1) Militaries change when they are forced to: military

innovation occurs when the civilian leadership of a country perceives a change in the security environment and then forces militaries to change. This approach assumes that militaries are resistant to any change that upsets their established routines. The civilian leadership is most likely to be successful when it finds allies, or "mavericks," inside the military to act as the agents of change.[94] The independent variable is the action of the civilian reformers.

The civilian leaders who perceive the security threats and the need to revamp radically and quickly the military will be hereafter referred to as "civilian reformers." While Posen is not exactly precise in his definition of a maverick - in one place they are generals who agree with civilian reformers, in another they are officers outside of, and seemingly out of favor with, the mainstream of officers who control the military[95] - military "mavericks" are here defined as having the following characteristics. They are held in disdain by, and irritate, their fellow officers; and, they are loners who favor quick, radical changes to reigning concepts upon which the military is organized.

2) Militaries change when they want to: militaries should be seen as "complex political communities." Individual members of those communities react to changes in the security environment by creating new approaches to waging war. Military change occurs as a result of "ideological" struggle between visionary groups and the traditionalist group which currently runs the military. The change becomes inculcated when senior leaders with an alternative vision of the future create pathways for promotion for their younger adherents.[96] Outside intervention by civilians is, therefore, not necessary and can be dysfunctional by inciting the military professionals to resist such intervention. The independent variable is the action of a visionary group within the service.

For the purposes of this book, "visionaries" are defined as officers who determine that changes in the security environment require the creation of new methods for waging war, but who have had conventional, mainstream careers, and are, therefore, acceptable in the eyes of their officer peers. Visionaries are not loners, and they favor slow, evolutionary change that does not radically upset the customs and traditions of their service.[97] The dominant group in the military, or "traditionalists," on the other hand, is the group identified with parochial organizational interests, the status quo, as normally described by the structural view of organizations (see above).

The similarities in these two approaches come from their treatment of the environment external to the military. Both Posen and Rosen see this environment as providing the initial impetus for change. The mechanisms through which change is wrought, however, differ drastically between the two.

For both theorists, the impetus for organizational change derives from changes external to the military in such things as technology (the internal combustion engine, precision guided munitions, etc.), changes in international structures (Posen refers directly to increases in threats; Rosen refers more obliquely to such things as the change in the U.S. international position after the Spanish-American War), and more implicitly, changes in the domestic environment within which military organizations exist (budgets, societal support, changes in governing political views, etc.). As noted above, these external forces function as permissive causes, but are not determinant by themselves.

In both models, the sufficient cause is the change process that leads from the external environment to military innovation. Where Rosen focuses on the political struggle between contending groups within the organization and the institutionalization of change, Posen's key variables are the actions of the non-military civilians, and when possible, their maverick allies.

OPERATIONALIZING THE VARIABLES: THE DEPENDENT VARIABLE

Posen and Rosen define the dependent variable, military innovation, in slightly different ways. In an early journal article, Rosen's original view of "innovation" was broader than that of most theorists. For an innovation to be genuine for Rosen, the military organization had to reorganize itself from top to bottom along a completely new set of principles.[98] Rosen calls this set of principles a "new way of war." In his later book Rosen sharpened this definition: a "major innovation is defined as a change in one of the primary combat arms of a service in the way it fights or alternatively, as the creation of a new combat arm."[99] Rosen offers as examples the combat arms of artillery, armor, infantry, and combat aviation. Posen's cases exhibited such "new ways of war," but Posen is not as specific in his definition of change as Rosen. Posen says that "innovation must be judged in terms of the general military and technological environment."[100] Posen talks specifically about changes in military "doctrine," but implies in the events he describes a broad view of the word "doctrine" which includes forces, plans, and equipment among other things.[101]

This study adopts a definition of change more in accordance with Rosen. Even though not all military innovations are major in the sense that Rosen means them, some of them are still worthy of investigation for what they might signal about the organization's future behavior. That signal could indicate 1) future major changes, or 2) a defensive tactic by organizations seeking to thwart outside interventions into their inner workings, their organizational essence.

In this study, we can discover fundamental and peripheral

change in the same manner - as changes in the Army's repertoire. Allison defines an organizational repertoire as a "list of programs relevant to a type of activity, e.g. fighting...."[102] Programs are themselves clusters of standard operating procedures for dealing with common situations. Changes in U.S Army force structure, formal doctrine,[103] and training programs offer good indicators of the development of this new repertoire, and hence, of the changes in Army behavior as a result of the action of the independent variables.[104]

Fundamental change will be noticeable because of the restructuring of the Army. An example might be the replacement of tanks with the attack helicopter, an event which would necessitate broad changes in command, control, communications, force structure, and tactical relationships between the various parts of the Army.[105] A peripheral mission would be identifiable as the addition of a new "repertoire" subordinate to the dominant mission of the military organization which was mid-intensity warfare for the Army in the period of this study. In this study, the new repertoire that signals the adoption of the peripheral mission is the cluster of Army programs, measured in terms of forces, doctrine, and training, necessary to engage in low intensity conflict.

CASES

From 1961 to 1993, the Army dealt with peacetime low intensity conflict in three ways: it ignored it; responded to it grudgingly with a plethora of studies, training programs, force structure, and doctrinal changes; and elevated it to a status near equal to other mission categories. In the period 1961-1964, under civilian pressure, the Army responded energetically to one facet of low intensity conflict, counterinsurgency. From 1965 to 1979, the Army first placed its counterinsurgency programs of the previous period into a decidedly secondary category as it moved to wage the Vietnam war in a traditional fashion, and after 1972, largely ignored low intensity conflict. The period 1979 to 1989 was another period of growth in Army efforts to deal with low intensity conflict. In the early 1990s, the Army elevated the status of low intensity operations by bringing this category of conflict directly into its operational doctrine and theory of war.

1961-1964: ACCEPTING THE PERIPHERAL MISSION I: COUNTERINSURGENCY

Although the Army had dealt with low intensity missions several times in the previous 100 years - the Indian Wars, the Philippine Insurrection, and the support for the Greek and Filipino government counterinsurgency programs after World War II - the Army did not develop a comprehensive set of doctrine, training programs, and forces to deal with these conflicts. This was changed by the advent of the Kennedy administration and the personal determination of President Kennedy to respond to the challenge of insurgency then threatening to rend the decolonizing Third World.[106] The Army was the principal agent assigned to develop the capabilities to wage counterinsurgency. The crucible for testing the counterinsurgency capability became Vietnam. Counterinsurgency rhetoric and programs drove much of the Army effort in the early years of the Vietnam conflict.

1965-1979: YEARS OF DENIAL

With the introduction of conventional units in 1965, the Army seriously downgraded the importance of its counterinsurgency programs in Vietnam. After the American withdrawal from Indochina, the Army shifted its focus almost entirely to the clash of heavily armored forces in central Germany. Absent civilian pressure to the contrary, the Army leadership intentionally turned from the Vietnam experience to focus on the one mission that enjoyed the widest agreement within the service and the most political support: the U.S. commitment to NATO. Doctrine and training programs reflected this shift. A consistent theme in force structuring in this period was the upgrading of anti-armor capability through the introduction of anti-tank missiles and armored personnel carriers into formerly non-mechanized infantry units.

1980-1989: ACCEPTING THE PERIPHERAL MISSION II

In 1979, the Iranian hostage crisis, the Soviet invasion of Afghanistan, and the onset of troubles in Central America pointed up the weakness of the U.S. military in general, and of the Army in particular, for responding to crises on the peripheries of the U.S.-Soviet competition. As in the early 1960s, this weakness prompted civilian attempts at reform.

With the appointment of General Edward C. Meyer and General John Wickham as Army Chiefs of Staff, Army light and special operations forces received new emphasis which was justified, in part, in terms of enhancing Army capabilities to engage in low intensity conflicts. However, from 1987 until 1989, the Army emphasis on low intensity conflict slackened as the Army leadership shifted attention back to Europe despite continued civilian concern.

1990-1993: ELEVATION

In the waning days of the Cold War, the Army fought in another "half war" - the Gulf War against Iraq. Within a few months of the end of that war, the Soviet Union fell apart. As a consequence, the new national security strategy, and the subordinate national military strategy, shifted the focus of U.S. security policy from the primary mission of defending Central Europe. The new mission was to combat regional instability and uncertainty. With its primary mission changed, the Army had to face the challenge of low intensity conflict as a mission equal to armored conflict. The Army responded by writing low intensity missions into its basic operational doctrine, and by changing Army training to more fully replicate low intensity environments.

These four cases provide good tests for the competing research propositions. In the first three cases, the Army's organizational essence was dominated by the mission of defending Central Europe. In the last case, the primary mission changed. In three of the cases, 1961-1964, 1979- 1989, and 1990-1993, there was civilian pressure for change. In the remaining case, 1965-1979, there was little civilian pressure. Thus, the cases allow for the comparison of the relative influence of intraorganizational squabbles with the impact of civilian reformers.

LIMITATIONS

An investigation of the relative explanatory power of the two approaches detailed above hinges on identifying the impetus for change and the path that change takes within a military organization. In the cases which are the subject of the following chapters, I will attempt to do exactly this.

There are certain crucial limitations to such a study within the field of political science. As mentioned above, several of the variables most commonly studied in the fields of civil-military relations or military affairs - leadership, interservice rivalry, budgeting, and technology - are downplayed, ignored, or combined in this analysis. The Rosen and Posen models are in themselves very simplified, or parsimonious - organizations appear as monoliths; international and domestic variables which are necessary, but not sufficient causes are rolled into the "environment" within which the sufficient causes operate; and individuals are treated only as members of groups.

However, social scientific models have to be simpler than

the phenomena which are their subjects. As Kenneth Waltz put it, "Explanatory power...is gained by moving away from 'reality,' not by staying close to it."[107] Furthermore, "Simplifications lay bare the essential elements in play and indicate the necessary relations of cause and interdependency...."[108] Consequently, this book mutes much of the descriptive richness of the Army's actions, and the actions of officers and civilian officials connected with the Army in the period 1961-1993 in favor of identifying and focusing on the most likely explanations for the Army's behavior with respect to low intensity conflict.

This book is also limited to one organization in one nation. Its conclusions, though, should serve as a stepping stone for studies of other military organizations within the United States, or to other foreign policy organizations within the United States government. A logical next step would then be an expansion to comparative studies of other militaries that have faced, or still do, the challenge of low intensity conflict, such as the British or French armies. The amount of time and other resources involved in learning the intricacies of more than one domestic military organization and its relationships with other governmental organs, let alone foreign organizations and governments, preclude such a broad-based study here. What, then is the value of this study? The value falls within Stanley Hoffman's "islands of theory" concept.[109] Given the lack of an overarching paradigm in the study of international relations or foreign policy, the best researchers can do is continue working in each subfield on specific research projects that are worthwhile and important."[110] These various projects ultimately produce the various theoretical islands - what others have called "middle range theories." As part of this process, researchers must attempt to build bridges between the various islands in an attempt "to reforge the elements of a larger integrating theory...."[111]

My study attempts to build, or strengthen, a bridge between

the structural and the human resources schools of organizational theory and the study of military organizations. Further, the study is linked to the explanation of U.S. foreign policy behavior to the degree that an understanding of how sub-governmental organizations behave is one small step toward understanding why governments act internationally in the manner that they do.[112] Connecting these islands to others, such as the study of the peaceful interaction between democratic states - for example, do the militaries of democratic states behave and change differently than those of authoritarian or totalitarian states? - awaits further research.[113]

POLICY RELEVANCE

In 1962 President Kennedy warned of "another type of war, new in its intensity, ancient in its origin - war by guerrillas, subversives, insurgents, assassins.... It requires a whole new kind of strategy, a wholly different kind of military training."[114] Thirty years later, the internal strife in Yugoslavia, Azerbaijan, and the West Bank, the simmering insurgencies in Guatemala and Peru, and the international relief effort in Somalia, suggested the continuing relevance of what had come to be called low intensity conflict. One could reasonably argue that with the demise of the Cold War, the relative importance of low intensity conflicts as a challenge to U.S. interests became greater than at any time since World War II. One author, Martin Van Creveld, made this very argument by boldly proclaiming the demise of warfare as we have known it - that is, interstate warfare. Van Creveld believed that the future wars that would dominate our security concerns would be of the internal variety: "As war between states exits through one side of history's revolving door, low-intensity conflicts among different organizations will enter through the other."[115] The first decades after the Cold War have borne out much of Van Creveld's prediction.

For the United States to respond adequately to these continuing challenges, the U.S. Army must think about, organize and train for the conduct of operations in a low intensity environment. The study of how and why the Army responded to low intensity conflict in 1961-1993 will provide a better intellectual roadmap for the future for this vital instrument of U.S. foreign policy as we face the possibility of more conflicts like those in Iraq, Afghanistan, Libya, and Syria.

ORGANIZATION OF THE STUDY

Since one goal of this study is to contribute to the historical knowledge of this phenomenon, this book will proceed chronologically, rather than thematically. The next chapter will provide a more complete description of what low intensity conflict is and how it appeared in scholarly literature of the period. The purpose of this chapter is to provide an intellectual background for understanding the definitions and controversies associated with low intensity conflict. The subsequent chapters are devoted to development of the cases for historical purposes and for the tracing of the causal connections, if any, between the variables in the approaches of Rosen and Posen. The final chapter will address the shortcomings of the Rosen and Posen approaches, provide a synthesis of their arguments in light of the evidence, and suggest future avenues of inquiry based on the application of this study's findings to other military organizations and other periods of history.

Chapter 1 Endnotes

1 Barry Posen, *The Sources of Military Doctrine* (Ithaca: Cornell University Press, 1984). Stephen P. Rosen, *Winning the Next War: Innovation and the Modern Military* (Ithaca: Cornell, 1991).

2 Howard Lee Dixon, *Low Intensity Conflict: Overview, Definitions, and Policy Concerns* (Langley Air Force Base, VA: Center for Low Intensity Conflict, 1989) 20.

3 FM 100-20 *Military Operations in Low Intensity Conflict* (Washington, DC: Headquarters, Department of the Army, March 1990) 1-1.

4 Colonel D. Dennison Lane and Lieutenant Colonel Mark Weisenbloom, "Low-intensity Conflict: In Search of a Paradigm," *International Defense Review*, no. 1, 1990, 37. See also Harry G. Summers, Jr., "A War Is a War Is a War Is a War," *Low Intensity Conflict: The Pattern of Warfare in the Modern World*, ed. Loren B. Thompson (Lexington, MA: 'Lexington Books, 1989) 27-50.

5 Summers 45; Eliot Cohen, "Constraints on America's Conduct of Small Wars," *Conventional Forces and American Defense Policy*, revised edition, eds. Steven E. Miller and Sean M. Lynn-Jones (Cambridge, MA: MIT Press, 1989) 325-327. See also Lane and Weisenbloom 37.

6 For the original concept behind U.S. Army Special Forces, see Aaron Bank, *From OSS to Green Berets* (Novato, CA: Presidio Press, 1986) 163. Bank was an early OSS Operative, and instrumental in the founding of Army Special Forces.

7 Donald M. Snow, *Distant Thunder: Third World Conflict and the New International Order* (New York: St. Martin's Press, 1993) 58.

8 The Army adopted the latter phrase in the early 1990s to replace "low intensity conflict;" See FM 100-5 *Operations* (Washington, D.C.: Department of the Army, June 1993) chapter 13.

9 Dr. Mike Perlman of the U.S. Army Command and General Staff College suggests that the earliest use of the phrase low intensity conflict by a high-ranking Army officer was in a lecture by Chief of Staff of the Army General George Decker on 8 June 1961. See Mike Perlman, Draft Memorandum, SUBJECT: Origins of the Term "LIC," 28 October 1961. Contained in Center for Low Intensity Conflict Reference File 2 General 40, Center for Low Intensity Conflict, Langley Air Force Base, VA. Dr. Perlman confirmed these findings in a telephone interview in March 1993.

10 *Webster's New Collegiate Dictionary* (Springfield, MA: G. and C. Merriam Company, 1977) 237.

11 Carl von Clausewitz, *On War*, ed. and trans. by Michael Howard and Peter Paret (Princeton: University of Princeton Press, 1976) 75.

12 See for example Melvin Small and J. David Singer, "Patterns in

International Warfare, 1816-1980," *International War*, ed. Melvin Small and J. David Singer (Homewood, IL: Dorsey, 1985) 8-9.

[13] Robert J. Art and Kenneth N. Waltz, "Technology, Strategy, and the Uses of Force," *The Use of Force: International Politics and Foreign Policy*, ed. Robert J. Art and Kenneth N. Waltz (Boston: Little, Brown, 1971) 3.

[14] Carl H. Builder, *The Masks of War: American Military Styles in Strategy and Analysis* (Baltimore: Johns Hopkins, 1989) 9.

[15] One author goes so far as to call the entire Cold War a low intensity conflict. See John M. Collins, *America's Small Wars: Lessons for the Future* (Washington, D.C.: Brassey's, 1991).

[16] In this one campaign, 23 October-26 November 1965, the fighting resulted in more than 1000 soldiers killed in action. See Dave R. Palmer, *Summons of the Trumpet: U.S.-Vietnam in Perspective* (Novato, CA: Presidio Press, 1978) 93-103.

[17] For an interesting discussion of the differences between combat, engagements, battles, and war, see Michael Howard, *Clausewitz* (Oxford: Oxford University Press, 1983) chapter 3, especially pages 36-37.

[18] Stephen Sloan, "Introduction," *Low-Intensity Conflict: Old Threats in a New World*, ed. Edwin G. Corr and Stephen Sloan (Boulder, CO: Westview Press, 1992) 7.

[19] There were advocates within the Navy and the Air Force who argued for much expanded roles for these services in low intensity conflict. For the debate on Air Force roles see Alan L. Gropman and Noel C. Koch, "Is There a Role for Air Power in Low-intensity Conflict?" *Armed Forces Journal International*, May 1985. For the view of the Air Force as supporter, see David J. Dean, *The Air Force Role in Low Intensity Conflict* (Maxwell Air Force Base, AL: Air University Press, 1986). At least one soldier argued that the Navy and the Marine Corps were the "logical choice" for use in counterinsurgency missions. See Major Thomas X. Hammes, "Insurgency. The Forgotten Threat," *Marine Corps Gazette*, Vol. 72, No. 3, March 1988. It is illuminating to note that the Air Force and the Army established a joint Center for Low Intensity Conflict in 1986. The Navy and Marines refused the invitation to join.

[20] The Marines were the force of choice for use in the period of U.S. interventionism in Central America and the Caribbean in the first three decades of the Twentieth Century. At least one author, Larry E. Cable contends that the Marines developed true expertise in "small wars" in this period. Moreover, he contends that the U.S. performance in Vietnam would have been more successful if the Army and Marines had heeded those lessons. See Larry Cable, *Conflict of Myths* (New York: New York University Press, 1986) chapters 6, 9. In the last few years of this period, the Marines reissued their manual on small wars that was developed in the earlier interventionist period. They also devoted a portion of their *Marine Corps Gazette* to the

subject of low intensity conflict.

[21] The Marines have had a special relationship with Congress which has resulted in maintaining the Corps with a strength of three active duty divisions. The Marines remain strongly wedded to the amphibious concept, which by necessity is a technology-intensive, coastal enterprise. On the strength of this commitment, see Gordon W. Keiser, *The U.S. Marine Corps and Defense Unification, 1944-1947* (Washington: National Defense University, 1982) 56, Chapter 9; Martin Dinkin, *Where Does the Marine Corps Go From Here?* (Washington: Brookings, 1976) chapter 2.

[22] See Dean, who was much more confident of the utility of the U.S. Air Force in low intensity conflicts than others. He based his belief in this utility on the British RAF experience of policing parts of the British empire in the 1920s and 1930s. Yet, in his concluding chapter, Dean focused on training Third World air forces, supporting friendly regimes against external aggression, or applying force to achieve U.S. political objectives. As he says, "There likely will be little 'glory' for low-intensity warriors and no great air campaigns." See chapter 2 and 7 in particular.

[23] Another ancillary Marine mission might be to conduct amphibious raids against insurgent positions. The Marines conducted these types of missions in the early months of their engagement in Vietnam. See Shelby L. Stanton, *The Rise and Fall of an American Army: U.S. Ground Forces in Vietnam, 1965-73* (Novato, CA: Presidio Press, 1986) 29-44.

[24] Colonel Howard Lee Dixon, *Low Intensity Conflict Overview, Definitions, and Policy Concerns* (Langley Air Force Base, YA: Center for Low Intensity Conflict, 1989) 25. Dixon, an Air Force colonel, noted that the Army was the service with the main responsibility for low intensity conflict in the late 1980s. Andrew Krepinevich reports that this was also the view of the Kennedy administration with respect to counterinsurgency-one facet of low intensity conflict - in the early 1960s. See Andrew Krepinevich, *The Army and Vietnam* (Baltimore: Johns Hopkins, 1986) 30-36.

[25] James Q. Wilson, *Bureaucracy* (New York: Basic Books, 1989) 91.

[26] Morton H. Halperin and Arnold Kanter, "The Bureaucratic Perspective," in *International Politics: Anarchy, Force, Political Economy, and Decision Making*, 2d ed., ed. Robert J. Art and Robert Jervis (Boston: Scott, Foresman, 1985) 444.

[27] See Builder, chapter 1.

[28] Wilson 91. Builder 7.

[29] Wilson 222.

[30] Wilson 222.

[31] Wilson does not deal directly with the concept of peripheral change in a process that leads eventually to fundamental change, but does imply it in his examples. Wilson tells us that often peripheral change comes as a response to the organization's external environment, or as a result of "organizational entrepreneurs." In the long run, these changes can become fundamental. As

examples, Wilson cites the U.S. Air Force's acceptance of the intercontinental missile in response to political demands, and the U.S. Navy's original acceptance of the airplane as a reconnaissance tool, despite the Navy's internal "entrepreneurs" who wanted aviation to become a primary naval weapon. See Wilson 225-226.

[32] The concept of peripheral change as a defensive strategy is derived from Philip Selznick, *TVA and the Grass Roots: A Study in the Sociology of Formal Organizations* (Berkeley: University of California Press, 1953). See particularly the section "The Co-optative Mechanism," 259-261.

[33] Kurt Lang, "Military Organizations," *Handbook of Organizations*, ed. James G. March (Chicago: Rand McNally, 1965) 838-878.

[34] Posen 40.

[35] See Posen 35-36, 40-47.

[36] Max Weber defined bureaucracies as organizations with hierarchy, internal division of labor across tasks, and the application of standardized rules to similar situations. See Donald E. Klingner, *Public Administration: A Management Approach* (Boston: Houghton Mifflin, 1983) 45-46.

[37] One of the earliest studies of the effects of the desire for control in organizations can be found in R.K. Merton, "Bureaucratic Structure and Personality," *Social Forces* 18, 1940, 560-568. Cited in Herbert Simon and James March, *Organizations* (New York: John Wiley, 1958) 37-38.

[38] See Charles E. Lindblom, "The Science of 'Muddling Through,'" *Public Administration Review*, 19, 1959. Incremental change is James Q. Wilson's "add-on change," or what I am calling peripheral change. Wilson also tells us that the predilection for routine order leads organizations to consider information selectively. They only look for the information that their routines tell them is important. See Wilson 101-102.

[39] That is, organizations "satisfice" instead of maximize. The classic argument on this point is Robert Cyert and James March, "A Behavioral Theory of Organizational Objectives," *Modern Organization Theory*, ed. Mason Haire (New York: John Wiley, 1959) 76-90. Cyert and March expanded on these concepts in *A Behavioral Theory of the Firm* (Englewood Cliffs, NJ: Prentice-Hall, 1963).

[40] Posen 38.

[41] Posen 39.

[42] Posen makes these arguments 43-46. Furthermore, Posen argues that if left to themselves, military organizations will often favor offensive doctrines because such doctrines allow the military to impose a standard situation on the enemy. Operating offensively outside the boundaries of the state also increases the autonomy of the military. See Posen 46.

[43] I borrow these classifications from Jay M. Shafritz and J. Steven Ott, ed. *Classics of Organizational Theory*, 3d ed. (Pacific Grove, CA: Brooks/Cole, 1992). Neoclassical organizational works include Simon and March, and Selznick. Modern Structuralists include Peter M. Blau and W. Richard Scott,

Formal Organizations: A Comparative Approach (San Francisco: Chandler, 1962), and Tom Burns and G.M. Stalker, *The Management of Innovation* (London: Tavistock, 1961). I acknowledge a debt to Shafritz and Ott for categorizing much of the often disparate thought on organizations and making it intelligible.

[44] Jay M. Shafritz and J. Steven Ott, "'Modern' Structural Organization Theory," *Classics of Organization Theory*, 3d ed., ed. Jay M. Shafritz and J. Steven Ott (Pacific Grove, CA: Brooks/Cole, 1992) 201.

[45] Shafritz and Ott, "'Modern' Structural Organization Theory," 202.

[46] Scholars have described these contending forces variously as "division of labor" v. "the need for centralizing authority" and "differentiation" v. "integration." I prefer to use the terms "delegation" and "integration" because the former term is one often used in military settings. See the discussion in Shafritz and Ott, "'Modern' Structural Organization Theory," 203.

[47] Posen 57.

[48] Posen 120, 174.

[49] Posen 25.

[50] According to Allison, many of the propositions derived from organizational theory amount only to "tendencies" which "must be hedged by modifiers like 'other things being equal' and 'under certain conditions.'" To Allison, these modifiers reduced to a question of whether the tendency holds or not for the organization in question. See Graham T. Allison, "Conceptual Models and the Cuban Missile Crisis," in *International Relations; Contemporary Theory and Practice*, ed. George A. Lopez and Michael S. Stohl (Washington, D.C.: CQ Press, 1989) 114. Posen's model proposes a "general tendency" which holds that military organizations require external intervention to promote fundamental change.

[51] Tom Burns and G. M. Stalker, *The Management of Innovation* (London: Tavistock Publications, 1961)119-125. Burns and Stalker argue that when the environment external to the organization undergoes rapid change, the organization can deal with it best by becoming flexible - that is, by allowing leadership to flow to those who prove themselves the most capable of dealing with the change. This implies the creation of new power centers within the organization. These pages were reprinted in Shafritz and Ott, ed., *Classics of Organization Theory*, 207-211.

[52] A good example of this is the Office of the Inspector General in the Army. Any soldier, no matter the rank, has the right to complain directly to the Inspector General, outside any formal chain of command. The Inspector General must formally reply to the soldier's complaint. Since the Inspector General works directly for the highest ranking commander on any given Army installation, the soldier can be confident that his complaints have been considered at the highest level.

[53] Posen 173-175.

[54] Posen 200.

[55] Posen 120.

56 Posen 233.

57 See Posen 43-46 for the influence of the domestic environment on the organization. See 30, 231-236 for the influence of relative economic power, geography, technology and international threats. Leadership is implicit in the civilian reformers' willingness to intervene, and the willingness of the military maverick to act as an agent of change.

58 These questions come from the preface to J. Steven Ott, ed., *Classic Readings in Organizational Behavior* (Pacific Grove, CA: Brooks/Cole, 1989) v.

59 Stephen F. Rosen, "New Ways of War: Understanding Military Innovation," *International Security*, Summer 1988, 140.

60 The classic statement of this is Robert Dahl, *Who Governs: Democracy and Power in an American City* (New Haven: Yale, 1961). See also Rosen, *Winning the Next War*, 19-22. See also Wilson 105-106, and 110 for the possibility of multiple cultures within organizations, some of which may be linked to peripheral missions.

61 Rosen, *Winning the Next War*, 57.

62 Rosen, *Winning the Next War*, 57-58, 102.

63 Rosen, *Winning the Next War*, 66.

64 Rosen, *Winning the Next War*, 68-71.

65 Rosen, *Winning the Next War*, 58.

66 Rosen, "New Ways," 140.

67 See Rosen, *Winning the Next War*, chapter 3.

68 In the case of U.S. Naval aviation, the process took about 25 years. The fastest case Rosen addresses - the introduction of helicopters into the U.S. Army - took 11 years. See Rosen, *Winning the Next War*, 80, 105.

69 Jay M. Shafritz and J. Steven Ott, "The Organizational Behavior Perspective, or Human Resource Theory," *Classics of Organization Theory*, 3d ed. Jay M. Shafritz and J. Steven Ott (Pacific Grove, CA: Brooks/Cole, 1992) 143.

70 See Richard M. Cyert and James G. March, "A Behavioral Theory of Organizational Objectives."

71 See Jeffrey Pfeffer, *Power in Organizations* (Cambridge, MA: Ballinger, 1981) 27-29, 31.

72 M. Sherif, et al, *Intergroup Conflict and Cooperation: The Robber's Cave Experiment* (Norman, OK: University Book Exchange, 1961); See also Edgar K. Schein, *Organizational Psychology* (Englewood Cliffs, NJ: Prentice-Hall, 1965) 80-87.

73 Rosabeth Moss Kanter, *The Change Masters* (New York: Simon and Schuster, 1983).

74 Kanter 279. Note that as "organizational reality" changes, so must the organizational culture or essence which revolves around the organizational behavior - the tasks it must accomplish to fulfill its mission. See Wilson 222,225.

75 Kanter 278.
76 Kanter 299.
77 A number of technology-based studies exist. For one such application to the Army, see Frederic A. Bergerson, *The Army Gets an Air Force* (Baltimore: Johns Hopkins, 1980).
78 See Arnold Lee Kanter, *Defense Politics: A Budgetary Perspective* (Chicago; University of Chicago, 1979).
79 Asa A. Clark IV, "Interservice Rivalry and Military Reform," *The Defense Reform Debate* (Baltimore: Johns Hopkins, 1984).
80 The Army experience with low intensity conflict also suggests that these other potential determinants would not carry much explanatory power. Army forces devoted exclusively to low intensity conflict never numbered more than a few thousand, most of them contained in the special operations community. Hence, the use of low intensity conflict as a means of propping up or expanding the Army budget is not worthy of investigation. Similarly, Army efforts at low intensity conflict were not technology dependent. Finally, as already explained above, the bulk of the low intensity missions and forces involve the Army, and no other service was seeking a greatly expanded low intensity role in the period of this study.
81 For a lucid general summary of this method as applied to political science, see Jack Snyder, "Richness, Rigor, and Relevance in the Study of Soviet Foreign Policy," *International Security*, Winter 1984-5, 89-108; also Jack Snyder, "Science and Sovietology: Bridging the Methods Gap in Soviet Foreign Policy Studies," *World Politics*, Vol. XL, #2, January 1988, 169-193;
82 Arend Lijphart, "Comparative Politics and the Comparative Method," *The American Political Science Review*, vol. 65, 1971, 685.
83 Alexander L. George, "Case Studies and Theory Development," unpublished paper presented to the Second Annual Symposium on Information Processing in Organizations, Carnegie-Mellon University, October 15-16, 1982 (Reprinted at USMA with the author's permission) 14.
84 George 40.
85 This critique is sharpest in Rosen, "New Ways."
86 See Lijphart 687-690.
87 Lijphart 687.
88 Focusing on "the really key variables" is what Lijphart calls "parsimony." See Lijphart 690.
89 Lijphart 687.
90 Lijphart warns that this method is not perfect because "the same country is not really the same at different times." See Lijphart 689. Nonetheless, despite the sacrifice of some descriptive accuracy, the number of potential variables is much reduced by this method.
91 Three works on the U.S. response to counterinsurgency have at the core of their arguments the constancy of Army response in terms of doctrine despite the period of consideration. See Larry Cable, *Conflict of Myths* (New York: New York University Press, 1986); Andrew Krepinevich, *The Army and*

Vietnam (Baltimore: Johns Hopkins, 1986); D. Michael Shafer, *Deadly Paradigms* (Princeton: Princeton, 1988). Although the content of counterinsurgency doctrine, one facet of low intensity conflict, appears to have changed little from 1961 to 1993, these works do not do a good job of explaining why the emphasis on such missions has waxed and waned.

92 Harry Eckstein, "Case Study and Theory in Political Science," *Handbook of Political Science*, Volume 7; *Strategies of Inquiry*, ed. Fred I. Greenstein and Nelson W. Polsby (Reading, MA: Addison-Wesley, 1975) 99. The disciplined-configurative case study is also useful for this project in that it allows theory to illuminate the historical case. Lijphart suggests a similar approach - the "interpretive case study." However, Lijphart's approach is focused on theoretical illumination of the case's events and does not admit to using the case to suggest modifications to theory.

93 As Mill described the Second Canon: "If an instance in which the phenomenon under investigation occurs, and an instance in which it does not occur, have every circumstance in common save one, that one occurring only in the former; the circumstance in which alone the two instances differ, is the effect, or the cause, or an indispensable part of the cause, of the phenomenon." John Stuart Mill, *A System of Logic, Ratiocinative and Inductive*, ed. J. M. Robson (Toronto: University of Toronto, 1973) 391.

94 Posen 174-175, chapter 7.

95 Posen 120, 174.

96 Rosen, *Winning the Next War*, 19-22

97 This definition is congruent with Rosen's descriptions of visionaries. See Rosen, *Winning the Next War*, 76-80, for a good example in his description of Rear Admiral William Moffet's role in the development of carrier aviation in the U.S. Navy.

98 See Rosen, "New Ways," 134.

99 Rosen, *Winning the Next War*, 7. See also Wilson's view of fundamental change above, which is essentially the same. For Wilson, the mere replacement of horse-drawn carts with trucks was not a military innovation because it just made the existing tactics more efficient. However, the introduction of the machine-gun forced a wholesale restructuring of infantry tactics. See Wilson 22. By logical extension, the original use of tanks as an infantry support vehicle - a mobile pillbox - was not really an innovation. On the other hand, the use of the tank as a deep exploitation vehicle in blitzkrieg tactics was an innovation.

100 Posen 29.

101 See Posen 29-32.

102 See Graham T. Allison, *Essence of Decision* (Glenview, IL: Scott, Foresman, 1971) 33.

103 By formal doctrine I mean those operational and organizational concepts embodied in the Army's field manuals and pamphlets. This is a much more restricted definition than Posen's.

104 See Builder, 128, on indices of change in militaries: "how the services

perceive the next major war they must fight is an important determinant of the types of forces they try to acquire, the doctrine they develop, and the training they follow for the use of those forces in combat."

[105] As an example of such futuristic thinking, see Robert Holzer and Vago Muradian, "Will Choppers Chop Tanks?" *Army Times*, 2 August 1993, 30.

[106] On 6 January 1961, Khrushchev declared that the USSR would support "wars of national liberation" as a means of combatting imperialism. Roger Hilsman records that President Kennedy ordered all members of his administration to read Khrushchev's remarks. From his first National Security Council meeting until his death, the development of counterinsurgency capabilities was a top priority for Kennedy. See Roger Hilsman, *To Move a Nation* (New York: Doubleday, 1967) 414.

[107] Kenneth N. Waltz, *Theory of International Politics* (New York: Random House, 1979) 7.

[108] Waltz 10.

[109] Stanley Hoffman presented this idea orally at a seminar at Harvard, 28 February, 1980. Howard J. Wiarda describes this event and elaborates on the concepts in "Future Directions in Comparative Politics," *New Directions in Comparative Politics*, ed. Howard J. Wiarda (Boulder: Westview, 1985) 208-211.

[110] Wiarda 210.

[111] Wiarda 210.

[112] The gap between intended policies and the actual implementation of policies is a persistent theme of studies that seek explanation for foreign policy behavior at the state level or below. For a general discussion of the value of using these levels for understanding this problem, see Asa A. Clark IV, Thomas F. Lynch III and Rick Waddell, "The Subsystemic Lens," *Understanding International Relations*, ed. Asa A. Clark IV, Thomas F. Lynch III and Rick Waddell (New York: McGraw-Hill, 1992) 392-397.

[113] One scholar, Kimberly Marten Zisk, investigated changes in Soviet military doctrine using competing independent variables focusing on forces external to the military and others which were internal. She found that civilian academics also had an impact if they gain entrance to the wider defense policy community. However, it is not apparent that her findings are applicable in a U.S. setting. Yet, future efforts might focus on building a bridge between her study and mine. See "Soviet Reactions to Shifts in U.S. and NATO Military Doctrine in Europe: the Defense Policy Community and Innovation," Ph.D. dissertation, Stanford, 1991.

[114] Speech given at the West Point graduation ceremonies, 6 June 1962.

[115] Martin Van Creveld, *The Transformation of War* (New York: The Free Press, 1991) 229.

CHAPTER 2

DEFINITIONS AND MISCONCEPTIONS

Kill one, frighten ten thousand.
                                    —Sun Tzu[1]

"To meet future challenges, America's Army must turn from the warm and well-deserved glow of its Persian Gulf victory and embrace, once more, the real business of regulars, the stinking gray shadow world of 'savage wars of peace,' as Rudyard Kipling called them."
                                    —Daniel P. Bolger[2]

Low Intensity Conflict is a subject that suffers from definitional and conceptual ambiguity. This chapter will lay out the framework of the debate about the nature and content of this phenomenon. Many of the organizational problems that plagued the U.S. government and military in general in this period, and the Army in particular, flowed from this ambiguity. While the ambiguities and misconceptions underlie all of the cases in this study, this chapter will only touch on those issues; their impact will be explored in more depth in the subsequent chapters.

The Army and others in the national security establishment insisted on dealing with low intensity missions as a single category of conflict. While doing so, however, the Army and other governmental organizations, over time, provided several different definitions of the phenomenon. In the previous chapter, I offered a definition that established low intensity conflict as an autonomous category of conflict worthy of study. This chapter will expand on that definition by presenting definitions for the various manifestations of low intensity conflict. Next, the chapter will present a brief background history of some earlier periods in which the Army's institutional adaptation to low intensity missions was difficult. Then the chapter will address the official definitions which were in themselves indicators of the modern Army's behavior in response to low intensity conflict. Finally, the chapter will proceed to discuss common misconceptions about low intensity conflict found in scholarly literature and military thinking.

DEFINITIONS AND CATEGORIES GUERRILLAS, REVOLUTIONARIES, AND INSURGENTS

For most of the Cold War, the United States was concerned with countering Marxist-led, often Soviet-backed, insurgencies. In the 1980s, while the United States embarked on new counterinsurgency efforts in El Salvador and Honduras, the U.S. efforts expanded to include the fostering of insurgencies in Nicaragua, Afghanistan, and Angola. But, "insurgency" as a concept often suffered from the same ambiguity as low intensity conflict, as it was too easily confused with guerrilla warfare and revolutionary warfare.

Using Snow's definition from above, it is clear that guerrilla tactics can be used quite effectively in mid- or high intensity war, and are generally the necessary tactics of partisans who operate as adjuncts to combat between standing armies. The original concept, for example, behind the creation of U.S. Army Special Forces in 1952 was to support partisan operations behind enemy lines in any future European conflict.[3] Because guerrilla warfare can be seen as a tactical choice - much as a frontal attack or a turning movement - it need have no political overtones. Revolutionary warfare, in contrast, is inherently political. The goal of revolutionary warfare is wholesale social or political change of the state affected.[4] Revolutionaries often use guerrilla tactics, but not always. Maoist-inspired revolutionary doctrine treats revolution as a process with intermediate stages which include guerrilla war as an intermediate step, and finishes with open combat between a standing revolutionary army and a standing governmental army.[5]

What, then, is insurgency? Sam Sarkesian says that it is somewhere between guerrilla war and revolution.[6] This, however, is too imprecise. Adam Roberts suggests that insurgency has "a largely political element and is opposing an established government and trying to create a new order."[7] He goes on to err, though, by equating it with the broader concept of revolutionary warfare. The definition of insurgency that this book will use is an armed movement using guerrilla tactics that seeks political change in its host society. Thus, an insurgency may seek something less than the wholesale replacement of the established order - it may only seek the recognition of minority rights or the redress of some political grievance. Or, insurgency may be a subordinate component of "revolutionary warfare," which does seek the wholesale replacement of the existing political and social order. To the extent that insurgencies or revolutions do not create the trappings of sovereignty - the control of a populace within a definable territory by some governmental apparatus - then they remain non-state actors, and remain subjects of study in low intensity conflict. If they attain de facto sovereignty, and battle deaths exceed 1000, "war" would be the appropriate category of study.[8] Partisan guerrilla warfare conducted in the context of a wider mid- or high-intensity war is also not low intensity conflict.

Governments of nation-states may act to foster insurgency or revolutionary war to weaken or replace the governments of their rivals. This is pro-insurgency. When a nation-state seeks to thwart an insurgency, or support another state's attempts to do so, this is counterinsurgency.

TERRORISM

Terrorism, too, suffers from definitional ambiguity. Yet, it forms an indelible part of the challenge that low intensity conflict poses. The term is too often used to characterize any violent act with which the describer disagrees. Hence, marital violence is "domestic terrorism." The violence of urban criminal gangs becomes "street terrorism." Governments facing an insurgency often term their adversaries "terrorists." State-conducted military action against internal or external foes is also called "state terrorism" by those opposed to it. Like unconventional warfare and guerrilla warfare, terrorism connotes certain techniques of action. On the other hand, like insurgency, it also connotes violent action in the name of political change. Gordon C. Schloming offers the following definition - "*random* acts of violence employing *fear* or intimidation and aimed at coercing, persuading, or gaining public attention. This would exclude acts of violence against official or military targets in an ongoing conflict between two declared opponents, no matter how unconventional the means or supposedly illegitimate the cause."[9] While this definition is fairly restrictive, the acts need not be random, and the definition should be restricted further to say that the perpetrators are non- state actors. States often find it necessary or expedient to attack unofficial or non-military targets, but there is a political difference between the acts of a state and those of a non-state actor. The targets of state action know against whom to retaliate. The elusive nature of non-state actors, though, such as an ethnic group or an insurgent movement, makes them hard to find; thus, they are not so easy to target for retaliation.[10]

Hence, terrorism ought to be seen as a violent attack by a non-state actor against an unofficial or non-military target with the purpose of changing the political behavior of one or more governments. Clearly, terrorism can be an adjunct to partisan warfare, insurgency, or revolutionary warfare. If guerrilla war is "war on the cheap" used by the militarily weak, terrorism is often the act of very weak guerrillas.

As with insurgency, a state may seek to support a non-state group which chooses to use terrorism. This is known as "state-sponsored terrorism." Such support can open the state to retaliation from other states, given the sensitive nature of such attacks. States which are the frequent targets of terrorist attacks can take defensive measures, or can seek to retaliate.

SMALL-SCALE COMBAT OPERATIONS

While the challenge of low intensity conflict includes such categories as insurgency and revolutionary warfare, and terrorism, it also includes operations which require the very short-term application of violence. One historical name for these operations is *coup de main* - usually direct combat action in the form of a surprise attack. The direct action may be undertaken as part of a rescue operation, such as the attempted rescue of the U.S. hostages from Iran in 1980, or it may be done for punitive reasons, as was the U.S. occupation of Vera Cruz in 1914. These small-scale combat operations have particular saliency as a tool to punish or preempt terrorist acts, as was demonstrated by the U.S. bombing of Libya in 1986 in retaliation for that country's support of terrorist groups. These operations are characterized by rapidity of execution and acute political sensitivity which generally constrains the type of forces and firepower used.

OPERATIONS INVOLVING THE POTENTIAL OF COMBAT

As acts of deterrence or indications of national resolve, military demonstrations and shows of force are as old as recorded history. Hans J. Morgenthau lists such operations as one of three principal ways that any country engages in the use of power. He called such usage of the military the "policy of prestige."[11] The deployment of military forces to areas of potential conflict is a show of force. Once those forces arrive, if they carry out maneuvers simulating their wartime missions, these are demonstrations. Since these forces are operating in close proximity to their potential adversaries, the possibility of initiating combat and a wider conflict is great. While the U.S. Navy has been the force designated for most shows of force, the placement of troops on the ground carries particular significance because of the greater danger of casualties and the greater difficulty of withdrawal. Thus, the Army-dominated exercises that occurred at irregular intervals in Honduras during the 1980s, several of which included operations along the borders of Soviet-supported Nicaragua, were a very strong indicator of U.S. resolve to defend the region.

Also included in this category of operations would be those missions which rely more on the protective, logistical, or medical capabilities of the armed forces than on their combat capabilities. These include non-combatant evacuations and humanitarian interventions. The overseas protection of one's citizen's in a war zone is not a new military mission. Often forces are dispatched to evacuate such non-combatants. Additionally, military forces prove useful to ameliorate widespread suffering after natural or man-made disasters. In both evacuation and intervention missions - as opposed to a pure humanitarian relief mission - combat is still a potential liability of the sort that comes from getting caught in the crossfire of belligerents, bandits, or looters. The August 1990 evacuation of non-combatants by the U.S. Marines from Liberia and the international relief mission to Somalia in 1992 and 1993 are examples of these operations. Again, the forces tend to be of the lighter, more mobile variety, and operating under severe restrictions on the use of firepower.

Also falling under this category are peacekeeping, peace

enforcement, and peacemaking. As in the other missions just described, the forces employed are often more lightly armed than forces employed in other military missions. Combat is still a distinct possibility, and may be a necessity in peace enforcement and peacemaking, but a short-term nature is not guaranteed.

Once thought of as side shows to the Cold War, peacekeeping operations underwent a rapid expansion at the end of the 1980s. At the beginning of 1993, the United Nations (UN) had peacekeeping troops deployed in 12 countries. The U.S. Army also maintained a reinforced battalion of such troops in the Sinai as part of a non-UN mission. In the early 1990s there were calls for the establishment of a permanent UN "army" of peacekeepers to replace the current ad hoc arrangements.[12] There were also calls for the United States to place some of its forces on permanent stand by for use by the UN for these operations.[13]

Peacekeeping developed out of the United Nation's inability to establish an effective system of collective security during the Cold War. Dag Hammarskjold, as Secretary General of the United Nations, called these operations "preventive diplomacy." As he described the intent of peacekeeping, the United Nations temporarily "enters the picture on the basis of its noncommitment to any power bloc... so as to provide to the extent possible a guarantee in relation to all parties against initiative from others."[14] However, peacekeeping operations in Cyprus, Lebanon, and the Sinai have lasted decades.

Peacekeeping is defined in this study as the policing by the forces of non-involved parties of some agreement arrived at by diplomacy between belligerents and/or mediators, such as a truce, ceasefire, or armistice. These forces provide a buffer, or tripwire, against a renewal of hostilities.[15] Any combat that the peacekeepers engage in is purely self-defense. "Peace enforcement" can then be defined as the threat, or use, of offensive force by non-involved powers to ensure compliance with the provisions of such agreements. "Peacemaking" may be defined as the threat or use of offensive force by non-involved powers to coerce belligerents to cease hostilities and enter into negotiations.[16]

Definitional controversies aside, by the 1980s low intensity conflict was acknowledged to be a persistent problem for the U.S. The 1980s was a growth period for writings on various low intensity conflict topics both in professional military journals and in the academic presses. As noted in the first chapter, Martin Van Creveld went so far as to claim that low intensity conflicts may, in fact, replace large scale conventional wars as mankind slips into a kind of new Dark Age.[17]

Van Creveld was not alone in such sentiments. One scholar from within the Army ranks, then-Lieutenant Colonel Dan Bolger, proclaimed, controversially, that the grand armored sweep through the Iraqi desert that finished the Gulf War held no more relevance to the future of warfare in our age than the successful British cavalry charge at Omdurman held at the end of the 19th century. The Mahdi's dervishes had chosen to fight a set-piece battle on European terms with disastrous results. The same British Army that won so spectacularly at Omdurman fared poorly soon after when facing the guerrilla tactics of the Boers. In the Gulf War, Saddam Hussein was the Mahdi and his troops suffered the fate of the dervishes. Carrying this analogy to its conclusion, Bolger surmised that the British lancers "did not overawe Afrikaners, nor will a U.S. armored division much concern the [Filipino] New People's Army."[18]

Despite the difficulties in definition, the Army and others in the national security establishment insisted on dealing with low intensity missions as a single category of conflict, which, as the definition offered above demonstrates, can be done. But, to fully understand the Army's responses to the low intensity challenge from 1961 to 1993 requires an exploration of the Army's history with respect to low intensity missions before 1961. Next, it is useful to explore the definitional controversy within the service for the light it can shed on the Army's responses over time. Finally, the chapter will turn to enduring misconceptions of low intensity conflict that flowed from the Army and the nation's history, that underlay the change in definitions, and that continued to plague our understanding of the phenomena that composed low intensity conflict.

THE ARMY AND LOW INTENSITY CONFLICT PRIOR TO 1961

The Army had long experience with many of the missions included within low intensity conflict before 1961. However, the Army of the earlier eras was much smaller than the Cold War Army. It was an organization without a central mission for most of this time. It was, as Samuel Huntington once described it, the nation's "obedient handyman" - a fire brigade that built ports, forts, railroads and roads, fought the Indians, put down strikers and rebellions, and acted as a law enforcement agency.[19] And for a few years every so often, it expanded and fought the nation's civil and foreign wars. What patterns can the researcher discern that might give clues as to the roots of the Army's behavior in the periods of concern? What effects might this have had on civilian policy makers in the eras under consideration in this study?

For most of the first 125 years of the nation's existence, the enemies were internal, mainly the Indian tribes. Despite fighting more than a thousand engagements against Indians, which included one protracted guerrilla conflict against the Florida Seminoles from 1835 until 1841, the Army never institutionalized a method for handling such conflicts.[20]

As one writer put it, "The period of the Indian wars, following the Civil War, established the patterns of how America would deal with its 'lesser conflicts' until World War II, i.e., ad hoc, without doctrine, training, force structure or equipment designed for these environments."[21] The Army was never numerous, averaging only a few thousand regulars before the Civil War, and some 25,000 men in the decades after 1865 until the Spanish American War.[22] Training was done locally to meet local needs. Force structuring in the Indian wars was the most rational of all the processes. Even so, after 1865, the less useful infantry regiments outnumbered cavalry regiments by two-to-one.[23]

Regardless of the era, intellectually, the officers studied primarily the wars of Europe. The few books on tactics that existed prior to the Civil War were wholly conventional. After the Civil War, the Army experienced an explosion of military education. The Army established branch schools for officers of artillery, engineers, infantry and cavalry. But, as one scholar described this period, "The gathering currents of military professionalism, centering on conventional wars of the future, left almost wholly untouched the unconventional wars of the present."[24]

Nonetheless, the local experimentation in the Indian Wars produced rudimentary techniques which the Army would employ several more times. Against the Seminoles, and again against the Plains Indians, the principal Army method was to establish a fort and saturate the surrounding area with patrols. When the Indians misbehaved, patrols became punitive expeditions. Because the Plains Indians were so mobile, the Army learned to lighten its pack trains, and, as a precursor to the later use of helicopters, to use railroads to shift units across wide stretches of territory. When the Indians refused to fight superior forces, the Army learned to operate in winter when the Indians were tied to their villages. The Army also used converging columns to chase down roving bands, a style of operations not unlike the "block and sweep" of a century later.

The Army also acted as a force to bring civilization to the areas surrounding the fort. Towns of settlers grew in close proximity. Indians who were not "hostile" settled onto reservations where they received education, medical care, and food. This "civilizing mission" of the Army was a foreshadowing of its future experience with foreign "nation-building" in support of counterinsurgency.[25] Since the Army as an organization spent so little time studying these experiences, the Army kept relearning old lessons when it began to face foreign insurgents. The ad hoc approach continued throughout the first foreign experience at counterinsurgency - the Philippine Insurrection. The U.S. Army which had been raised and trained to fight the conventional Army of the Spanish found itself fighting an unexpected insurgency. Sometimes the transition proved difficult, as the Army even employed at least one cavalry charge against the insurgents.[26] As in the Indian wars, the Army established fortified outposts in hostile territory in an attempt to pacify the areas. The forts would then conduct aggressive local patrols to destabilize the insurgents. The Army troops also used infiltration and subversion of guerrilla groups, the most famous instance of which led to the capture of the insurgent leader Aguinaldo. Furthermore, the Army expended many efforts at what would eventually be called civic action, or nation-building. Army engineers built sewers, roads, and bridges. Army units opened and ran schools and provided medical aid. Once again, this process was less rationally directed than one of trial-and-error learning which owed much to the initiatives of the local commanders.[27]

The following patterns emerge from these early conflicts: 1) a consistent focus on future conventional conflict, generally centered in Europe, despite any other missions at hand; 2) an ad hoc approach to low intensity missions with little serious study conducted for future reference; 3) a consistent pattern of the use of incentives and punishment when dealing with insurgents. The incentives were almost always in the form of improved living conditions - something at which the Army happened to be adept, given its role in the development of U.S. infrastructure. The punishment was by combat.[28]

The Army had little engagement in low intensity conflict after the Philippine Insurrection until the 1940s. It occasionally participated in putting down a rebellion, as in Cuba in 1906, or in punitive expeditions as at Vera Cruz in 1914, and in the chase after Pancho Villa in 1916. Still, the focus remained on future European wars.

In World War II, the creation of the Office of Strategic Services (OSS) in 1942 furnished the opportunity for many Army officers to experience what came to be known as unconventional warfare (UCW). The OSS experience had a profound impact on these officers, many of whom would go on to found the Army's Special Forces. Unlike previous Army experience which had been earned fighting native and foreign insurgents, the OSS functioned to collect strategic intelligence, to carry out raids and promote or support partisan activity behind enemy lines in occupied Europe and Asia. These operations functioned strictly in support of conventional wartime missions. Since the OSS was the brainchild of a personal friend of President Roosevelt, William J. Donovan, it enjoyed a high level of civilian support, but earned the jealousy of conventional officers and units.[29]

Immediately after the war, with its protector, President Roosevelt, dead, the OSS was disbanded. In 1948, the Joint Chiefs of Staff decided that the newly created Central Intelligence Agency - the successor to the intelligence-gathering sections of the OSS - could also have any peacetime UCW missions that arose since most of them would have to be conducted covertly in conjunction with intelligence gathering activities. However, the

Army was to be responsible for wartime UCW missions. No peacetime military resources, though, were to be dedicated to preparing for such missions.[30] This split in responsibilities set up a sometimes confusing arrangement that has still not been totally resolved.

From the late 1940s through the mid-1950s, the Army got fresh opportunities to learn about counterinsurgency and guerrilla warfare. In Greece in the late 1940s, several hundred soldiers were sent as advisers to support the Greek government's war against communist rebels supported originally from Yugoslavia. During the Korean War, the Army also had to contend with irregular columns of North Korean forces which had been left behind after the Inchon invasion, or which had been sent to wreak havoc in the rear areas of South Korea.[31] In the Philippines in the 1950s, Army advisers supported the national army against home-grown insurgents.

These events established another pattern for the Army: since most of the advisers in these situations had experience from conventional operations in World War II, they taught what they knew. The units they helped organize were trained and equipped for conventional combat against similarly armed foes. Additionally, given that the insurgents in these situations were communist, they were treated as partisans of an expanding Soviet hegemony. As Larry Cable described this period, "Americans had a fixation on borders, the notion of an external sponsoring power... All guerrillas, whether of the partisan type or of the insurgent variety, were seen as being of the sponsored partisan stripe."[32]

The 1950s were also a time of growth in unconventional warfare. After the disbanding of the OSS, the Army found itself with very little capability to conduct unconventional warfare in the Korean War, although it did support some amphibious raids on the North Korean coast.[33] This lack of capability prompted the

Army to authorize the creation of a Special Forces group and a Psychological Warfare Training Center in May 1952 at Fort Bragg, NC. The focus of this effort, though, was not to be Korea, but rather to recreate the operational capabilities of the OSS for any future conflict in Europe. This put the Army into direct competition with the CIA for the mission of raids and partisan activities. During the East German uprising of 1953, the original Special Forces Group was split with half being sent to Germany, and half remaining at Fort Bragg to form a new group.

In 1954, Special Forces were first introduced into Asia when the group at Fort Bragg sent a mobile training team to Thailand. Other missions followed to Taiwan and Vietnam. These original training missions were all designed to enhance the conventional and unconventional warfare capabilities of the host forces. In 1957, the Army activated a third Special Forces group in Okinawa. In the summer of 1959, the first Special Forces soldiers were sent to Laos to engage in a new endeavor - counterinsurgency.

It was in Laos that the OSS roots of both the CIA and the Special Forces reunited. Since 1959 was peacetime, the CIA had control, and the Special Forces augmented the agency. Since the operation was covert, the 107 Special Forces soldiers operated in civilian clothes from an organization called the Programs Evaluation Office (PEO) headed by an Army Major General, John A. Heintges, who was called "Mr. Heintges." The Special Forces teams sent to aid the training of the Royal Laotian Army in counterguerilla techniques were called "White Star" teams. In 1961, the PEO was converted into a standard military advisory group, ending CIA control.[34]

The Laotian experience highlights the last pattern to emerge from these earlier eras - competition between civilians and the military over control of unconventional operations, counterinsurgency, and other low intensity missions. The founders of OSS had included many citizen-soldiers called up for the war effort. After the war, many of these operatives returned to civilian life and formed the nucleus of the new CIA. When, in 1948, the CIA received the peacetime mission of unconventional warfare, it also fought to be given the wartime mission, thus cutting the military entirely off from such activities.35 In situations such as Laos and the early years in Vietnam, the CIA initially exercised control because of the need for secrecy and the confusion over peacetime and wartime responsibilities. As the missions grew in size and were no longer secret, interagency squabbles ensued.

CONTROVERSY, CONFUSION, AND OFFICIAL DEFINITIONS

Before the 1960s, the Army did not seek to define low intensity conflict as a separate category of concern. The 1962 edition of the Army's *Field Service Regulations: Operations* was the first major field manual to introduce the concept of a "spectrum of war" that "ranged from cold war - 'a power struggle between contending nations' - through limited war to general (nuclear) war."36 Even after this introduction, the various categories of low intensity conflict were treated functionally, if at all, in manuals devoted specifically to the topic, such as counterguerilla operations, or the broader topic of counterinsurgency. For the entire decade of the 1960s, the "power struggle" in the Cold War became almost synonymous with "counterinsurgency."37 In the years after the U.S. withdrawal from Vietnam, the Army and the U.S. government expended little effort attempting to fashion a response to low intensity conflict.38 When such a response seemed necessary after the surge in terrorism in the 1970s, and the Soviet invasion of Afghanistan and the renewal of Central American instability in 1979, the Army responded by issuing a manual in January 1981 devoted to the topic. However, as the definition clearly demonstrated, the Army was still focused on counterinsurgency.

The 1981 definition of low intensity conflict was either "low intensity conflict Type A":

> "Internal defense and development assistance operations involving actions by U.S. combat forces to establish, regain, or maintain control of specific land areas threatened by guerrilla warfare, revolution, subversion, or other tactics aimed at internal seizure of power."

Or, "Type B":

> "Internal defense and development assistance operations involving U.S. advice, combat support, and combat service support for indigenous or allied forces engaged in establishing, regaining, or maintaining control of specific land areas threatened by guerrilla warfare, revolution, subversion, or other tactics aimed at internal seizure of power."[39]

By the mid-1980s, political pressures to provide a response to Soviet threats in Southwest Asia, continued terrorist attacks, and both U.S.-backed and Soviet-backed insurgencies, prompted many definitional efforts. In 1985, the Army's definition of low intensity conflict became:

> "A limited politico-military struggle to achieve political, social, economic, or

psychological objectives. It is often protracted and ranges from diplomatic, economic, and psychological pressures through terrorism and insurgency. Low intensity conflict is generally confined to a geographic area and is often characterized by constraints on the weaponry, tactics, and the level of violence."[40]

However, in the Army's primary doctrinal manual of 1986, low intensity conflict was defined as a "form of warfare [that] falls below the level of high- and mid- intensity operations and will pit Army forces against irregular or unconventional forces, enemy special operations forces, and terrorists."[41] Unfortunately, the manual did not define mid- or high-intensity conflict which would have allowed a clear distinction of the phenomenon, and further confused the reader by stating in a separate section that enemy special operations forces, "guerrillas, terrorists, and saboteurs" would operate in all forms of conflict.[42] The paragraphs following the definition also clearly indicated that operations such as demonstrations, raids, and rescues were also included, despite the fact that many such operations would take place against conventional forces. The Army was not alone in its definitional confusion. In an attempt at creating a single definition broadly acceptable to all members of the national security policy community, the National Security Council convened an interagency working group in March 1986.[43] Two years later, this effort resulted in the following definition of low intensity conflict:

"Political-military confrontation between contending states or groups below conventional war and above the routine, peaceful competition among states. It frequently involves protracted struggles of competing principles and ideologies. Low-intensity conflict ranges from subversion to the use of armed force. It is waged by a combination of means employing political, economic, informational, and military instruments. Low-intensity conflicts are often localized, generally in the Third World, but contain regional and global security implications. Also called LIC."[44]

This interagency definition also did not satisfy everyone, but there the matter rested until the Army and the Joint Chiefs of Staff once again redefined the phenomenon. In the 1993 version of the Army's primary doctrinal manual, low intensity conflict underwent not only another definitional change, but also a name change:

"The Army classifies its activities during peacetime and conflict as *operations other than war*. During peacetime, the U.S. attempts to influence world events through those actions that routinely occur between nations. *Conflict* is characterized by hostilities to secure strategic objectives. The last environment - that of *war* - involves the use of force in combat operations against an armed enemy."[45]

The official definition was too broad to be truly useful. This imprecision led critics to charge:

"[s]o deliberately broad and ambiguous is the official description of low-intensity warfare that it embraces drug interdiction in Bolivia, the occupation of Beirut, the invasion of Grenada, and the 1986 air strikes on Libya. Also included are a wide range of covert political and psychological operations variously described as 'special operations,' 'special activities,' and 'unconventional warfare.'"[46]

These critics were correct. The official definition was deliberately broad and ambiguous, but not for the reasons they offered. The official definition was too broad and ambiguous simply because it did not characterize the dividing line between war, low intensity conflict, and combat. In the first of the two definitions above, "conventional war" is not defined. In the latter, "conflict" requires hostilities, but seems differentiated from "war" only to the extent that war is combat against an armed enemy. This leaves the reader wondering against whom the hostilities in conflict are directed. As for the operations since the 1970s in Bolivia, Beirut, Grenada, Libya, Panama, Somalia, the Balkans, Iraq, or Afghanistan, these all can fit under the low intensity definition I offered above - that is, to the extent that the operations have less than 1000 battle deaths from interstate combat per year, or are directed by states against non-state actors regardless of casualties.

The official definitions of low intensity conflict provided a shifting, confusing view of the phenomenon. What did these definitions mean in terms of missions that the Army was expected to accomplish? In 1981, the Army was clearly preparing to wage counterguerrilla campaigns (Type A) or security assistance and nation-building as a part of a wider counterinsurgency effort (Type B). By 1986, the menu of missions had expanded to include "countering an insurgency," "peacetime contingency operations," "peacekeeping," and "antiterrorism" and "counterterrorism."[47] By 1990, "support for an insurgency" was also added, and the Army had complete definitions for each category that it published in a new edition of Field Manual 100-20 *Low Intensity Conflict*.

These mission categories and their definitions are important for they indicate what the U.S. Army considered to be in the realm of low intensity conflict during the period of study. In light of the constant redefinition and the constant ambiguity, the best positive definition for the Army was, perhaps, the laundry list of events covered in the various manuals - at least tactical operations might be understood even if their context was not.

MISSION CATEGORIES: OFFICIAL DEFINITIONS
SUPPORT FOR INSURGENCY AND COUNTERINSURGENCY[48]

According to the 1990 edition of FM 100-20, insurgency "is an organized, armed political struggle whose goal may be the seizure of power through revolutionary takeover and replacement of the existing government."[49] Furthermore, "Insurgency and counterinsurgency are two aspects of the same process."[50] Fostering or supporting an insurgency requires an analysis of the situation obtaining in the country or region of concern, and building upon the political groupings and grievances that naturally exist. Fostering insurgency often proceeded in a covert manner.[51] Conversely, counterinsurgency "uses principally overt methods and assumes appropriate change within the existing system is possible."[52] This mission included "all military and other actions taken by a government to defeat insurgency."[53] Counterinsurgency programs are founded on an Internal Defense and Development (IDAD) Strategy. The IDAD strategy included societal development, military and police operations to secure the property and the lives of citizens in a country threatened by insurgency, and political operations to neutralize the insurgents and to mobilize the citizens to rally to the sitting government.[54]

COMBATTING TERRORISM
The official Department of Defense definition of terrorism in 1990 was "the unlawful use of - or threatened use of - force or violence against individuals or property to coerce or intimidate governments or societies, often to achieve political, religious, or ideological objectives."[55] Combatting terrorism involved two missions. The first was "antiterrorism" which was officially defined as "defensive measures taken to reduce vulnerability to terrorist acts." The second was counterterrorism which was "offensive measures taken to prevent, deter, and respond to terrorism."[56]

PEACEKEEPING OPERATIONS
Peacekeeping was defined as "military operations which maintain peace already obtained through diplomatic efforts."[57]

PEACETIME CONTINGENCY OPERATIONS
Peacetime contingency operations (PCOs) were officially defined as "politically sensitive military activities normally characterized by short-term, rapid projection or employment of forces in conditions short of war."[58] They were often conducted under crisis situations. The missions include rescues, raids, noncombatant evacuations, humanitarian relief, and interestingly, peacemaking. This last operation is defined as the use of military force "in the national interest to stop a violent conflict and to force a return to political and diplomatic efforts."[59]

ANALYSIS

How do these official definitions compare to the autonomously defined components of low intensity conflict offered at the beginning of the chapter? The definitions of peacekeeping and peacemaking are essentially the same, while the definition of insurgency is a close match. The official definition of insurgency is deficient only because it does not offer a sharp enough distinction between guerrilla war and revolutionary war. The official definition of terrorism is far too broad, because it does not clearly identify the actors, nor does it sufficiently define "unlawful." [See Table 2 for a comparison of the autonomous definitions and the various official definitions.]

Finally, peacetime contingency operations are the "all other" category of low intensity conflict, which itself is quite easily considered an "all other" category of conflict. It is an overbroad lumping of combat missions with those which involve the potential of combat, and those which are basically noncombat. Conceptual clarity would suggest considering these categories of missions separately, as I did above. Simplicity would also suggest that peacekeeping is not a distinct category for the use of force, but rather the use of force in a situation that might result in combat.[60] Nor is antiterrorism purely a military operation. Rather, it is passive self-defense that could be performed by a variety of organizations - guard details, security checks, fences, hardened structures, and road blocks among other techniques. Counterterrorism operations are indistinguishable from the raids included in the peacetime contingency category.

Why do the official definitions of the subordinate low intensity missions make peacekeeping, anti-terrorism, and counterterrorism separate and distinct missions? Why is there a broad and ambiguous "catch-all" category such as peacetime contingency operations? One has to recognize that these definitions are part of the dependent variable of this study - a reflection of how the Army responded to the challenge of low intensity conflict. As noted in the opening chapter, the findings of this study indicate that the Army's responses to low intensity conflict were not simply the result of organizational whims. Nor were they simply a result of external pressures applied by civilian officials. The Army's behavior was a result of the blending of organizational desires and civilian pressure.

Consequently, "low intensity conflict" means different things to different people at different times. Due to the efforts of the Kennedy administration civilians, counterinsurgency became the primary peripheral mission of the Army in the early 1960s. In the 1970s, with neither civilians nor soldiers caring about low intensity missions, the only definitions or thought on the subject was what had been left from Vietnam. When civilians again demanded a response in the early 1980s, the Army gave them what it had handy - another counterinsurgency manual officially called a low intensity conflict manual, despite the fact that the civilians were also concerned about countering terrorism, rapid deployment to Southwest Asia, the new Sinai peacekeeping mission, and even fostering insurgency on the periphery of the Soviet sphere of interest.

TABLE 2: Comparison of Definitions for Low Intensity Conflict

Autonomous Definition:
The use of armed force internationally between states that produces less than 1000 battle deaths per year, or the use of force internationally between a nation-state and non-state actors such as a terrorist group or insurgent movement regardless of the casualties produced.

Official Definitions:

1962: "Cold War:" a power struggle between contending nations.

1981: Internal defense and development assistance involving actions by U.S. forces.

1985: A limited politico-military struggle to achieve political, social, economic, or psychological objectives. It is often protracted and ranges from diplomatic, economic, and psychological pressures through terrorism and insurgency.

1988: Political-military confrontation between contending states or groups below conventional war and above the routine, peaceful competition among states. It frequently involves protracted struggles of competing principles and ideologies. Low-intensity conflict ranges from subversion to the use of armed force. It is waged by a combination of means employing political, economic, informational, and military instruments.

1993: The Army classifies its activities during peacetime and conflict as *operations other than war*. During peacetime, the US attempts to influence world events through actions that routinely occur between nations. *Conflict* is characterized by hostilities to secure strategic objectives. The last environment - that of *war* - involves the use of force in combat operations against an armed foe.

As the civilians kept pushing for responses in the mid-1980s, the Army did respond, but in a piecemeal fashion. As one former Senate Armed Services Committee Staff member described civilian efforts at the time, "We were convinced that in the absence of [legislative action], there would be no significant change."[61] In response, definitions were fashioned, and chapters added to doctrinal manuals, to deal with, respectively, antiterrorism, counterterrorism, peacekeeping, and support for insurgency without regard to conceptual clarity, depending on the specific pressure received. As one retired general put it, "After the Arab-Israeli War of 1973, we (the Army) tended to categorize modern mechanized warfare as 'real war'....In doing so we kept our attention on the NATO scenario and the majority of our intellectual and analytical effort on that scenario."[62]

Since the Army and NATO faced the "real war," any other missions were indeed placed into an "all other," residual category which could be treated as manifestations of the same phenomenon - low intensity conflict. Here lies the explanation for peacetime contingency operations - it became a mission area composed of all possible Army missions for which civilian officials did not require specific treatment. The civilians did not get all the change that they wanted, and the Army had to divert some of its focus from NATO. The following chapters will explore in detail these political and organizational processes.

MISCONCEPTIONS ABOUT LOW INTENSITY CONFLICT

This study's findings identified enduring misconceptions about the phenomenon known as low intensity conflict. These misconceptions affected civilian officials and military officers alike, and flowed out of the Army's and the nation's experience with low intensity conflict prior to 1993. They underlie all of the cases in this study, contributing to the definitional and policy confusion.

1. **Low intensity conflict is limited war**. The concept of limited war is an old one - war waged with some intention other than the complete overthrow and subjugation of the enemy. Clausewitz speaks of wars of limited aims - "minimal wars" - meaning war waged for definable political goals that are not likely to bring ruin to any of the participants.[63] Although most wars, including most American wars, have been limited, the concept of limited war took on increased saliency in the aftermath of World War II, the creation of the atomic bomb, and the advent of the Cold War. Scholars and policy makers perceived that total victory of the style sought in World War II was no longer possible among nuclear powers. For Thomas Schelling, nuclear weapons meant that "[m]ilitary strategy can no longer be thought of...as the science of military victory. It is now equally, if not more, the art of coercion, of intimidation and deterrence."[64] Military power could still be used, but always under the threat of escalation to the nuclear holocaust. Many writers have suggested that the use of terrorism or insurgency is one way to get around the restrictions of the nuclear age.[65]

However, limited wars can be quite costly. The Korean War was limited, at least for the major powers involved, but it killed tens of thousands of Americans and more than a million Chinese and Koreans. This is equally true of the Vietnam War after 1965 and the Gulf War. The fact that all manner of weaponry was used in these wars, except for weapons of mass destruction, allows us to draw a line between mid-intensity and high intensity wars. The latter would involve the weapons avoided in the former. Seeing low intensity conflicts as just limited war invites intellectual confusion, and this confusion can have serious consequences. More than a few scholars have noted that the United States response in Vietnam and other counterinsurgency efforts was warped by its experiences in Korea: fear of a cross border invasion by an outside power and seeing all insurgents as the equivalent of partisans.[66] A persistent criticism of the U.S. counterinsurgency efforts in Central America in the 1980s was that the United States had difficulty seeing the political, economic, and social sources of insurgency and therefore had difficulty establishing programs that directly addressed those sources as well as addressing any meddling by the Soviets and their clients. There is also a vast difference between a raid or a rescue and the Gulf War.

The phrase "limited war" is also not precise in that it does not refer to the actions of all parties involved. The mid-intensity limited wars of Korea and Vietnam were not limited for the Koreans or the Vietnamese, only for the outside powers. Similarly, while the U.S. counterinsurgency efforts in El Salvador were limited, the continued existence of the El Salvadoran government and the various insurgent organizations was at stake for the El Salvadorans involved. The phrase "low intensity conflict" suffers from the same inexactness. Nonetheless, low intensity conflicts should be seen as a variety of limited international conflict, but a variety that is quite distinct from mid-intensity conflict where the stakes and the efforts involved are higher for all participants. It is also distinguishable from mid-intensity wars by the political context - the constrained use of force between states resulting in less than 1000 battle deaths, or the use of force between states and non-state actors.

2. **A War is a War is a War...** [67] The roots of this misconception lie in the failure to properly distinguish between combat and war. To the soldier in the mud, getting shot at from unknown directions, no combat is of low intensity. At the tactical level of war,[68] combat operations are much the same, regardless of the level of conflict of the wider war in which the tactical battle is but a small piece. A combat patrol, on foot or mounted in a vehicle or aircraft, is conducted in similar fashion whether it occurs during a raid, counterinsurgency operation, or in a mid-

intensity conflict.

Where the differences between combat, low intensity conflict, and higher forms of conflict are sharpest is at the operational and strategic levels. At these levels, all wars and conflicts are not the same. The political implications of all low intensity actions affect the operational and strategic levels. Those political considerations color all actions at the tactical level. In mid- or high intensity conflict, military means dominate the achievement of operational and strategic goals - this is the traditional American way of war.[69] In low intensity conflict, military force almost always acts as an adjunct to other means - political, economic, and diplomatic.

Of all of the misconceptions, this had perhaps the most dramatic effect on the way the Army girded for low intensity conflict. One of the first such sentiments was uttered in the early 1960s by General George H. Decker, Chief of Staff of the Army: "Any good soldier can handle guerrillas."[70] If any application of force is war, then generic military training should suffice for all contingencies.

This fallacy stems from a tactical view of low intensity conflict. LTG General Victor H. Krulak, USMC (Ret) felt that "each guerrilla conflict is a tactical, not a strategic undertaking."[71] At the tactical level one could argue that a dismounted patrol is a dismounted patrol. Logistics, communications, medical services, all remain the same under this misconception, whatever the style of conflict. While those who support military operations may be able to simply concentrate on lower level manual or technical task accomplishment, this is surely not the case with combat soldiers in a low intensity conflict.

If committed to combat or potential combat in low intensity conflict, in any of the many varieties, to be truly effective the soldiers will have to operate in full cognizance of the requirements of the political environment. Even in the case of the support services, it is doubtful that task accomplishment alone is enough. For an engineer or medical unit conducting civic action, problems can arise if the personnel of that unit are not attuned to local customs and needs, or if they are not sure of the mission.[72]

Most low intensity conflict missions require a surgeon's finesse and a scalpel-like tool. Most U.S. soldiers trained in the period of the Cold War, though, were trained in the use of heavy firepower to accomplish tactical victory. It is unreasonable to assume that without further training, such soldiers could shift easily into the difficult political conflict environment of low intensity missions. During the Just Cause operation, infantry soldiers went from the mission of combating the Panamanian Defense Forces to the mission of vehicular traffic and refugee control literally overnight. That rapid transition proved fatal to some Panamanians. The infantry men were trained only for combat.

American forces trained in the concepts of traditional war with its emphasis on the application of massive destructive power may be less capable of carrying out operations that require very subtle applications of force. The differences between low intensity conflict and higher forms of conflict, and the checkered history of U.S. attempts to deal with this challenge, make the topic worthy of separate investigation.

3. **Low intensity conflict equals Special Operations**. Most writings on low intensity conflict get to a discussion of Special Operations Forces (SOF) very quickly.[73] If, as argued above, the soldier trained as a generalist is not good enough for low intensity conflict, superficial logic suggests that one needs specially-trained troops. Since the U.S. Army has units designated Special Forces, the connection is easily, if erroneously made. This misconception arises from the counterinsurgency era

of the early 1960s when President Kennedy assigned the Army Special Forces, the Green Berets, to lead the military's efforts in combating Soviet- and Chinese-backed wars of national liberation. The misconception was reinforced by the legislative creation in 1987 of the position of Assistant Secretary of Defense for Special Operations and Low Intensity Conflict (ASD SO/LIC) and the directly related creation of the unified Special Operations Command (SOCOM). Note that the unified command was not named SOLICCOM.

Special operations missions reach across the entire spectrum of conflict, and do not necessarily focus at the lower end. In the period under consideration, Special Operations missions came to include unconventional warfare, foreign internal defense, direct action, special reconnaissance, and counterterrorism.[74] These categories included explicitly low intensity missions: insurgency, counterinsurgency, and the conduct of raids or rescues. Support for insurgency falls under unconventional warfare.[75] Foreign internal defense is synonymous with counterinsurgency.[76] Special operations doctrine also included a set of missions known as "collateral activities," among which were the low intensity missions of security assistance, humanitarian assistance, and counternarcotic operations.[77] Yet, special operations forces also functioned to support conventional operations by performing direct action commando-style operations and special reconnaissance.

While special operations forces had clearly specified low intensity missions within their purview, the most numerous bodies of troops that engaged in low intensity conflict from 1961 to 1993 were not special operations forces, but regular troops. In Vietnam in the early 1960s, most of the Americans involved were advisors drawn from the regular Army and placed on special duty. In the 1980s, most of the troops engaged in low intensity conflict were from the supporting branches, not from the combat branches: signal, medical, engineering, logistics, transportation. The U.S. Army conducted numerous humanitarian and civic action projects throughout Latin America and Africa in this decade in the name of "nation-building."[78] In the 1990s, the nation-building deployments continued. Additionally, the troops sent on the humanitarian relief mission to Somalia were almost all light infantry from the Army and Marine Corps, as well as the support troops necessary for the relief effort.

Seeing low intensity conflicts as the special province of special operations forces can lead to the devaluing of the contributions made by regular forces. To create forces that can engage in low intensity missions with a high degree of success, it is necessary to identify those forces in advance in order to train them. Both special operations forces and regular forces are needed; in the period considered, only the former put much emphasis on training for low intensity conflict.

4. **Low intensity conflict is revolutionary war, or low intensity conflict is counterinsurgency.**

In attempting to come to grips with the challenge posed by this form of conflict, one tendency is to simplify the problem by transforming low intensity conflict into one form or another of revolutionary conflict.[79] Revolutionary warfare, or internal war as some call it, is the most difficult of all of the forms of low intensity conflict, but that is a poor reason to ignore the other low intensity conflict missions.[80]

Focusing only on revolutionary warfare because it is the most difficult form of low intensity conflict is akin to focusing on defending NATO's Central Front to the detriment of other missions because this mission was the most difficult task facing the western allies. While the United States has been involved at various levels of effort in many revolutionary conflicts, we have also found it necessary to conduct numerous contingency, peacekeeping, and counterterrorism operations. Because of U.S. experience in Laos in the late 1950s, and in fashioning a response to the challenge posed by Castro in Cuba in the early 1960s, but most importantly because of the Vietnam War, low intensity conflict quickly, and too easily, became synonymous with counterinsurgency.

Much of the emphasis on the study of military uses in nation-building focused on the necessity of such activities to prevent or remove the conditions spawning insurgencies.[81] The Army's low intensity conflict manual in 1981 was devoted entirely to counterinsurgency. Much of FM 100-20 of 1990 was still devoted to countering the Maoist mass insurgency.[82] Even among authors that treated low intensity conflict as revolutionary war, the emphasis was often on countering the phenomenon. Max G. Manwaring, for example, refers alternately to "uncomfortable wars," or "small wars," and in the essay where Manwaring presents a new paradigm for such conflicts, low intensity conflict becomes simply "Insurgency Wars."[83]

Yet, in the 1980s, the United States engaged as much in fostering insurgency as in countering it. Only in El Salvador did the United States undertake a traditional counterinsurgency program. In Honduras and a few other Latin American countries, the United States engaged in what might be called "preventive nation-building" - activities designed to prevent insurgencies from growing. On the other hand, the United States supported insurgencies in Afghanistan, Angola, and Nicaragua. During and in the aftermath of the Gulf War, the United States encouraged the people of Iraq to oust Saddam Hussein, leading in part to the inconclusive Shiite and Kurdish uprisings.

Furthermore, low intensity conflict entails many activities divorced entirely from either fostering or countering insurgency. Seeing low intensity conflict as just revolutionary or insurgency warfare mutes the importance of those activities.

CONCLUSION

By listing the definitions and misconceptions I seek to provide an essential element of continuity for this project. The information above forms no part of the theoretical discussion of this project. However, the topics addressed were necessary to clarify the admittedly confusing issue of low intensity conflict. I have set out in this chapter how I define the subject and its subordinate concepts. I have also addressed the utility and exactness of the official definitions of the eras considered. However, this chapter provides material common to all the chapters that goes well beyond the definitions because it also addresses common errors in thinking about low intensity conflict. These errors crop up in defense policy and academic debate across all of the cases, though not all of the misconceptions are present in each case. Understanding these errors is a first step to understanding how and why the U.S. Army responded to low intensity conflict in the manner that it did in the period 1961-1993.

Chapter 2 Endnotes

[1] Field Manual 100-20/Air Force Pamphlet 3-20 *Military Operations in Low Intensity Conflict* (Washington, D.C.: U.S. Government Printing Office, December 1990) 3-0. Hereafter cited as FM 100-20.

[2] Daniel P. Bolger, "The Ghosts of Omdurman, " *Parameters*, Autumn 1991, 31-32.

[3] Aaron Bank, *From OSS to Green Berets* (Novato, CA: Presidio Press, 1986) 163. These forces were also to carry out unconventional operations in conjunction with partisans, or alone.

[4] See, for example, the necessary linkage between revolution and change in Theda Skocpol, *States and Social Revolutions*(New York: Cambridge University Press, 1979) 4-5. Skocpol does distinguish between revolutions that seek a change in the political order, such as the American Revolution, and those that seek complete social transformations as well, such as the French, Russian, and Chinese Revolutions.

[5] See Donald M. Snow, *Distant Thunder: Third World Conflict and the New International Order* (New York: St. Martin's Press, 1993) 73.

[6] Sam C. Sarkesian, *The New Battlefield: The United States and Unconventional Conflicts* (New York: Greenwood Press, 1986) 46-47. Sarkesian defines guerrilla warfare, insurrection, and revolution on pages 34-50. He finishes by suggesting a synthesis that he calls, simply, revolution. The opposite is counterrevolution. To Sarkesian, revolution, counterrevolution, and terrorism are the constituent elements of "unconventional conflict" - his term for low intensity conflict.

[7] Adam Roberts, *Nations in Arms* (New York: St. Martin's Press, 1966) 36.

[8] See the entries for "Sovereignty" and "Recognition: Belligerency" in Robert L. Bledsoe and Boleslaw A. Boczek, *The International Law Dictionary* (Santa Barbara, CA: ABC-CLIO, 1987) 55-56, 46-47. When internal conflicts take on this territorial character, they become "civil wars" as commonly understood, such as the American Civil War, or the civil war between Biafra and the rest of Nigeria.

[9] Gordon C. Schloming, *Power and Principle in International Affairs* (New York: Harcourt Brace Jovanovich, 1990) 484. Emphasis in original.

[10] For general discussions on international terrorism, see Charles W. Kegley, Jr., ed.. *International Terrorism: Characteristics, Causes, Controls* (New York: St. Martin's Press, 1990), and Walter Lacqueur, *The Age of Terrorism* (Boston: little, Brown, 1987). See particularly page 5 of Lacqueur where the author makes a careful differentiation between the terrorist and the guerrilla.

[11] See Chapter 6 of Hans J. Morgenthau, *Politics Among Nations: The Struggle for Power and Peace*, 6th ed., rev. Kenneth W. Thompson (New

York: McGraw-Hill, 1985).

[12] See the editorial "The New World Army," *New York Times*, 6 March 1992, A32.

[13] Ted Sorensen, speech to the Student Conference on United States Affairs, West Point, NY, 16 November 1992. Sorensen suggested that the United States place at least a brigade in readiness for these missions at all times. See similar suggestions in Bernard Adelsberger, "New Rules, New Roles for the 'Decade of Disorder,'" *Army Times*, 18 January 1993, 6," and the editorial "U.S. Troops for a UN Army," *New York Times*, 9 August 1993, A14.

[14] Quoted in Charles W. Kegley, Jr. and Eugene R. Wittkopf, *World Politics: Trend and Transformation*, 4th ed. (New York: St. Martin's Press, 1993) 518.

[15] See Joseph S. Nye. Jr., *Understanding International Conflicts: An Introduction to Theory and History* (New York: Harper Collins, 1993) 147.

[16] However, peace enforcing or peacemaking could become war under the definitions above if the battle deaths exceed 1000. For general works on peacekeeping, see William J. Durch, ed., *The Evolution of UN Peacekeeping* (New York: St. Martin's Press, 1993); Alan James, *Peacekeeping in International Politics* (New York: St. Martin's Press, 1990); F. T. Liu, *United Nations Peacekeeping and the Non-use of Force* (Boulder: Lynne Reiner, 1992); Augustus Richard Norton and Thomas G. Weiss, *UN Peacekeepers: Soldiers with a Difference* (New York: Foreign Policy Association, 1990).

[17] 17 See Martin Van Creveld, *The Transformation of War* (New York: Free Press, 1991).

[18] Bolger 31.

[19] Samuel P. Huntington, *The Soldier and The State: The Theory and Politics of Civil-Military Relations* (Cambridge, MA: Harvard, 1957) 261.

[20] The Army fought 943 engagements against the Indians after 1865, and one presumes, numerous ones before. See Russell F. Weigley, *History of the United States Army* (New York: Macmillan, 1967) 160-161, 267.

[21] Lieutenant Colonel Gerald B. Thompson, "History and Current Status of LIC Doctrine," unpublished paper prepared for presentation at New York University lecture series entitled "New Threats to Peace: Low Intensity Conflict in the Third World," 11 May 1988, contained in Center for Low Intensity Conflict Reference File 2 General 31, Langley Air Force Base, VA.

[22] Weigley 267, 292. Robert H. Utley, *Frontier Regulars: The United States Army and the Indian, 1866-1891* (Bloomington, IN: Indiana University Press, 1973) 12.

[23] Weigley 267.

[24] Utley 44.

[25] The information above represents a summary of material found in Utley Chapter 3, and Weigley 160-163, 170-171, and 274-278.

[26] Edward L. Katzenbach, Jr., "The Horse Cavalry in the Twentieth Century," *The Use of Force*, ed. Robert J. Art and Kenneth N. Waltz (Boston: Little, Brown, 1971) 282.

[27] For an exhaustively researched volume on the Army's activities in the Philippine Insurrection, see John M. Gates, *Schoolbooks and Krags: The United States Army and the Philippines, 1898-1902* (Westport, CT: Greenwood Press, 1973). For a good account of the Army's similar efforts at military government in Cuba immediately after the Spanish- American War, see Ivan Musicant, *The Banana Wars: A History of United States Intervention in Latin America from the Spanish-American War to the Invasion of Panama* (New York: MacMillan, 1990). In Cuba, the Army also practiced civic action extensively. Musicant says of the officer in charge of the city of Santiago, a Harvard-educated doctor who had participated in the capture of Geronimo, Colonel Leonard Wood, "His tasks were clear: feed the hungry, bury the dead, nurse the sick, and clean up the city." Musicant 38. The Army also used force to maintain order when necessary, horsewhipping even Cuban notables for violating sanitation laws. See Musicant chapter 2.

[28] On the role of punishment by combat, see Thomas C. Schelling, *Arms and Influence* (New Haven: Yale University Press, 1966) 1-34. On pages 5-6, Schelling specifically addresses the use of combat to punish Indians.

[29] Donovan was a hero of World War I who became a well-known attorney before World War II. Donovan formed the OSS in 1942. See Bank 3. See also Alfred H. Paddock, Jr., *U.S. Army Special Warfare: Its Origins* (Washington, D.C.: NDU, 1982). Paddock covers the period 1941-1952. See also Ray S. Cline, *The CIA: Reality vs. Myth* (Washington, D.C.: Acropolis, 1981) chapters 1-2.

[30] Bank 145. Cline chapter 3.

[31] Roy K. Flint, "An Entirely New War," *Selected Readings in Warfare Since 1945*, ed. Roy K. Flint, Peter W. Kozumplik, Thomas J. Waraksa (West Point, NY: U.S. Military Academy, 1981) 150. Charles M. Simpson, *Inside the Green Berets: The First Thirty Years* (Novato, CA: Presidio, 1983) 15. See also Paddock 71-75.

[32] Larry Cable, *Conflict of Myths* (New York: New York University Press, 1986) 134. See also D. Michael Shafer, *Deadly Paradigms* (Princeton: Princeton University Press, 1988) Chapter 7 for the U.S. counterinsurgency efforts in Greece, and Chapter 8 for the Philippines.

[33] Simpson 15.

[34] The Laotian information comes from Simpson 67-93.

[35] Simpson 17; Bank 147.

[36] Harry G. Summers, *On Strategy: A Critical Analysis of the Vietnam War* (New York: Dell, 1984) 104. Summers quoted from FM 100-5 *Field Service Regulations: Operations* (Washington, D.C.: Department of the Army, 19 February 1962) 4-5. One of the earliest references to the phrase "low intensity conflict" is *Study of Low Intensity Conflict* (Washington, D.C.: Headquarters, Department of the Army, 1964). See also Howard Lee Dixon, *Low Intensity Conflict: Overview, Definitions, and Policy Concerns* (Langley Air Force Base, VA: Center for Low Intensity Conflict, 1989) 5, 8-9.

[37] Roger Hilsman records that the President Kennedy actually preferred the

term "Subterranean War." Roger Hilsman, *To Move A Nation: The Politics of Foreign Policy in the Administration of John F. Kennedy* (Garden City, NY: Doubleday, 1967) 413.

[38] See chapter 4 below.

[39] Field Manual 100-20 *Low Intensity Conflict* (Washington, D.C.: Department of the Army, January 1981) 14. Hereafter cited as FM 100-20.

[40] Field Circular 100-20, *Low Intensity Conflict*, Final Draft (Fort Leavenworth, KS: U.S. Army Command and General Staff College, June 1985) 1-2.

[41] Field Manual 100-5 *Operations* (Washington, D.C.: Government Printing Office, 1986) 4. Hereafter cited as FM 100-5.

[42] FM 100-5, 3, 4.

[43] Colonel Albert N. Barnes, "Commander's Preface," *Historical Report of the Army-Air Force Center for Low Intensity Conflict, 1 January-30 June 1987*, ed. Thomas Crouch.

[44] Thomas Crouch, ed., *Historical Report of the Army-Air Force Center for Low Intensity Conflict, 1 January-30 June 1987*, 12.

[45] FM 100-5 *Operations* (Washington, D.C.: Government Printing Office, 1993), 2-0. Emphasis in original.

[46] Michael T. Klare and Peter Kornbluh, "The New Interventionism: Low-Intensity Warfare in the 1980s and Beyond," *Low-Intensity Warfare*, ed. Michael T. Klare and 46 Peter Kornbluh (New York: Pantheon Books, 1988) 7.

[47] FM 100-5, 1986, 5.

[48] The 1990 edition of FM 100-20 does not give separate chapters to the missions of supporting and combating insurgency. It lumps them together as different sides of the same coin.

[49] FM 100-20, 1990, 2-0.

[50] FM 100-20, 1990, 2-0.

[51] FM 100-20, 1990, 2-17, 2-18.

[52] FM 100-20, 1990, 2-0.

[53] FM 100-20, 1990, 2-7.

[54] FM 100-20, 1990, 2-7 through 2-22.

[55] FM 100-20, 1990, 3-0.

61 Telephone interview with Chris Mellon, 6 August 1993. Mellon was on the staff of Senator William Cohen at the time of these events.

[56] The definitions come from FM 100-20, 1990, g-2.

[57] FM 100-20, 1990, 1-7.

[58] FM 100-20, 1990, 5-1.

[59] FM 100-20, 1990, 5-7.

[60] At the time of writing in 1993, the U.S. government was considering redefining "peacemaking" to be the diplomatic action of forging a truce, ceasefire, or armistice. There was also discussion of replacing "peace" with "truce" in peacekeeping and peacemaking. Interview with Lieutenant Colonel

Anne Storey, Center for Low Intensity Conflict, Langley, VA, 16 March 1993. Also, this was confirmed in a telephonic interview with Major Rick Brennan, Office of the Assistant Secretary of Defense for Democracy, Human Rights, and Peacekeeping, 14 July 1993.

[61] Telephone interview with Chris Mellon, 6 August 1993. Mellon was on the staff of Senator William Cohen at the time of these events.

[62] Letter from General (Retired) John W. Foss to Rick Waddell, 1 August 1993. As a younger officer, General Foss drew up the initial post-Vietnam planning scenarios for the Army. He finished his career as the officer in charge of refashioning the Army's doctrine and training after the Cold War.

[63] "Suppose one merely wants a small concession from the enemy. One will only fight until some *modest quid pro quo* has been acquired, and a modest effort should suffice for that; consequently we must also be willing to wage such minimal wars, which consist *in merely threatening the enemy with negotiations held in reserve.*" Carl von Clausewitz, *On War*, Book VIII, chapter 3, ed. and trans. Michael Howard and Peter Paret (Princeton: Princeton University Press; 1976) 604 (emphasis in original).

[64] Thomas Schelling, "The Diplomacy of Violence," *International Politics*, 2d ed., ed. Robert Art and Robert Jervis (Boston: Scott, Foresman, 1985) 185. The classic work on limited war remains Robert Osgood, *Limited War: The Challenge to American Strategy* (Chicago: Chicago University Press, 1957).

[65] According to one study, the idea of a spectrum of conflict arose in the years immediately after the Korean War with the work of Sir F. Reginald Farmer who devised risk versus probability curves for nuclear safety, nuclear strategy, and eventually for all conflict. Low intensity conflict would involve high probability, but low risk to a nation. Nuclear war was the opposite. See the discussion in Dixon 4.

[66] See Larry Cable, *Conflict of Myths*; Andrew Krepinevich, *The Army and Vietnam* (Baltimore: Johns Hopkins, 1986); D. Michael Shafer, *Deadly Paradigms*.

[67] I borrowed this title from Summers 27.

[68] There are three levels of war: strategic, operational, and tactical. In the 1980s, strategy was defined as "the art and science of employing the armed forces of a nation or alliance to secure policy objectives by the application or the threat of force." The operational level of war was about "the employment of military forces to attain strategic goals in a theater of war or theater of operations through the design, organization, and conduct of campaigns and major operations." The operational level was generally the concern of commanders above corps level. The tactical level was where "corps and smaller unit commanders translate potential combat power into victorious battles and engagements." See FM 100-5, 1986, 9, 10.

[69] Robert Osgood felt that this tradition included turning the prosecution of the war largely over to the military. See Osgood 29. Similarly Morton Halperin has described the American tradition of war as that of a "moral crusade." See

Morton Halperin, *Limited War in the Nuclear Age* (Westport, CT: Greenwood Press) 1963) 19.

[70] Quoted in Krepinevich 37.

[71] LTG Victor H. Krulak, "Strategic Implications of 'the Little War,'" Student Text 100-39 *Low Intensity Conflict: Selected Readings* (Fort Leavenworth, KS: U.S. Army Command and General Staff College, 1985) 84.

[72] I have covered such inadequacies in the supporting services in Rick Waddell, *In War's Shadow: Waging Peace In Central America* (New York: Ivy, 1992).

[73] See, for example, Loren B. Thompson, ed., *Low Intensity Conflict: The Pattern of Warfare in the Modern World* (Lexington, MA: Lexington Books, 1989). Three of nine total chapters are devoted specifically to Special Operations Forces. In the opening chapter, the editor acknowledges that special operations forces and low intensity conflict are often confused, but then spends much of the next 15 pages contributing to that confusion by detailing the U.S. special operations capabilities, including a table listing all such forces. He only briefly mentions non-Special Forces. See Loren B. Thompson, "Low-Intensity Conflict: An Overview," *Low Intensity Conflict: The Pattern of Warfare in the Modern World*, ed. Loren B. Thompson (Lexington, MA: Lexington Books, 1989) 6-20.

[74] See Field Manual 31-20 *Doctrine for Special Forces Operations* (Washington, D.C.: Department of the Army, 1990). Hereafter cited as FM 31-20.

[75] See FM 31-20 chapter 9. This same category includes support for "resistance" - partisan operations behind enemy lines in a mid- or high intensity conflict.

[76] See FM 31-20 chapter 10.

[77] See FM 31-20 chapter 3.

[78] Aside from the thousands of regular soldiers who served in Latin America, one source indicates that in the period 1984-1990, more than 27,000 Army Reserve and National Guard engineers also served there. See Major General Daniel R. Schroeder, "Clear the Way," *Engineer*, March 1990, 2.

[79] See Max G. Manwaring, ed. *Uncomfortable Wars: Toward a New Paradigm of Low Intensity Conflict* (Boulder, CO: Westview Press, 1991). See also Richard M. Swain, "Removing Square Pegs from Round Holes: Low Intensity Conflict in Army Doctrine" *Military Review*, December 1987, 3-15. Swain notes that one of the first scholars to focus on low intensity conflict, Dr. Sam Sarkesian, came to believe that "LIC and revolutionary war are essentially identical." See Swain 15. See also Sarkesian chapters 1-4.

[80] Even among forces tasked with low intensity conflict missions, such as the Army Special Forces, there are more glamorous and less glamorous missions. In Special Forces doctrinal manual, FM 31-20 of 1990, support for insurgency rates only a piece of the unconventional war chapter. Yet, counterinsurgency and counterterrorism get chapters of their own. Most of the other low

intensity missions are ingloriously lumped together as "collateral activities."
[81] See John W. De Pauw and George A. Luz, ed., *Winning the Peace: The Strategic Implications of Military Civic Action* (Carlisle Barracks, PA: U.S. Army War College, 1990); Harry D. Train III, et al, *The Relations Between Democracy, Development and Security; Implications for Policy* (New York: Global Economic Action Institute, 1989) chapter 1.
[82] See FM 100-20, 1990, chapter 2, and Appendices A, C, D, E.
[83] Max. G. Manwaring, "Preface," *Uncomfortable Wars: Toward a New Paradigm of Low Intensity Conflict*, ed. Max G. Manwaring (Boulder, CO: Westview Press, 1991) xii. And Max G. Manwaring, "Toward an Understanding of Insurgency Wars: The Paradigm," *Uncomfortable Wars: Toward a New Paradigm of Low Intensity Conflict*, ed. Max G. Manwaring (Boulder, CO: Westview Press, 1991) 19-20. As late as the early 1990s, U.S. defense policy spoke of responding to the challenges of insurgency in terms of "defense against". For examples see Dick Cheney, *Annual Report to the President and the Congress* (Washington, D.C.: U.S. Government Printing Office, January 1990) 3, and George Bush, *National Security Strategy of the United States* (Washington, D.C.: U.S. Government Printing Office, August 1991) 8.

CHAPTER 3
THE COUNTERINSURGENCY ERA
1961-1965

"This is another type of war, new in its intensity, ancient in its origin - war by guerrillas, subversives, insurgents, assassins, war by ambush instead of by combat; by infiltration, instead of aggression, seeking victory by eroding and exhausting the enemy instead of engaging him....It requires a whole new kind of strategy, a wholly different kind of military training. "

> — John F. Kennedy, West Point graduation ceremonies, 6 June 1962.[1]

Some critics of the efforts at low intensity conflict in the 1980s claimed that the phenomenon is little more than a return to the failed policies of the early 1960s.[2] The fact that the heart of the Army's efforts in low intensity conflict still placed heavy emphasis on counterinsurgency suggested that the Army's experience of the early 1960s is worthy of review, simply for comparative value.[3] The fact that we are still looking at the same institution in the same country, although at an earlier time, allows this study to compare the counterinsurgency era and the later low intensity conflict cases, controlling for many cultural and institutional variables that might prove troublesome if I had chosen to make a cross-national study.[4] Moreover, since many of the officers who oversaw the growth in emphasis on low intensity conflict in the 1980s had their formative experiences in the Vietnam period, this case is quite important for historical value.

The methodology that I will pursue will entail a chronological review of the history of the case with heavy emphasis given to the explanatory works that already exist.

Finally, I will relate this information to the competing explanations for the Army's behavior with respect to the challenge of low intensity conflict.

For the case to support Posen's argument on military change and innovation, I should find three crucial items of evidence. First, the case should exhibit evidence of a change in the perceptions of U.S. civilian leaders with respect to international threats. Next, the case should exhibit considerable hostility by the Army as an organization to the idea of changing from its primary mission, waging high and mid-intensity warfare, to adopt a mission such as low intensity conflict. The changing perceptions then must lead the civilians to attempt to reform the military. Posen suggests that this reform process often requires the use of a military maverick that operates inside the military to advance the reforms.[5] Therefore, the final point of the investigation will be identifying the existence of any of these mavericks. To the degree that the three points above are provided by the cases, the argument for Posen's approach is strengthened.

For the case to support Rosen, the case must exhibit five things. First, a group of Army officers has to become convinced that the changing security environment of the United States requires a new defense capability. Second, they must conceptualize a vision of how the Army would provide that capability. Third, the officers have to translate the vision into combat tasks which would provide the basis for training soldiers and units. Fourth, this group must convert one or more very senior officers with impeccable mainstream credentials to their view. Last, those senior officers have to act to create viable pathways for the promotion of younger adherents to higher ranks.

What the evidence of this case shows is that a synthesis of these two approaches is necessary. In this case, the Army leadership responded to some of the demands made on it by civilians outside the organization and by groups within the Army – those officers who believed in creating a special capability for combating insurgency and those who sought to refashion the Army through the use of helicopters as primary fighting vehicles for all possible future combat. However, the Army's dominant group believed that the Army must devote most of its efforts to the mission of defending Europe. This caused all other efforts to be bent in that direction. The civilians acted to change the Army, but they chose members of this dominant group, not mavericks, as their agents for change. As a result, what the civilians got was peripheral change of the kind that could easily be reversed when civilian pressure disappeared.

THE SECURITY ENVIRONMENT: FLEXIBLE RESPONSE

The appearance of counterinsurgency cannot be understood apart from the political debate of the late 1950s concerning defense. The Eisenhower Administration was the focus of academic, military, and political criticism for perceived neglect of conventional forces and over reliance on nuclear retaliation as the means for strategic deterrence. Principal among the academic critics were William Kaufmann of MIT and Henry Kissinger of Harvard. To these critics, neither massive retaliation nor early use of tactical nuclear weapons was a credible doctrine. In their opinions it was not believable that the United States would risk total destruction over any confrontation, however minor. Hence, in reality, the United States had few capabilities to deal with much of the conflict that it might face, especially as instability was increasing in the former colonial areas.

The Democrat contender for the Presidency in 1960, Senator John F. Kennedy, and his campaign staff made this criticism a major campaign issue. Rather than rely on massive nuclear retaliation, they proposed a deterrent strategy of "flexible response." Reliance on nuclear weapons had not prevented the Soviet repression of the Hungarian uprising, nor had it kept the People's Republic of China from meddling with Quemoy and Matsu. In the former case, the U.S. had been left with little recourse other than diplomatic remonstrations. The latter case required nuclear threats and the deployment of U.S. naval forces to prevent the crisis from widening. The fear was that a future confrontation might leave the United States with a choice between "humiliation or holocaust" or "suicide or surrender."

The Kennedy campaign pledged to give the U.S. military the forces capable of dealing with lesser threats to peace and stability, threats that did not warrant nuclear retaliation, but ones that nevertheless fell within the purview of U.S. concerns. Such capabilities would, as well, strengthen the overall strategic deterrent posture by being more believable, and hence lessening the reliance on the early use of nuclear weapons.

Along with a general fear that strategic deterrence might fail in the face of gains in Soviet missile and bomber technology was the fear that smaller crises might provoke larger ones, especially crises arising from subversive threats to American allies or interests. Both the Eisenhower and Kennedy administrations perceived these threats to be quite real. American aid and advice appeared decisive in enabling the Greek and Philippine governments to defeat their communist insurgencies. By the end of French involvement in Indochina, the U.S. was financing a large portion of France's war effort. Eisenhower had also entered into an aid-and-advisory relationship in Laos near the end of his administration.

Critics charged, though, that despite the apparent success of many of these operations, the United States was still ill-prepared to counter subversion and insurgency. Hence, the particular fear was that one of these "brush-fire wars" might bring on a much larger, and much more dangerous confrontation between the

United States and the Soviet Union. Fidel Castro's victory in Cuba in 1959 exacerbated this fear precisely because Castro had used guerrilla tactics to defeat an American-equipped and American-advised conventional army.[6] This fear became especially acute when Khrushchev, in January 1961, declared "wars of liberation" necessary and inevitable in the historic struggle that communism would wage. This speech had such an impact on the new president that "President Kennedy directed that all the members of his new administration read the speech and consider what it portended."[7] Furthermore, U.S. Special Forces had been training Laotian forces since 1959, but in March 1961, it looked as if Laos might fall to communist guerrilla forces. The possibility of an early defeat presented the new president with what Walt W. Rostow called a "roaring crisis."[8] All of these events culminated in a search for some special answer to the challenge of insurgency.

President Kennedy, in charge of a new, enthusiastic administration full of the promise of change, entered office pledging America to "pay any price, bear any burden, meet any hardship, support any friend or oppose any foe to assure the survival and the success of liberty." He proposed to retool the U.S. military to give it the means to respond to any crisis with the appropriate level of force. The new administration aimed to strengthen the conventional component of NATO defense to keep the firebreak between confrontation and conflagration high. Also included in this retooling was the creation of capability to deal with the threat posed by Khrushchev's new wars.

Consequently, under the new Secretary of Defense, Robert McNamara, the budgets and force structures of all of the services increased. The Army increased from 12 to 16 divisions, while reorganizing for better command and control.[9] The Navy's surface fleet also grew and air and sealift capacities expanded. New generations of fighter jets emerged. The ultimate goal of this effort was to give the United States the ability to deal with two-and-a-half wars simultaneously: a large-scale conflict in Europe, another large-scale conflict against China, and then a "half-war" - a localized threat in any remaining region of the world. It was into the latter category that the Kennedy administration would place its counterinsurgency effort, as the new president fervently believed "that the most likely and immediate threat from the Communists was neither nuclear war nor large-scale conventional wars, as in Korea, but the more subtle, ambiguous threat of the guerrilla."[10]

In the first meeting of President Kennedy's National Security Council, the subject of guerrilla war surfaced.[11] The NSC then produced National Security Action Memorandum No. 2 to propose a preliminary response. The memorandum called for the development of forces to counter guerillas.[12] The scholars sprinkled through the Kennedy administration spoke of insurgency as a tactic used to reach ends other than the overthrow of the local government.[13] Kennedy himself made the point quite clear: "The message of Cuba, of Laos, of the rising din of Communist voices in Asia and Latin America - these messages are all the same."[14] In the early 1960s those ends were generally seen as the threat of Soviet and Chinese expansion. To combat this tactic required "developing a counter-revolutionary strategy which applies revolutionary strategy and principles IN REVERSE to defeat the enemy with his own weapons on his own battlefield."[15]

In 1962 the Kennedy administration produced the blueprint for the counterinsurgency doctrine. It was contained in National Security Action Memorandum 182 of 24 August 1962. The title of the memorandum was "United States Overseas Internal Defense Policy" (USOIDP). The aim of the document was to provide "basic policy guidance to diplomatic missions, consular personnel, and military commands abroad; [and] to government departments and agencies at home...."[16] The USOIDP defined the threat as "Communist inspired, supported, or directed insurgency." Such insurgencies posed "[a] most pressing national security problem...."[17]

Why did the threat exist? The USOIDP laid the blame on the pressures created by the development process in what came to be called the Third World. The often weak governments in these areas found these pressures difficult to confront. The combination of developmental pressures and weak governments provided fertile soil for exploitation by Soviet-sponsored subversives.[18]

What was the answer to the threat? The USOIDP specified several programs that have since become synonymous with counterinsurgency: land reform, community development, education, and reform of the host government so that it could more effectively meet the demands of its people, and training of local police and military officers. The latter programs were designed to create a cadre of public servants capable of directly affecting the nation-building process while physically protecting the people from subversive violence.

With the blueprint in place, the Kennedy administration began training its people. The State Department's Foreign Service Institute conducted the training in what came to be known as the Inter-Departmental Seminar on Counter-Insurgency.[19] The first class met in June 1962. The instructors included some of the best political scientists and diplomats in the nation. The students came from all of the agencies involved in national security and in areas of development and security assistance. Even Ambassador Henry Cabot Lodge attended before taking up residence in South Vietnam.

THE ARMY RESPONSE

On 6 September 1961, Secretary of Defense McNamara

designated the Army as the executive agent primarily responsible for counterinsurgency in the Defense Department.[20] How did the Army react to the pressures from the Kennedy Administration to become more flexible? To understand fully the Army response to the Kennedy administration requires investigation of three areas - force structure changes, the doctrine produced, and the training conducted.

FORCE STRUCTURE CHANGES

In 1956 the Army approved a reorganization plan that would provide it the ability to operate on the nuclear-dominated battlefield envisioned by the strategic planners of the massive retaliation era. With the strategic emphasis shifting to the delivery of nuclear weapons, the Army declined in strength from 1,025,778 in 1956 to 861,964 in 1959.[21] By 1959, however, the Army leadership became convinced that the reorganization of the Army for the nuclear battlefield, named the "Pentomic Army" had been overdone. Consequently, in 1959 a new study was prepared to explore the changes than would be necessary to enable the Army to function on a variety of battlefields.[22] This study called for the reorganization of the Army yet again, this time to increase the ability of units to act independently. Increased independence required enhancements in firepower and tactical mobility.

Thus, even before the advent of the Kennedy administration with its emphasis on flexible response, the Army was searching for the means to respond to a variety of contingencies. Yet, the focus of the reforms was still on armored warfare. In March 1961, the Army issued its next reorganization study, entitled "Reorganization Objectives Army Division (ROAD) 1965." The new president quickly accepted this plan in May 1961, with the reorganization to commence in 1962. The hallmark of the plan was the ability to tailor Army divisions and subunits to meet required missions, whether on a nuclear or conventional battlefield.[23] The reorganized Army met much of the concern of the Kennedy administration for a land force flexible enough to operate across a range of contingencies. What the reorganization did not do was satisfy the administration's desire for a means of fighting insurgency.

To satisfy the special needs of counterinsurgency, the Army proposed increases in its Special Forces as early as February 1961. What is remarkable about these proposed increases, given the president's personal concern for counterinsurgency capabilities, was that they numbered in the mere thousands. Three Special Forces Groups existed in early 1961, but all were severely understrength, with less than 400 men assigned to each. The total number of Special Forces on active duty was roughly 2000.[24] The Army proposed doubling the number of groups by 1963 and raising those to full strengths of 1262 each for a total increase of over 5000.[25] Moderate increases were also planned for counterinsurgency support units with missions in psychological warfare and civil affairs.

While the Special Forces increases seem minor, they must be compared to what the President had in mind for the Army as a whole. The Kennedy administration planned to increase the entire Army by only 5000 spaces in FY 62. Of those, the Special Forces were allocated 3000.[26] With the Berlin and Cuban Missile crises, though, the Army would swell to over 1 million during 1962, and would stay in the vicinity of 970,000 until 1965 when expansion for the Vietnam intervention began.[27] The number of Army divisions grew to 18 in 1962, and then dropped to 16 through 1966. Special Forces Groups numbered seven by 1965. As a percentage, then, of the total force, the Special Forces actually lost ground.

Under criticism for its efforts in 1961, the Army adopted a plan which assigned four regular Army brigades to assist Special

Forces efforts in regional insurgencies.[28] The primary mission of these brigades remained, however, devoted to mid-intensity warfare. "[F]orce structuring for counterinsurgency was viewed as very much a resource allocation problem, pitting the Army's need of and preference for conventional forces for its traditional contingency of war in Europe against the new requirements placed on the service to address the problem of Third World insurgencies."[29] Eventually, five infantry brigades were identified as back-ups to the seven existing Special Forces Groups.

In total, then, in the so-called "counterinsurgency era," the Army had less than 20,000 troops earmarked for counterinsurgency on the eve of intervention in 1965. Of those, less than 10,000 - those in the Special Forces - had counterinsurgency as their primary mission. This five-fold increase in counterinsurgency soldiers indicates that the Army responded to the guidance it received from civilian leaders. On the other hand, given that Vietnam was the theater of concern, three of the newly created groups had missions focused on Latin America, Africa, and the Middle East, respectively. Another remained focused on unconventional warfare in Eastern Europe.[30] This indicates that while the Army responded by creating groups, it did not necessarily create them for Vietnam, and in the case of Europe and the Middle East, maybe not even for counterinsurgency, but rather for unconventional operations. Therefore, the Army changed in response to civilian intervention, but not fully in the direction that the civilians desired.

THE DOCTRINE
Several Army doctrinal publications that dealt with counterinsurgency were in the production process prior to the arrival of the new administration. One can only speculate how the immediate emphasis of the President affected these 1961 releases.[31] However, in the process of reorganizing itself for

Flexible Response, the Army conducted two studies of the need for a counterinsurgency capability. The first, the Stilwell Report of 13 October 1961, chided the Army for the failure to provide clear, concise doctrine for counterinsurgency. The second report, the Howze Report of 28 January 1962, also emphasized the lack of suitable counterinsurgency doctrine, especially given that the "concept [of counterinsurgency] is foreign to fundamental Army teaching and practice."[32]

As a result of these studies and the president's personal interests, the Army issued a spate of counterinsurgency doctrinal manuals by the close of 1963 that covered a range of subjects from the level of general Army operations down to company level tactics.[33] These manuals did indeed bear the mark of the new administration's emphasis on counterinsurgency.[See Table 3]

Field Manual 100-5 *Field Service Regulations: Operations* served the same role in the early 1960s as its modern counterpart does now - the capstone doctrinal statement for the Army from which all other field manuals (FMs) are supposed to derive. The 1962 edition of this manual contained, for the first time, a chapter devoted to counterinsurgency, Chapter 11, "Military Operations Against Irregular Forces." Other insights into counterinsurgency operations were contained in Chapter 10, "Unconventional Warfare Operations." The following excerpts from these chapters demonstrate a concern for the peculiar political nature of counterinsurgency, but quickly descend to a focus on guerrilla destruction. This emphasis on aggressive offensive actions is consistently followed in all the derivative manuals, and becomes one of the foci of later criticism of the doctrine.[34]

TABLE 3

1961 MANUALS
FM 31-15 *Operations Against Irregular Forces*
FM 31-21 *Guerrilla Warfare and Special Operations Forces*
FM 61-100 *The Division*

1962/1963 MANUALS
FM 7-20 *Infantry, Airborne Infantry and Mechanized Infantry Battalions* (1962)
FM 7-30 *Infantry, Airborne and Mechanized Division Brigades* (1962)
FM 31-16 *Counterguerrilla Operations* (1962, 1963)
FM 31-21 *Guerrilla Warfare* (1962)
FM 31-22 *U.S. Army Counterinsurgency Forces* (1963)
FM 100-5 *Field Service Regulations: Operations* (1962)
Counterinsurgency Operations: A Handbook for the Suppression of Communist Guerrilla/Terrorist Operations (1962)
FM 33-5 *Psychological Operations* (1962)
FM 41-10 *Civil Affairs Operations* (1962)

The 1962 edition of FM 100-5 did at least begin its chapter on unconventional operations with a genuflection to the politically sensitive nature of counterinsurgency:

> "The ideological nature of modern conflict gives an important role for all forms of war. Particularly in Cold War the struggle for influence over the minds of men makes unconventional warfare a key element. Successful conduct of unconventional warfare could be decisive in achieving national objectives. Counter unconventional warfare is equally

important."[35]

Additionally, the manual did place some emphasis on less violent means of countering the insurgent before rapidly turning to address offensive anti-guerrilla operations:

> "Enemy unconventional warfare operations must be countered. Measures include the use of consolidation psychological operations in conjunction with civil affairs, and the use of combat troops or friendly guerrillas in an antiguerrilla role."[36]

Army doctrine became quite explicit about the process of destroying the guerrilla forces in the field: "Operations to suppress and eliminate irregular forces are primarily offensive in nature."[37] When addressing the subject of anti-guerrilla operations the 1962 manual for infantry companies specified that "[t]he mission of the rifle company... is to close with the enemy by means of fire and maneuver in order to destroy or capture him..."[38] Later, the manual adds "[c]ontinuous pressure is maintained by vigorous combat patrolling."[39] Such pressure would deprive the guerrillas of their supply and support base, keep their operations off balance, and lower their morale. The counterguerrilla manual published in 1963 was specific about the means necessary to a carry out such operations:

> "Superior mobility is essential in counterguerrilla operations to achieve surprise and to successfully counter the mobility of the enemy force. The extensive use of airmobile forces will ensure the

military commander superior mobility."[40]

The emphasis on mobile operations to find and destroy insurgent guerrilla forces contained in the doctrinal field manuals of the day conjure up clear pictures of helicopters filling the sky and bring echoes of the Vietnam era operational phrases "search and destroy," "block and sweep," "search and clear." Because the manuals focus on combat operations, it is easy to forget that they at least paid lip service to the political environment of insurgency. FM 31-16 *Counterguerrilla Operations* cautioned: "The scope and nature of a commander's mission may emphasize political, economic and social considerations to a greater extent than in conventional operations."[41] Such admonitions were easily lost in the combat focus. Critics during the early 1960s and afterwards would point to this focus on military force as the principal weakness in the counterinsurgency efforts of the Kennedy and Johnson administrations.

TRAINING PROGRAMS
The Army had experimented with special forces during World War II and the Korean War. The Army had organized companies and battalions of Rangers which saw heavy action in the Italian and Normandy campaigns, and again in the Korean conflict. The Army also organized the 10th Special Forces Group in 1952 to wage unconventional warfare behind enemy lines in Europe in the event of a new war there.[42] The primary purpose of all of these special units was unconventional support to conventional operations.[43] The organization of guerrillas behind enemy lines was one option for supporting friendly operations. Other operations included deep reconnaissance patrols, raids, and ambushes. Doctrinal literature of the period also focused on dealing with the opposite: guerrilla threats behind our lines.[44]

What interest there was in unconventional warfare, let alone insurgent warfare, waned in the Pentomic era.

Given this background, how did the Army train itself for counterinsurgency in the era of Flexible Response? Training includes two very different functions: classroom-style teaching and hands-on practice of combat tasks by individuals and units. Yet in training for counterinsurgency, the Army faced a special problem: with only small numbers of U.S. soldiers serving in unconventional warfare units, most of the U.S. Army soldiers assigned to South Vietnam prior to 1965 came from conventional units. More than 4700 were assigned to ARVN units by 1964 primarily to train the ARVN in conventional tactics against the cross-border threat of the NVA.[45] The lesser included task was always to combat large groupings of Viet Cong. On the other hand, large numbers of Special Forces soldiers also operated in South Vietnam, training both ARVN and Montagnard tribes to combat the guerrillas.[46] The Special Forces controlled eighteen camps along the South Vietnamese border which utilized local tribes to maintain watch on the routes used by the Viet Cong and their North Vietnamese supporters. In 1964, the Army transferred the headquarters of the 5th Special Forces Group to Vietnam to control this aspect of counterinsurgency.[47] The United States did not have the leisure of a "train-up" period before commencing counterinsurgency operations; it had to train even as it fought.

TEACHING THE DOCTRINE

The first step in the training effort was the provision of new doctrine. As is seen in the preceding section, this occurred rapidly. The next step was teaching the doctrine. In his effort to capture the intellect of the Army, President Kennedy ordered "counterinsurgency training added to the curricula of military schools at all levels, from West Point all the way up to the Army

War College."[48] The president further directed the creation of "guerrilla warfare libraries" for use by all ranks.[49] Colonels and brigadier generals considered to have the best potential for higher responsibilities were also ordered to attend courses on counterinsurgency given at the Special Warfare Center at Fort Bragg, NC.[50]

The civilian impetus to expand the Special Forces, however, also led to diluted training. The Special Warfare Center increased its yearly graduates from 400 to over 3000 per year. To do this required reducing the attrition rate of trainees by more than 60%, resulting in Special Forces soldiers of lesser quality.[51]

Douglas Blaufarb records that in the eighteen months after Kennedy took office, war college instruction on counterinsurgency increased by 53 instructional hours. Instruction at the Command and General Staff College and officer advanced courses increased an average of 38 hours. In the same period, more than 500,000 enlisted men received some training on counterinsurgency topics.[52] Andrew Krepinevich, though, points out that much of what was reported as counterinsurgency instruction in fact dealt with operations against irregulars and partisans behind the lines of a mid- or high intensity war. Or, common subjects such as map reading and civil defense training were placed into counterinsurgency training programs to beef up the appearance of complying with the president's directives.[53] These subjects had always been taught; just their location within the program of instruction changed to reflect the new emphasis. As for the political and social aspects of counterinsurgency, these subjects apparently remained the near-exclusive province of training for Special Forces soldiers at Ft. Bragg. The revamped Special Forces Groups contained Civil Affairs and Psychological Operations soldiers who were trained to improve the lives of host nation citizens and distribute propaganda, both with the intention of strengthening the citizenry's support for the local government.[54]

TRAINING THE UNITS

The next step in the training process was the application of the new doctrine in unit training programs. Due to President Kennedy's intense personal interest in counterinsurgency, the Army revamped its Special Forces. Rather than focusing on operating behind enemy lines, they now concentrated on fighting insurgency. They would now train and utilize indigenous forces for counterinsurgency efforts. However, there were a few bizarre attempts to capitalize on the new notoriety that was the result of the President's personal attention. For the sake of good publicity, Special Forces soldiers were detailed to form a "Green Beret Drum and Bugle Corps," a precision military drill team known as the "Kennedy Rifles," a "Green Beret Chorus," and to present an average of five demonstrations per month of skills such as rappelling, sky diving, and snake skinning to dignitaries visiting Fort Bragg.[55] Without doubt, the training involved in such activities contributed little to the war effort.

For the vast bulk of the Army, counterinsurgency remained a distinctly secondary mission, even for the five brigades designated as back-up forces for the Special Forces Groups. The Army's view on the training necessary for counterinsurgency is best summed up by quoting the Army's Chief of Staff in the early 1960s, General George K. Decker: "Any good soldier can handle guerrillas."[56] In practical terms, what did this sentiment mean for the average soldier in conventional units? In the units where most of the enlistedmen were trained, the counterinsurgency exercises often were conducted as adjuncts to European war scenarios which involved multi-division assaults against similarly armed foes.[57] Conventional units underwent training for counterinsurgency that generally treated the subject at the lowest possible tactical level, that of a dismounted patrol.

This training technique had special appeal in that it required little change in conceptual focus for the conventional soldier. At the level of squads and platoons, all patrols are essentially the same, whether conducted in a counterinsurgency environment, or in an environment dominated by clashes of armored forces.[58] A telling comment on such thought comes from an Army Aviation School study in 1957 on the tactical utility of helicopters: "The required forces, then, for the small war appear to be much the same as those for the atomic war against the Soviet Union."[59] Given this tactical mind-set, a thorough reorganization of Army training to wage counterinsurgency appeared, therefore, unnecessary to the Army mainstream.[60]

ALTERNATIVE EXPLANATIONS

EXPLANATION I: CIVILIAN-MILITARY INTEGRATION AND THE SEARCH FOR A MAVERICK

The counterinsurgency era has much in it to suggest that civilians sought to force the Army to modify its preparations for war to meet changes in perceived strategic needs, particularly with respect to low intensity conflict. "President Kennedy entered office deeply impressed with the significance of this form of communist-inspired aggression...."[61] According to General Maxwell D. Taylor, Kennedy also "repeatedly emphasized his desire to utilize the situation in Vietnam to study and test the techniques and equipment related to counterinsurgency...."[62] On 11 May 1961, Kennedy signed National Security Action Memorandum 52 which authorized a significant increase in training and advisory strength in Vietnam, including the dispatch of 400 Special Forces soldiers.[63] The president's views had much support from other civilians within the administration, too. In June 1961, W. W. Rostow, then Deputy Assistant to the President for National Security Affairs, told Secretary of Defense Robert McNamara that "We shall need forces to support a counter-guerrilla war in Vietnam...." In Rostow's view, the forces required included Special Forces and "militia teachers."[64] Rostow's views were supported by other officials such as Roger Hilsman, Michael Forrestal, and the President's brother, Robert. On the other hand, the president also understood "that the Army is not going to develop in this counterinsurgency field and do the things that I think must be done unless the Army itself wants to do it."[65]

The civilian leadership of the United States had identified a new threat and sought to get the military to respond. The president and his advisors issued many directives concerning forces and training. As Posen suggests, the military resisted. Roger Hilsman records that newspapers in April 1961 carried stories that the Chairman of the Joint Chiefs, General Lyman Lemnitzer, feared that too much emphasis on counterinsurgency would impair efforts to make the South Vietnamese Army able to withstand conventional invasion from the north. Moreover, Lemnitzer "felt that the new administration was 'oversold' on the importance of guerrilla warfare...."[66] The Chief of Staff of the Army, General Earle G. Wheeler, after 22 months of emphasis on counterinsurgency by the Kennedy administration, stated in a speech at Fordham University on 7 November 1962 that the problems in South Vietnam were essentially military, and not economic or political, as the counterinsurgency specialists had maintained. Hilsman saw this as proof that "an important segment of the military did not accept the emphasis on political warfare."[67] Even though the president had clearly placed his faith in the Army Special Forces as counterinsurgency experts, by early 1963, of 22 generals assigned to Vietnam, none had a Special Forces background.[68]

From the discussion of doctrine and training above, it is obvious that the civilian administration applied a variety of pressures to get the Army to change more rapidly to face the counterinsurgent threat. After becoming dissatisfied with the Army's progress, the president even went to the extreme of speaking to the assembled ranks of all of the Army's major commanders to exhort them to greater efforts on 30 November 1961.[69] In a further attempt to ensure that his wishes would be obeyed, the President established the Special Group (Counterinsurgency), chaired by a former Army Chief of Staff, General Maxwell Taylor. The first function of the group, as listed in National Security Action Memorandum 124, was to "ensure proper recognition throughout the U.S. Government that subversive insurgency ('wars of liberation') is a major form of politico-military conflict *equal in importance* to conventional warfare."[70]

According to Posen's study, civilian intervention needs the cooperation of some military figure to have the highest chance of success. During the counterinsurgency era, though, no maverick appears. Nor did the Kennedy or Johnson administrations actively seek the use of such a person.

Potential mavericks were available. One of the most obvious was Brigadier General Edward Lansdale. Lansdale had cut his military teeth in the OSS and particularly in the Huk Rebellion in the Philippines. He also had two years of experience in South Vietnam after the French withdrew.[71] Here was a military officer without wide conventional experience, but one with long experience in "subterranean war." Despite attaining the rank of brigadier general without conventional experience, Lansdale's future as a military leader was severely circumscribed. As a U.S. Air Force officer with primarily experience in counterguerrilla land operations, it was unlikely that Lansdale would ever be called upon to command the larger formations of the military services at the divisional or higher level. On the other hand, the fact that he had spent much of his adult life in uniform, coupled with his recognized abilities in diplomacy and fighting guerrillas, would have given him the legitimacy unavailable to any civilian to lead a counterinsurgency revolution in the armed services.

Although he travelled to South Vietnam at the behest of the president, the Kennedy administration did not follow through with the advancement of Lansdale to a higher position of responsibility. According to Hilsman, Kennedy's failure to advance Lansdale was due to Pentagon opposition.[72] Rostow maintained that the reasons for Kennedy's rejection of advice from others, such as General Maxwell Taylor, to appoint Lansdale as the head of counterinsurgency efforts in Vietnam, "lay deep in the American military and the civil bureaucracy. The American ambassador and the ranking general in Saigon - and the departments backstopping them in Washington - did not want another American that close to Diem."[73] There is also evidence that even Taylor eventually found Lansdale "too unconventional, garrulous, and independent."[74]

General Maxwell Taylor, the officer credited with providing one of the strongest arguments for Flexible Response, was also available to act as a maverick in the sense meant by Posen. Recalled to active duty as the Military Representative of the President, he had enormous influence on the president.[75] His credibility within the military was unquestioned. His arguments had been responsible for getting the Army recognized as a viable strategic force after the dark years of Massive Retaliation. His efforts had brought increased resources and prestige to the Army.

GENERAL MAXWELL D. TAYLOR
U.S.A. (RET.)

★ ★ ★ ★

THE
UNCERTAIN
TRUMPET

GENERAL TAYLOR CONTENDS:

★ that the doctrine of massive retaliation has endangered our national security;

★ that our military planning is frozen to the requirements of general war;

★ that weaknesses in the Joint Chiefs of Staff system have left the planning of our military strategy to civilian amateurs and the budget-makers.

And General Taylor presents a new national military program to correct the resulting critical deficiencies.

Why consider Taylor a maverick? His views on the inadequacies of Massive Retaliation and on the Chiefs of Staff system had caused damage to the outgoing Eisenhower administration and fueled the Kennedy campaign's criticisms of Eisenhower's presumptive heir, Nixon.[76] Seeing Taylor as a maverick is, therefore, quite possible. Here was a general who had commanded an airborne division in World War II and the Eighth Army in Korea, and who served as Army Chief of Staff; yet, he found the moral courage to stand against the reorganization of the Army in particular and the military in general to wage the most unlikely of wars - high-intensity nuclear war. General Taylor's publication of *Uncertain Trumpet* in 1960 marks what one could see as his passage into the ranks of military maverick.[77] Taylor retired as President Eisenhower's Army Chief of Staff in July of 1959, and set about writing a book whose cover proclaimed "the doctrine of massive retaliation has endangered our national security" and "our military planning is frozen to the requirements of general war."[78] His public criticisms of Republican defense policy endeared him to the Kennedy campaign.

Kennedy sent Taylor to Vietnam to assess the counterinsurgency effort there. As mentioned above, Kennedy also gave Taylor the job of establishing and chairing the interagency Special Group (Counterinsurgency) to provide oversight for the various counterinsurgency programs that the administration had initiated.[79] After dealing with a recalcitrant military for a year-and-a-half, the president appointed Taylor Chairman of the Joint Chiefs of Staff on 1 October 1962.[80] In 1964, President Johnson would send him to South Vietnam as the U.S. ambassador. Much of the early U.S. effort in Vietnam can be laid at the feet of Taylor and the reports and studies he made of the situation in Indochina, particularly in his first year with the Kennedy administration.[81]

If Taylor was a maverick, however, it was only in the political sense that he had opposed what the Eisenhower administration's New Look had done to the Army.[82] In opposing the Eisenhower policies, Taylor was seeking to make the Army more capable of handling non-nuclear conflict. Thus, in this way, his opinions were in accordance with those of the Kennedy administration. Further, Taylor's views that the Army had greater strategic utility than was thought certainly would have coincided with the general view of most active duty Army officers. However, if Taylor sought to increase the Army's capabilities, he did so only for mid-intensity conflict. It was

Taylor's views on counterinsurgency that most limited his usefulness to Kennedy. When asked about the Army's capabilities to handle the special problem of counterinsurgency, Taylor responded, "We good soldiers are trained for all kinds of things. We don't have to worry about special situations."[83]

Posen had touted Air Chief Marshall Dowding of RAF Fighter Command as a prime example of a military maverick.[84] However, Rosen argued that anyone who had a career as successful as that of Dowding *before* the advent of British air defense, could not be considered a maverick in the true sense of the word.[85] Seeing Taylor as a maverick suffers from the same problem. In superficial form, Taylor resembles a maverick. Yet, given his pattern of assignments, particularly his service as Army Chief of Staff under Eisenhower, no officer could have been more mainstream. Certainly his advocacy of Flexible Response against the military strategy of Massive Retaliation is the one basis for labeling Taylor a maverick, but a maverick only as seen from outside the military organization. Within the Army, his advocacy of flexibility which would entail greater resources for reorganization, re-training, and rearming for a future ground conflict in Europe would not have been greeted skeptically by the Army officer corps and would certainly have satisfied Army claims to a special and enduring expertise in land warfare - an expertise in need of protection from other services.

Hence, he was not a maverick of the sort needed to embed new thinking for counterinsurgency. Furthermore, Taylor does not appear instrumental to the changes that did occur. In all likelihood, the Kennedy administration's counterinsurgency efforts, continued by President Johnson until the commitment of conventional units in 1965, would have happened without Taylor. Taylor himself records President Kennedy's desires "to utilize the situation in Vietnam to study and test the techniques and equipment related to counterinsurgency..."[86] It is highly likely that Kennedy would have pursued these ends without the aid of Taylor.

One other potential maverick existed in the Kennedy administration - Roger Hilsman. Hilsman made trips to South Vietnam and made direct comments to the president about what he perceived as the errors of the counterinsurgency efforts. Hilsman's views should have had wide credibility within the administration because he was a West Point graduate who had served in the China-Burma-India theater training guerrillas to operate behind Japanese lines. Certainly Hilsman's writings reflect a high degree of sensitivity to the problems of waging guerrilla warfare.[87] Hilsman did not like the large force conventional operations he observed on his visits to Vietnam. He preferred the strategic hamlet program advocated by such experts as Sir Robert Thompson.[88] Hilsman was instrumental in getting the president to accept the hamlet program as the key to the Vietnamese counterinsurgency effort.[89]

But, by the time Hilsman served in the Kennedy administration, he had been out of the military for more than a decade. Therefore, he would have had little legitimacy within the military ranks which surely hampered his abilities to make the kind of changes expected of a true maverick. President Kennedy perceived that Hilsman's views would be so unpopular with the Army that he even mentioned ensuring that Hilsman be protected from their wrath.[90]

This is a similar problem with other potential mavericks from within the military ranks, men such as Brigadier General William P. Yarborough, the commander of the Special Warfare Center. He could have been quite useful to the Kennedy administration's effort to inculcate counterinsurgency thinking and tactics in the Army. However, the Kennedy administration "rejected advice that (it) reach down into the lower ranks for a counterinsurgency-oriented officer...to command in Vietnam because of the shock this would have administered to the Army's career expectations..."[91] The Kennedy administration's counterinsurgency programs and Vietnam policies had already provoked significant opposition within the services. Roger Hilsman suggests in his memoirs that the president refused to push further for fear of creating open "political civil war" over Vietnam.[92] In conclusion, in this case, no maverick is apparent.

EXPLANATION II: INTRAORGANIZATIONAL INTERGROUP CONFLICT

In Rosen's case on the development of amphibious warfare doctrine within the U.S. Marine Corps, the visionary conceptualizer was Major Earl H. Ellis. Ellis's vision was that the Marine Corps should be the force given the mission of seizing island bases in any future war in the Pacific. Such an amphibious force would have to be much larger than the Marine Corps then was, and would need new equipment - in short, the Marines would become a major service like the Army or the Navy. Ellis's ideas were adopted and advanced by two Marine Commandants, first General John A. Lejeune in the early 1920s and then General John Russell in the mid-1930s. Russell inculcated the new doctrine by having it widely taught in Marine Corps schools. He created pathways for promotion by persuading the Navy to create a Fleet Marine Force permanently stationed with the fleet, and most importantly, by getting permission to retire older officers whose positions could be filled with young adherents to the amphibious doctrine.[93] Rosen's other cases of successful innovation exhibited a similar process.

Intergroup conflict within the Army lies embedded in the background of the counterinsurgency era. As the Army revitalized under Flexible Response, that conflict sharpened. That no "revolution" in military matters occurred suggests that the then dominant group remained in power. That this conflict continued in many ways into the early 1990s suggests that Rosen's approach to military change has substantial relevance. Furthermore, his view that the group dynamics of military change take a generation or more to come to fruition provides a possibly direct link between the counterinsurgency era and the subsequent time periods under consideration.

Three groups are worthy of mention. The first group was composed of those, of all ranks, who became convinced of President Kennedy's belief that counterinsurgency required a "whole new kind of strategy, a wholly different kind of military training." The second group was composed of aviation advocates. The last group was composed of those officers who led the Army in the counterinsurgency era - men with command experience on World War II and Korean battlefields. The evidence of these groups' existence has been noted previously and frequently lies in the background comments of observers, commentators, and scholars.[94] These groups did exist, and the debates within the Army over defense policy in this era can be defined by reference to the competition of these groups for power within the Army hierarchy.

There is evidence of a group of counterinsurgency advocates within the Army of this period. Hilsman concluded that "many people in the Pentagon, in the Special Forces, and elsewhere in the armed services - especially among company and field grade officers - became enthusiastic believers in the concept as a result of their personal experiences in the field...."[95] This group existed at the margins of the Army effort. As Hilsman suggested, the members of the group were probably soldiers directly involved in carrying out counterinsurgency programs.[96] One retired general officer reflected that this group came from the "light stream" within the Army - those people with backgrounds in airborne, ranger, and unconventional operations during World War II and the Korean War.[97] Members of this "stream" moved easily into counterinsurgency operations. Sitting atop this group were probably officers such as Yarborough and Brigadier General William B. Rosson, the Army Chief of Staff's Special Assistant for Special Warfare.

The influence of the counterinsurgency advocates was sharply delimited by their superiors' attitudes and by the lack of a powerful patron. General Decker, the Army Chief of Staff in 1961, had opposed the creation of Rosson's position. He acted immediately to place the bulk of Army activities and units outside of Rosson's purview.[98] President Kennedy, who might have elevated members of this group to prominence, chose not to do so. The effort to get the Army to create a sufficient number of counterinsurgency experts was derailed, as Hilsman put it, by Kennedy's failure to put personnel "blue chips" into the counterinsurgency programs. In this failure, Kennedy was actively supported by the traditionalists within the Army. One officer described the difficulty of getting "blue chips": "in that time frame the prevailing attitude of...Career Management Officers was to advise a good guy to avoid Special Forces like the plague."[99] Another officer recalled that Special Forces officers "weren't guys with great career expectations. If they were lucky, they were going to get their 20 years.... There was nobody that had any expectation of making colonel."[100] It was unlikely that officers in branches other than Special Forces would have found advocacy for counterinsurgency any healthier for their careers.

The other group that "lost" during the counterinsurgency era was the aviators. The Army used helicopters extensively in Korea for the evacuation of wounded. The Army also used helicopters for limited resupply, command and control, and transport of soldiers in Korea.[101] By the mid-1950s, the aviators had at least one senior leader, General James Gavin, a hero from World War II airborne operations, as their principal enthusiast. Their other principal senior leader was Lieutenant General

Hamilton Howze, who chaired two Army boards on aviation (1957 and May-October 1962) and one on special warfare (January 1962).

In the report from his first aviation board, Howze put forth the idea that helicopters could give the Army the mobility it required on the atomic battlefield. This same report also claimed that this same mobility would be useful in small wars, too. The report of the Howze Board on Special Operations of January 1962 made the dramatic recommendation that Special Forces be considered as ancillary to counterinsurgency. The primary forces would be conventional units. The Board's suggestions were dramatic: three divisions and three brigade battle groups should be given counterinsurgency as their primary mission. Moreover, these units should be restructured by introducing large numbers of helicopters, making them in effect, airmobile divisions.[102] The Howze Board of May-October 1962, which was accompanied by tests of the airmobile concepts by several units, was more modest. This board too studied counterinsurgency as a special subject.[103] The results of this board, though, were a major factor in convincing Secretary of Defense McNamara to authorize a more comprehensive test of air mobile units. This led to the creation of the 11th Air Assault Division (Test) that would eventually deploy to South Vietnam as the 1st Cavalry Division (Airmobile).[104]

The aviation advocates, much more than the counterinsurgent group, got a fair hearing of their views. Under Gavin and Howze, the group staked a claim to the transforming ability of helicopters before, and several times during, the Kennedy administration. Some scholars, including Rosen, point to the inclusion of helicopters in Army units as evidence of a fundamental innovation in warfare.[105] The experience of the counterinsurgency era, however, belies the notion of fundamental change.

Perhaps the most distinguishing characteristic of the Vietnam War was the helicopter. The thump-thump-thump of helicopter rotors is now standard fare as background noise for TV shows and movies about the era. Helicopters were touted as ushering in a new way of war - the sky cavalry, air mobile, or air assault operations. Eventually, the Army would acquire more than 12,000 helicopters.[106] In Vietnam alone, the Army would have 3500 more aircraft than the U.S. Air Force.[107]

The need for increased mobility on a nuclear battlefield gave rise to the first calls for expanded use of helicopters. The budgetary restrictions, though, of the Eisenhower years allowed for little except conceptualizing.[108] Two things changed this: first, the Kennedy administration's emphasis on revitalizing the armed forces; next, the Taylor-Rostow mission to Vietnam in 1961. The report from the Vietnam mission called for the expansion of the use of the helicopter as a means of overcoming the mobility differential which generally favors guerrilla forces.[109] Consequently, several hundred helicopters were sent to Vietnam. The Secretary of Defense, Robert McNamara, who had initially proposed cutting Army aviation spending, also became interested in air mobility as a cost effective means of increasing combat power for all forms of conflict.[110]

Yet, did the introduction of large numbers of helicopters fundamentally change the way the Army fought in Vietnam? For the individual infantryman who otherwise would have walked into battle or rode in ground transportation, or for the wounded soldier awaiting evacuation, the change was drastic. For the Army as a whole, despite the claims of Army aviation advocates, the advent of helicopters did not revolutionize the waging of counterinsurgency.

Early advocates of the helicopter foresaw warfare conducted entirely from the air.[111] General Howze had grandiose dreams for the helicopter. When commanding the XVIIIth

Airborne Corps in 1962, Howze "felt that these aircraft could effect a tactical revolution 'as profound as the mechanization of warfare by the introduction of the gasoline engine'...."[112] That was not to be. In fact, the addition of the helicopter to the battlefield required the average soldier to learn little beyond safety tips for mounting and dismounting. Planning for their use required little more of officers, too. Although helicopters were expensive, they premised rapid increases in battlefield mobility at little cost to the organization's established repertoires. Such mobility was thought crucial to overcome the advantage that guerrillas have on home terrain. Additionally, they greatly strengthened the Army's autonomy by reducing the need to call upon the Air Force for close air support and short-range transport.[113]

Despite the benefits of the helicopter to counterinsurgency, the limits of the helicopter for counterinsurgency became apparent early on. The second Howze Board on aviation, officially titled the Tactical Mobility Requirements Board, concluded that cargo helicopters could not completely replace the jeep. Nor could anti-tank helicopters completely replace ground anti- tank weapons.[114] The helicopter, far from ushering in a completely new style of warfare, became ancillary to established operations. Indeed, the Army's test of airmobility was decidedly set in mid-intensity, European- style scenarios.[115] As one critic of helicopter use in counterinsurgency put it, Army units in Vietnam became "air-mobile; [but] the troops they carried were not necessarily ground-mobile."[116] Other critics suggest that it was the helicopter that made possible the often misused "search and destroy" missions. Furthermore, helicopter mobility led the South Vietnamese Army to abandon its outlying bases to cluster around helicopter fields in the more urbanized areas, thus increasing the separation of the South Vietnamese people from their government's protectors.[117]

The final picture left to us by the expanded use of helicopters in the counterinsurgency era is one of, at best, an unfinished revolution. Helicopters became more of an infantry support vehicle, much like the use of the tank in the first twenty years of its existence.[118] By the time the "test" of the airmobile concept was concluded in the summer of 1965, the counterinsurgency era was over, and the war of conventional units began.[119] Even though helicopters were added to all divisions in the Army, the aviation group "lost" in that they failed to revolutionize the Army. Aviation did not become a separate branch within the Army until the 1980s. Only one division was created along airmobile lines (and one gets the impression that even this was done grudgingly). And, helicopter forces did not become the arm of decision as the horse cavalry once had been and armored forces still are.

The Army leadership of this period, the third group, is the group that can be said to have "won." The Army that emerges from the counterinsurgency era in 1965 was clearly this group's creation. What the Army leaders knew of guerrilla warfare came from World War II and Korea, and this knowledge was reinforced by the experiences of aiding and advising the governments of Greece and the Philippines as they fought off communist-inspired insurgencies in the decade after World War II.[120] In short, these leaders thought they knew how to wage war generally and how to handle guerrillas in particular.[121]

According to Hilsman, the Korean War had indelibly shaped this group's attitude toward limited war. They chafed at the restrictions the civilian administrations had placed on the use of force in that war. As a whole they were disinclined to get involved with another land war in Asia, but if they did, they wanted authorization to use to the utmost the military resources they had. Hilsman said that people in Washington began to refer to this group as the "Never Again" Club.[122]

Although individual Army leaders, such as Chiefs of Staff Decker and Wheeler and certainly General Taylor, were influential, the men who led the Army are better taken as a group with a strong, unifying common background. Because the Army leaders are better taken as a group, Rosen's explanation gains in credence. Although the Army leadership has been criticized for an ossified approach to war and counterinsurgency, the period 1961-1965 shows amazing willingness to adapt - the introduction of helicopters, reorganization of the basic divisional structure, mobilization of reserves for the Berlin and Cuban crises, and the various counterinsurgency programs.[123] Revolution may not have happened, but change certainly did, but only within the parameters established by the leadership group's view of warfare.

This group led the reorganization of the Army along the lines of the ROAD concept. This reorganization harked back to the glory days of the Army in World War II. As Major General (later Chief of Staff of the Army) Harold K. Johnson put it, "The basic fighting structure to which we are returning is one with which most of us have a reasonable familiarity."[124] This was so because the ROAD division "represented a logical extension of the armored division and its combat commands which had evolved from World War II through the post-Korean War years."[125]

The Army leadership bent all other suggestions for revamping the Army to fit within the ROAD concept. Thus, because the Army needed responsive close air support and much greater mobility to operate in dispersed units under tactical atomic threat, the leadership agreed to expand Army aviation by doubling the number of aviation assets in ROAD divisions as compared to Pentomic divisions.[126] They agreed to establish an entire airmobile division as a test case to prove their point. They did not, however, let aviation take over the Army. When the president contended that counterinsurgency was a "special art," the leadership responded by requiring "[a]ll infantry units...to be made proficient in counterinsurgency as *an added* duty."[127] As for the growing conflict in Vietnam, "the Chiefs envisioned 'a peninsula and island-type of campaign - a mode of warfare in which all elements of the Armed Forces of the United States have gained a wealth of experience and in which we have excelled both in World War II and Korea.'"[128] The Army that deployed in large numbers to fight in Vietnam in 1965 was the creation of this group, but it was not structured and trained for the kind of war it was sent to fight.

CONCLUSION

The period 1961-1965 has been the special focus of academics and policy makers because of the U.S. strategic failure in Vietnam. Many of the leaders of government, academe, and the military in the 1980s and 1990s cut their political teeth either in the counterinsurgency phase of the Vietnam conflict, the conventional phase, or both. Consequently this focus was understandable in human terms. The increased tensions of the Cold War in the early 1980s, and the return of insurgencies as troubling arenas of U.S. foreign policy, reinforced this understanding. Hackneyed though the phrase may be, nobody wanted "another Vietnam." The similarities between the early 1960s and the early 1980s made the counterinsurgency era worthy of comparison.

Central to this case were the notions of "change" and "revolution" in military organizations. Both events can have serious policy consequences. The Rosen and Posen models focused on wide military transformations. I have argued that peripheral changes are also worthy of investigation, and are amenable to explanation using models such as Rosen's and Posen's. While the Army did not revolutionize itself, it did change in the early 1960s by adding counterinsurgency to its repertoire, albeit in a subordinate ranking to the main mission of defending Europe.

Of the two competing explanations under investigation, Posen's approach should have worked well. This case had an external threat in the form of Khrushchev's "wars of national liberation." The case had a civilian executive committed to radical military change in that the president and his civilian advisers sought to make counterinsurgency "equal in importance to conventional warfare."[129] There were a few maverick officers available to lead the change from within. These factors made it a good case for testing Posen's contentions.

Yet, Posen was strangely silent in his work on when the external-internal alliance of civilians and maverick should work, and when it should not. In Posen's case on French doctrine of the 1920s and 1930s, he notes that civilian governmental leaders in the 1920s had forced a defensive doctrine on the military. That doctrine no longer matched French national strategy in the mid-1930s when the French diplomats were forging alliances with East European countries, and particularly after 1936 when Belgium declared its neutrality. Those alliances and the Belgian declaration required a French offensive capability that did not exist.[130] Posen notes that there were even officials and officers who recognized these needs, and consequently some measures were taken to strengthen the French military.[131]

What kept the civilians from intervening more vigorously? It was a combination of fears about the internal political conflict that a mobilization would generate, fears that it was too late to disrupt the armed forces with wholesale change, and fears of upsetting allies such as Britain.[132] In the case of counterinsurgency the civilian intervention did not work because of 1) civilian acceptance of superficial indicators of change; 2) poor choices of personnel to lead a transformation of the Army;

3) the strength of the group that led the Army; and 4) fears of upsetting the bureaucratic status quo within the government.

The president himself had ordered the Army to change. His civilian administrators demanded evidence of change, and evidence they got. Yet, they were often naive, as demonstrated by Robert Kennedy's comment to General Taylor, "Why can't we just make the entire Army into Special Forces?"[133] Within eighteen months of the order, the Joint Chiefs of Staff reported that hundreds of thousands had been trained; that officer education on counterinsurgency had been dramatically increased; that additional Special Forces units had been created.[134] Yet, as then-Brigadier General Yarborough would later recall, "this was obviously an attempt to give the President what he kept demanding of the military. And yet it wasn't - it wasn't done properly.... "[135] Perhaps because of the sheer numbers involved, the administration civilians too readily accepted such reports.

Where a Posen-style "maverick" was called for, President Kennedy chose officers with views that did not match his own. He chose Maxwell Taylor who clearly felt that any good soldier could handle guerrillas. While quickly easing out General Decker - the Chief of Staff that Kennedy inherited from Eisenhower - the president replaced him with another non-believer, General Earle Wheeler. What kept the president from utilizing those, such as Lansdale or Yarborough? Apparently it was the fear of upsetting established bureaucratic norms and relationships. The State Department objected to suggestions that Lansdale or Yarborough be put in charge of the effort in Vietnam for fear that such a move would diminish the U.S. ambassador's role.[136] The Defense Department, and particularly the leadership of the dominant group in the Army, also opposed any such action, and Hilsman reports that Kennedy heeded their protests out of a desire to avoid "political civil war."[137]

In similar fashion, the president also had difficulty deciding between the CIA and the Army over control of Special Operations. National Security Action Memorandum 52 had sent 400 Special Forces soldiers to Vietnam in late 1961, but to function under the CIA which still had ostensible control over unconventional activities in peacetime.[138] In National Security Action Memoranda 57 and 162, Kennedy again returned to this unclear delineation: "Where such an operation is to be wholly covert or disavowable, it may be assigned to the CIA, provided that it is within the normal capabilities of the agency."[139] Operations not wholly covert, or too large to be covert, were to be under control of the Defense Department. The controversy continued until 1964 when the Army regained control of the Special Forces. In trying to please all agencies, the president severely weakened his own programs.

Rosen's vision of a military organization as a collection of contending communities fares better. Three main groups are identifiable in this case: counterinsurgents, aviators, and the Army leaders then in power - the traditionalists. A telling blow to Posen's external-sources-of-change explanation is also that the Army itself had undertaken some changes in counterinsurgency programs prior to the advent of the Kennedy administration. The advocates of airmobility had set forth their challenge on innovative tactics for both mid-intensity conflicts and "small wars" in the 1957 Howze Board report. In 1960, General Lemnitzer had ordered U.S. advisors in South Vietnam to switch from training the ARVN for conventional war to training for antiguerrilla war.[140] In early 1961, several doctrinal manuals associated with counterinsurgency appeared, suggesting that their genesis predated President Kennedy's arrival. Perhaps these changes reflect the early influence of the counterinsurgency advocates, but more probably they reflect willingness of the Army leaders to accept missions clearly subordinate to the main mission. In this light, one might fairly argue that the Kennedy administration's efforts merely spurred on a process already underway, rather than being the primary source of change.

On the other hand, Rosen's approach does not give enough credit to the impact of civilian pressure from outside the military. As Harry Summers put it in the late 1970s, "Twenty years later, it is hard to envision the force with which the concept of counterinsurgency struck the Army."[141] The Army did expend enormous effort to comply with the wishes of the Kennedy administration. Army leadership was also acutely aware of the administration's perspective, as a memorandum from General Lemnitzer, Chairman of the Joint Chiefs of Staff, to General Taylor clearly demonstrates:

> "With respect to training the Vietnamese Army for the "wrong war" it seems clear that in recent months the insurgency in South Vietnam has developed far beyond the capability of police control. All of the Vietnamese army successes this past summer have met Viet Cong opposition in organized battalion strength."[142]

While aware of the administration's views, and while, by virtue of their constitutional positions, the Army leaders were willing to respond to civilian pressure, the leaders disagreed with the civilians and their views on what was necessary. Most of the Army efforts to comply, as General Yarborough pointed out, were not expended exactly in the direction that the civilians wished. The Army's efforts at counterinsurgency were filtered through the requirements of the organization's main mission. Consequently, neither the Posen nor the Rosen model adequately explains the exact course of events in this case.

A synthesis of civilian pressure and organizational group conflict is necessary. In this case, the Army adapted to the counterinsurgency mission in the manner that it did because the Army was dominated by the traditionalists. This group accepted some of the demands made on it by outside civilians and their counterinsurgent or aviation allies inside the organization. However, the traditionalists' belief that the Army must devote most of its efforts to the European mission caused all other efforts to be bent in that direction. The civilians acted to change the Army, but they chose traditionalists as their agents for change. As a result, what the civilians got was peripheral change of the kind that could easily be reversed when civilian pressure disappeared.

Chapter 3 Endnotes

[1] Roger Hilsman, *To Move A Nation: The Politics of Foreign Policy in the Administration of John F. Kennedy* (Garden City, NY: Doubleday, 1967) 411.

[2] See in particular Michael T. Klare and Peter Kornbluh, "The New Interventionism: Low-Intensity Warfare in the 1980s and Beyond," *Low-Intensity Warfare*, ed. Michael T. Klare and Peter Kornbluh (New York: Pantheon Books, 1988) and D. Michael Shafer, *Deadly Paradigms* (Princeton: Princeton, 1988) ix.

[3] In the 1980s, three extensively researched works appeared that do a fine job of describing and explaining the origins of U.S. counterinsurgency doctrine. Much scholarly work has thus already been accomplished. I will extract from these works and others the material necessary to test the Posen and Rosen models. See Shafer as well as Larry Cable, *Conflict of Myths* (New York: New York University Press, 1986) and Andrew Krepinevich, *The Army and Vietnam* (Baltimore: Johns Hopkins, 1986). Other secondary works which figure prominently in this chapter are Richard K. Betts, *Soldiers, Statesmen, and Cold War Crises* (Cambridge, MA: Harvard University Press, 1977), and Leslie H. Gelb and Richard Betts, *The Irony of Vietnam: The System Worked* (Washington, DC: Brookings, 1979). Where necessary I will incorporate primary sources to clarify or expand on points relevant to the competing explanations.

[4] One of Shafer's cases is a study of counterinsurgency doctrine in 1950s France. He uses this case appropriately to exclude one of his competing explanations. It also lends some credence to the approach he favors in the U.S. cases.

[5] For Posen, Air Chief Marshall Sir Hugh Dowding was the prime example of the maverick. At other times, Posen refers in the same vein to General Heinz Guderian in Germany in the 1930s. See Barry Posen, *The Sources of Military Doctrine* (Ithaca: Cornell University Press, 1981) 174-175, 207-213.

[6] Betts 48.

[7] Hilsman 414.

[8] W. W. Rostow, *The Diffusion Of Power: An Essay in Recent History* (New York: Macmillan, 1972) 265.

[9] Amos A. Jordan and William J. Taylor, ed., *American National Security: Policy and Process*, revised edition (Baltimore: The Johns Hopkins University Press, 1984) 72.

[10] Hilsman 53.

[11] Shafer 104, cites Hilsman 413. See also Krepinevich 29. Kennedy passed out copies of Khrushchev's "wars of national liberation" speech for NSC members to read.

[12] Shafer 104.

[13] For the impact of insurgency as a tactic in the bipolar confrontation, see Shafer 240-242. For the influence of academics within the Kennedy administration, see Shafer 110-115.

14 "Address before the American Society of Newspaper Editors, 20 April 1962," *Public Papers of the President, 1961* (Washington, D.C.: USGPO, 1962) 306. In the same address, Kennedy said that the armies and nuclear weapons of the adversaries of the United States "serve primarily as the shield behind which subversion, infiltration, and a host of other tactics steadily advance...."

15 Lieutenant Colonel John J. McCuen, *The Art of Counter-Revolutionary War: The Strategy of Counter-Insurgency* (Harrisburg, Pa.: Stackpole Books, 1966) p. 78. Emphasis in original. Quoted in Shafer 110. Shafer cites this as a representative example of conventional wisdom in the early 1960s. See also Charles M. Simpson, *Inside the Green Berets: The First Thirty Years* (Novato, CA: Presidio, 1983) 67: "Why couldn't a team developed and trained to organize and advise a guerrilla battalion be used to organize and advise a paramilitary counterguerrilla battalion?" Simpson entered the Special Forces in 1959. He eventually served as the Deputy Commander for the 5th Special Forces Group which controlled all Special Forces in Vietnam from mid-1965 on.

16 *The Pentagon Papers*, Senator Gravel ed., vol. II (Boston: Beacon Press, 1972) 688.

17 Quoted in Shafer 112. Note how these phrases are similar to the phrases used to describe the threat posed by low intensity conflict 20 years later. See Chapter 5 below.

18 The genesis of this paragraph and the next is Shafer 112- 113. Shafer took this material from the USOIDP 14-17.

19 Douglas S. Blaufarb, *The Counterinsurgency Era: U.S. Doctrine and Performance, 1950 to the Present* (New York: Free Press, 1977) 72-73.

20 Krepinevich 105.

21 These figures come from Major Robert A. Doughty, *The Evolution of U.S. Army Tactical Doctrine, 1946-76* (Ft. Leavenworth, KS: U.S. Army Command and General Staff College, 1979) 19.

22 This was the "Modern Mobile Army 1965-1970" (MOMAR I) study. Doughty 19.

23 Doughty 20-21.

24 Colonel Francis J. Kelly, *U.S. Army Special Forces, 1961- 1971* (Washington, D.C.: Department of the Army, 1973) 6-7. This was the early official Army history of the use of Special Forces in Vietnam. Colonel Kelly commanded the 5th Special Forces Group in Vietnam, 1966-1967.

25 These figures come from Krepinevich 103-5.

26 Krepinevich 103.

27 Center for Military History, "Historical Perspective on Force Structure Reductions, 1946-1988," undated briefing slides.

28 See Krepinevich's discussion of the Stilwell Report and the Howze Board, 105-110.

29 Krepinevich 110-111.

30 Simpson 70.

[31] FM 31-21 *Guerrilla Warfare and Special Operations Forces* (Washington, D.C.: Department of the Army, 1961); FM 31-15 *Operations Against Irregular Forces* (Washington, D.C.: Department of the Army, 1961).

[32] Quoted by Krepinevich, 44. The Howze Board, named after Lt. Gen. Hamilton Howze who chaired the proceedings, was also known as the Special Warfare Board.

[33] See FM 100-5 *Field Service Regulations: Operations* (Washington, DC: Department of the Army, 1962) and FM 7-10 *Rifle Company, Infantry and Airborne Battle Groups* (Washington, DC: Department of the Army, 1962).

[34] It is interesting to note that in the revision of the 1993 edition of FM 100-5, low intensity conflict once again appeared as a special chapter.

[35] FM 100-5, 1962, 127; quoted by Cable 119.

[36] FM 100-5, 1962, 130; quoted by Cable 119.

[37] FM 100-5, 1962, 139; quoted by Cable 120.

[38] FM 7-10, 1962, -1-5; quoted by Cable 115.

[39] FM 7-10, 1962, 179; quoted by Cable 123.

[40] FM 31-16, 1963, 21-22; quoted by Cable 125.

[41] FM 31-16, 1963, 22; quoted by Cable 127.

[42] For an account by one of the founders of U.S. Army Special Forces, see Aaron Bank, *From OSS to Green Berets* (Novato, CA: Presidio Press, 1986). Also, Doughty 25.

[43] Other examples of the use of guerrilla-style warfare to support larger conventional goals are Merrill's Marauders and the Chindits in the China-Burma-India Theater in World War II. Also, note that these operations behind enemy lines were often designed to incite popular resistance against invading forces, which is in accordance with Clausewitz's notions of "People's War." See Carl von Clausewitz, *On War*, ed. and trans, by Michael Howard and Peter Paret (Princeton: Princeton University Press, 1976) 479-483.

[44] See FM 31-20 *Operations Against Guerrilla Forces* (Washington, DC: Department of the Army, 1951).

[45] Shelby L. Stanton, *The Rise and Fall of an American Army: U.S. Ground Forces in Vietnam, 1965-1973* (Novato, CA: Presidio, 1985) 5.

[46] The Special Forces had also been operating in similar capacity in Laos since 1959. They operated first under covert civilian cover under the control of the Programs Evaluation Office (PEO), which itself was under the direction of the Central Intelligence Agency (CIA). More than 100 Special Forces soldiers operated in small groups known as "White Star" teams, training the Royal Laotian Army. In 1961, the training program was put under the control of the military advisory group in Laos, thus ending CIA control. See Simpson 67-93.

[47] Kelly 14, 46-47. Stanton 10.

[48] Krepinevich 32. The State Department was also ordered to develop and teach a counterinsurgency course to "everyone who was going to the underdeveloped countries...no matter what department they came from or how high they ranked." Henry Cabot Lodge attended the course before

assuming ambassadorial duties in Saigon. Hilsman 415.

49 Doughty 26. Krepinevich also lists useful information on the number of hours the various Army schools expended on counterinsurgency subjects in early 1960s. See Krepinevich 46-53.

50 Krepinevich 33. This mandatory schooling of "top notch" officers in the ways of counterinsurgency at the direct behest of the president is similar to the 1986 Defense Reform Act's requirement for joint education and service as a prerequisite for promotion to brigadier general in the current military.

51 Simpson 68. Simpson also notes that by 1965 the Army ordered the Special Forces to accept first-term enlistees and Second Lieutenants. Previously, the Special Forces chose only volunteers who were already veterans.

52 These figures come from Blaufarb 70-71. Blaufarb took them from a July 1961 report to General Taylor from the Joint Chiefs of Staff.

53 Krepinevich 46-47, 51. It is also interesting to note that Blaufarb records that the July 1961 report touts the number of soldiers given language training, but no languages are specified. Clearly, the Army had officers in language training before the Kennedy initiatives, and some of those languages - Spanish and French, for example - could easily have been counted as having counterinsurgency value without the Army having changed its program at all. The same is true of Blaufarb's note that of the half-million enlistedmen trained, some had been trained in underwater demolitions, psychological warfare, and air rescue. Again, these programs are not specifically counterinsurgency oriented. See Blaufarb 70-71.

54 Simpson 69, chapter 15.

55 Simpson 68-69.

56 Quoted in Krepinevich 37.

57 Krepinevich 51, 53-55.

58 The Army still used this training technique for many of its forces intended to participate in low intensity conflict in the 1980s and1990s. As the Assistant Commandant of the John F. Kennedy Special Warfare Center and School described to me in an interview, most of the tasks required of soldiers in low intensity conflict reinforce what the soldier would have to do in "warfighting" - that is, in a mid- or high intensity conflict. Interview with Colonel Mack Dorsey, Fort Bragg, NC, 10 February 92. It was also common in the Corps of Engineers in the 1980s to refer to the "fantastic training opportunities available in Latin America." What the Army engineers were actually doing in Latin America was a form of nation assistance, or nation-building, which clearly fell within the purview of low intensity conflict doctrine. However, the focus remained on the experience derived from deploying and operating in such undeveloped theaters. This experience was seen as useful just in case a "real war" should break out. The Army shied away from using the word "operating" in favor of the word "training" to describe these Latin American efforts. See the author's *In War's Shadow: Waging Peace in Central America* (New York: Ivy, 1992).

[59] Quoted in Doughty 28. This is analogous to the humorous aphorism "the dog we keep to lick the cat can lick the kittens."

[60] Shelby Stanton described the early training: "Although units were still expected to fight on a conventional European battlefield, their training was applicable to any combat situation." Stanton 25.

[61] Maxwell D. Taylor, *Swords and Plowshares* (New York: W. W. Norton, 1972) 200.

[62] Taylor 202.

[63] *Pentagon Papers*, vol. 11, 50 At the end of Kennedy's first year, troop strength in Vietnam went from 700 to over 3200. See Gelb and Betts 80.

[64] *Pentagon Papers*, Vol. II, 67.

[65] Quoted in Krepinevich 31.

[66] Hilsman 415-416.

[67] Hilsman 426.

[68] Hilsman 455.

[69] Krepinevich 31.

[70] *Pentagon Papers*, Vol. II, 660. Emphasis added.

[71] See Hilsman 419-420. For a general account of Lansdale's background, see Edward G. Lansdale, *In the Midst of Wars* (New York: Harper and Row, 1972).

[72] Hilsman 419.

[73] Rostow 278-279.

[74] Betts 132-3.

[75] Taylor 197.

[76] Douglas Kinnard, *The Certain Trumpet: Maxwell Taylor and the American Experience in Vietnam* (New York: Brassey's, 1991) 52.

[77] Maxwell D. Taylor, *The Uncertain Trumpet* (New York: Harper Brothers, 1960.

[78] See the image of the cover of *The Uncertain Trumpet* at http://www.amazon.com/gp/product/images/B0027NM0AG/ref=dp_image_0?ie=UTF8&n=283155&s=books, accessed 11 October 2012.

[79] The Special Group contained representatives from the Defense Department, State Department, Central Intelligence Agency, National Security Council, and U.S. Information Service, among others. See Krepinevich 31.

[80] Rostow 161.

[81] Taylor himself admitted, that as the Military Representative of the President, he exerted enormous influence on the president. Taylor, *Swords and Plowshares*, 197.

[82] Cable 116. Cable cites *The Uncertain Trumpet* 23.

[83] Quoted in Krepinevich 30.

[84] Posen 175-175.

[85] For a discussion of the problem of seeing Dowding as a maverick, see

Stephen P. Rosen, "New Ways of War: Understanding Military Innovation," *International Security*, Summer 1988, 134-168.

[86] Taylor, *Swords and Plowshares*, 202.

[87] See Hilsman 425 and 435-6 on the correct manner of fighting guerrillas. He provides a list of five tasks necessary for good counterinsurgency.

[88] *Pentagon Papers*, vol. II, 132, 142.

[89] William J. Rust, *Kennedy in Vietnam* (New York: Charles Scribner's Sons, 1985) 68. This is a paraphrasing of Rust's points.

[90] Hilsman 438.

[91] Blaufarb 82.

[92] Hilsman 508.

[93] See Rosen, *Winning the Next War*, 66-67, 82-84.

[94] See Betts 127, and Frederic A. Bergerson, *The Army Gets an Air Force: Tactics of Insurgent Bureaucratic Politics* (Baltimore: Johns Hopkins, 1980).

[95] Hilsman 578-579.

[96] Hilsman's point about contending groups can be illustrated by reference to Army publications of the era. The Association of the United States Army, an association led by retired officers and whose members are largely active and retired soldiers, acts as the Army's lobby. *Army* magazine, the association's monthly publication, should be considered as having quasi-official status as a voice of the Army, at least on the same level as *Military Review* and *Parameters*, the periodic publications, respectively, of the Command and General Staff College and the U.S. Army War College. In March 1962, *Army* published "Big Push in Guerrilla Warfare," which asserted that the thrust of President Kennedy's ideas was not all that different from General Decker's belief that any good soldier could handle guerrillas. In August 1962, *Army* published "Retooling for Guerrilla War," a rejoinder by Major Charles K. Nulsen, an officer with years of experience teaching at the Special Warfare Center. Major Nulsen contended that, on the contrary, the Army was not ready to fight the Viet Cong, or any other communist-inspired insurgency, because staff officers and commanders did not understand the essentially political nature of this style of conflict.

[97] Interview with General (Retired) John R. Galvin, West Point, NY, 21 July 1993. As a young officer, General Galvin had been part of the "light stream." He eventually served in Vietnam in both armored and air mobile units, and was one of the Army officers detailed to compile what became known as the "Pentagon Papers".

[98] Krepinevich 43.

[99] John C. Woolshlager, oral history interview with Major General (retired) John K. Singlaub, page 98, Senior Officer Oral History Program, U.S. Army Military History Institute, Carlisle, PA. Singlaub commanded the Military Assistance Command, Vietnam, Studies and Observations Group (MACVSOG), 1966-1968. Galvin gave a similar impression of Special Forces soldiers in his 27 July 1993 interview.

[100] Edward A. Fitzsimmons, Jr., oral history interview with Colonel (retired) J. H. Crerar, Special Operations and Low Intensity Conflict Oral History Project, U.S. Army Military History Institute, Carlisle, PA.

[101] Bergerson 71. See also John R. Galvin, *Air Assault: The Development of Airmobile Warfare* (New York: Hawthorn, 1969).

[102] See Krepinevich 108-109.

[103] "Irwin School's Summer Term: How the 'Howze Board' Did Its Work," *Army*, September 1962, 76.

[104] Bergerson 112-116.

[105] This is the point of Bergerson. See also Kevin Patrick Sheehan, "Preparing for an Imaginary War? Examining Peacetime Functions and Changes of Army Doctrine," Ph.D. dissertation, Harvard, 1988, and Rosen, *Winning The Next War*, 71-75, 85-95. Although all three scholars deal with organizational change, in these works heavy emphasis is placed on the impact of technology. Sheehan's study dealt with changes in the governing army doctrine found in the Field Manual 100-5 series. He concluded that technology was the primary cause of changes in Army operational doctrine. His view is that the U.S. Army has changed rather incrementally to adapt to enhanced, rather than revolutionary, technology. Rosen, *Winning The Next War*, 72, concluded that Army changes were prompted "by technology rather than increased international political commitments." Technology can thus be seen as part of the general security environment.

[106] Bergerson 82.

[107] Bergerson 1.

[108] Doughty 28. The first Howze Board on aviation was held in 1957. There simply was not enough money in the Army budget to act on the recommendations.

[109] Krepinevich 109.

[110] Krepinevich 115. Galvin 276. Doughty 27-29.

[111] Krepinevich 113.

[112] Galvin 278. In the 27 July 1993 interview, Galvin noted that those in the "light stream" always hoped that technology would provide the firepower and mobility to win battles and survive on a battlefield of any intensity.

[113] Sheehan's findings tend to indicate that doctrine changes to incorporate new technology into existing missions - the same conclusion that Vincent Davis reached with respect to nuclear technology and the changes to U.S. Naval doctrine in the 1950s. Rosen cites this conclusion of Davis's in footnote 1, page 134 of Rosen, "New Ways of War". It comes from Vince Davis, *The Politics of Innovation: Patterns in Navy Cases* (Denver: University of Denver Press, 1967) 7, 15. Posen also advances this idea, attributing it to Bernard Brodie and Edward L. Katzenbach. See Barry Posen, *The Sources of Military Doctrine* (Ithaca: Cornell, 1984) 55. This certainly seems to be the case with the helicopter in the Army.

[114] "Irwin School's Summer Term," 78.

[115] Doughty 29.

[116] Krepinevich 113.

[117] The British expert on counterinsurgency, Brigadier Sir Robert Thompson held the first view. The other views are the assessment of Betts. For both, see Betts 137.

[118] Non-aviators in the Army still often refer derisively to Army and Air Force cargo pilots as nothing but "glorified truck drivers." By extension, attack helicopter pilots are just "glorified artillery." However, the vision of the helicopter as the arm of decision for the Army, replacing the tank, was still around in the 1980s. Chris Demchak cites Brigadier General Huba Was de Czege as holding this view. Was de Czege was one of the principal authors of the 1982 edition of AirLand Battle. See Chris C. Demchak, *Military Organizations, Complex Machines: Modernization in the U.S. Armed Services* (Ithaca: Cornell, 1991) 43.

[119] McNamara ordered the conversion of the 11 Air Assault Division (Test) to the 1st Cavalry Division on 28 June 1965. On 2 August, the lead elements of the division left for South Vietnam. See Galvin 287. Krepinevich notes with some irony that the Special Forces, which were structured especially for counterinsurgency in this period, never deployed their augmented groups to South Vietnam as intended. Instead, when the Army went into Vietnam in large numbers, the first unit to go was the airmobile unit which was devoted to mid-intensity European warfare. It was followed by even more conventional ROAD divisions. One can easily see the influence of the school of thought that held "any good soldier can handle guerrillas."

[120] The ramifications of this collective experience form the basis for the explanations of Shafer, Krepinevich, and Cable.

[121] See Chief of Staff of the Army Decker's quote on any good soldier above.

[122] Hilsman 129. This view of the disinclination of the military to fight in Asia contrasts sharply with many of the, often superficial, views of this period and after of the military as an organization "chompin' at the bit" to get into the Vietnam War. Oliver Stone's *JFK* is a veritable gold mine of such stereotypes. If any "chompin'" was going on, it is likely that it was being done over how the war should be fought - by an elite cadre of counterinsurgency specialists, or by firepower heavy, standard units.

[123] General Taylor records in his memoirs a rarely emphasized fact of the period - that the Army taught counterinsurgency and practiced civic action in more than a dozen countries during this era. Taylor, *Swords and Plowshares*, 202.

[124] Address to the U.S. Army Command and Staff College in May 1961. Quoted in Doughty 21.

[125] Doughty 21.

[126] Doughty 21.

[127] Blaufarb 80. Emphasis in original.

[128] Rust 63. This is a cite from JCS MEMORANDUM 36-42 to the Secretary

of Defense, entitled "The Strategic Importance of the Southeast Asia Mainland."

[129] National Security Action Memorandum 124, 18 January 1962, *Pentagon Papers*, vol. II, 660.

[130] See Posen 121-127.

[131] Posen 128-129.

[132] Posen 127, 129, 133, 139. French diplomats feared that any preparations that appeared too aggressive might cause the British to fear being dragged into a war.

[133] Quoted in Krepinevich 35.

[134] Blaufarb 70-71.

[135] John R. Meese and Houston P. Houser III, oral history interview with Lieutenant General (retired) William P. Yarborough, Senior Officer Debriefing Program, U.S. Army Military History Institute, Carlisle, PA.

[136] Rostow 278-279; Betts 131-132 Gelb and Betts 85.

[137] Hilsman 419, 439, 508.

[138] *Pentagon Papers*, vol. II, 445.

[139] Quoted from National Security Action Memorandum 162, 19 June 1962, *Pentagon Papers*, vol. II, 683

[140] Krepinevich 42.

[141] Summers 100.

[142] Memorandum for General Taylor, SUBJECT: Counterinsurgency Operations in South Vietnam, 12 October 1961, from General L. L. Lemnitzer, Chairman, Joint Chiefs of Staff, *Pentagon Papers*, vol. II, 651.

CHAPTER 4

DISTASTE AND IGNORING PERIPHERAL CONFLICTS: YEARS OF DENIAL, 1965-1979

It is also of importance that we should understand in what way our power, great as it is, can be challenged by a few thousand ragged jungle fighters armed with a dedicated leadership, a tested theory, and great patience. Too many have fallen back on the easy excuse that we failed in Indochina because our power was constrained and leashed, that more bombs, more destruction, more firepower was the answer.

— Douglas S. Blaufarb[1]

While U.S. performance in Vietnam is most notable for sheer conventionality and slowness to adapt, it would be misleading to ignore the many examples of adaptive change designed to meet felt needs. Naturally, most of these were the sort of relatively modest, evolutionary, or frequently technological changes that the institutions involved could fit into their existing repertoires without much destabilizing impact.

— Robert M. Komer[2]

For almost the entire Vietnam War we believed and acted on the enemy's people's war propaganda even in the face of considerable evidence to the contrary. . . . The guerrillas in Vietnam did not achieve decisive results on their own. Even at the very end there was no popular mass uprising to overthrow the Saigon government.

— Colonel Harry Summers[3]

Stephen Rosen argued that innovation in peacetime is drastically different from innovation during war. Rosen noted that militaries,

> "exist in order to fight a foreign enemy, and do not execute this function every day. Most of the time, the countries they serve are at peace....Instead of being routinely 'in business' and learning from ongoing experience, they must anticipate wars that may or may not occur."[4]

As a necessary consequence, most of the learning and changing that militaries do in peacetime is speculative. On the other hand, in wartime, militaries are "in business" and are presented with daily examples of what does and does not work. Additionally, because of casualties and the political implications of failure, the military organization is under extreme pressure to fix any problems as rapidly as possible.[5]

Since organizational failure is often said to provoke organizational change, what about the learning potential from a lost war? According to Rosen, this potential has been overstated: "Defeat by itself does not tell a military organization what future wars will look like, only that its preparations for the war just ended were not adequate."[6] Rosen also noted that learning after defeat is hampered by the composition of the officer corps, which only knows the methods that failed.

This chapter will address the impact of the strategic defeat in Vietnam on the U.S. Army in the years immediately after the war. To understand fully this impact it is necessary to explore the climate created within the Army by the Vietnam experience. While this project is about changes in the Army during peacetime, the experience gained by many Vietnam-era soldiers in the arenas of counterguerrilla operations, internal defense and development (IDAD) programs, and unconventional warfare missions affected their willingness to deal with non-standard missions in the years after the war.

Consequently, this chapter will address the significant Army developments in these mission areas after the advent of the main force war in 1965, and in the years immediately after the U.S. withdrawal from Southeast Asia.

All of the misconceptions discussed in chapter 2 above undergird much of the debate in this era: 1) low intensity conflict is limited war; 2) A war is a war is a war; 3) low intensity conflict equals special operations; and 4) low intensity conflict is revolutionary war, or low intensity conflict is counterinsurgency. These misconceptions flow out of the patterns of Army history for dealing with insurgents, guerrillas, and unconventional warfare operations, which were also discussed in chapter 2. The first three were solidified during the counterinsurgency era when policy makers sought to treat the war as possibly another Korean-style conflict, or sought to handle it as an undertaking akin to OSS operations, in World War II, or sought to utilize soldiers trained for the conventional conflict in Europe. All of the misconceptions were strengthened after the introduction of North Vietnamese and U.S. regular forces. They hardened in the period immediately thereafter, thus strengthening the resolve particularly of the dominant group within the military.

In this period, civilians external to the military exerted less influence on military reform than they had in the early 1960s. Civilians were, nevertheless, quite active in changing the sociological basis of the military primarily through the creation of the All-Volunteer Army and by the expansion of opportunities for women and minorities. Other than setting broad budgetary constraints, civilian activism regarding the specific organization and equipping of the forces for future conflict was weak, with the notable exception of President Jimmy Carter's request in 1977 that the Army create a special counterterrorism capability.

In the absence of imposing demands by civilians, Posen's structural view of organizations indicates that militaries would seek maximum simplicity and autonomy, often through the crafting of an offensive military posture. For this case to support the Posen model, the Army would have to fashion, in the wake of Vietnam, an offensive posture in terms of forces, training, and doctrine, to handle the future requirements of its main mission. In very strong terms, Posen said, "There is little in organization theory or the civil-military relations literature to suggest that modern militaries will prefer anything but offensive doctrines, if such doctrines are in any way feasible."[7]

Rosen's human resources view of organizations does not require civilian intervention to provoke change. It proceeds by investigating the sources and outcomes of conflict among the groups composing the organization. While Rosen claims that "in bureaucracies the absence of innovation is the rule, the natural state," the human resources approach remains useful to describe and explain the dynamics of organizational behavior even in the absence of major change.[8] For this case to support Rosen, it would have to exhibit group conflict, and the ultimate behavior of the Army must reflect the expected patterns of behavior of the group that wins.

The evidence of this case offers substantial support for Posen's model. The Army refashioned itself zealously to wage war in Europe. The Soviet threat in the European theater offered the Army maximum autonomy: because of the distance from the United States, and because of the complexity of the operations, once a war began, the military commanders would control events. While domestic and international political factors made the basic Army doctrine defensive at the *strategic* level, the Army made its *tactics* as offensive as possible. However, Posen's view of organizations is too monolithic in that it misses the dynamics internal to the Army.

On the other hand, the human resources view of organizations is inherently grounded in the internal dynamics. Hence, once again, the evidence suggests that a synthesis of the two models is best. The Posen model explains best the broad policy constraints and their impact on the Army, while the Rosen model better explains the inner workings of the Army.

A synthesis of the strong points of the two models suggests another pathway: changes in the security environment - the surging Soviet conventional threat in Europe and U.S. domestic distaste for further involvement in Vietnam-style conflicts - combined with a lack of civilian activism allowed group conflict within the Army to decide the path that the Army of the 1970s would take. Because the defeat in Vietnam put into disfavor the "counterinsurgency group," identified in the previous chapter, the "traditionalist group" decisively won the internal debate, and enshrined its view of warfare: an updated version of the war that had provided the formative experiences of this group - the armored sweep across Europe in World War II.

THE DEPTHS OF VIETNAM, 1965-72: REJECTING CIVILIAN GUIDANCE: COUNTERINSURGENCY AND NATION-BUILDING ON THE PERIPHERY

The groundwork for Army reactions to low intensity conflict in the mid- to late-1970s was established during the eight years of major U.S. ground combat in Vietnam. In this period, as is often stated nowadays, the Army lost no major ground battle, but still lost the war.[9] Post hoc analysis of Army performance in Vietnam falls into two camps: the counterinsurgency war waged incorrectly, and the conventional war waged incorrectly. The latter view prevailed within the ranks. The critics in this particular school identified the efforts expended on counterinsurgency and nation-building programs to be largely ancillary to the conventional force operations if not purely distracting and wasteful.[10]

On the other hand, counterinsurgency programs continued throughout this entire period of the Vietnam War, experiencing resurgence in the era of Vietnamization. While not peacetime low intensity conflict, the Army experience with counterinsurgency as a sideshow to main combat operations is important to understanding the re-making of the Army in the 1970s. The purpose of the following section is to discern and illuminate organizational patterns of behavior in the Vietnam War that influenced the development of Army training, doctrine, and force structure after the return to peacetime in the mid- to late 1970s.

The major conceptual problem with respect to the Vietnam War is to differentiate the continuation of counterinsurgency programs from the counterguerrilla operations of conventional units. While counterinsurgency programs continued after 1965, they were eclipsed in perceived importance by the introduction of conventional ground and air forces. Working with the definitions established in chapter 2 above, counterguerrilla operations focus on the destruction of guerrilla combat and support forces, regardless of the intensity of the overall conflict.

Counterinsurgency, on the other hand, is broader. Counterinsurgency may focus on the destruction of guerrilla combat capability, but it is also designed to undercut the political support the guerrillas receive from the local populace, the support without which the insurgency will not survive.

In Vietnam, the bulk of U.S. Army forces were devoted to counterguerrilla operations. Such operations were necessary because the North Vietnamese Army and the main force units of the Viet Cong utilized guerrilla tactics - emphasizing small units, stealthy movement, and surprise attacks - even when operating without much popular support. However, a few thousand U.S.

personnel were also devoted to counterinsurgency. By investigating the operations of Army personnel and units assigned to the Civilian Irregular Defense Group (CIDG), the Civil Operations and Revolutionary Development Support (CORDS), the Military Assistance Command Vietnam Studies and Observation Group (MACVSOG), as well as conventional operations, the essential elements of both counterguerriila and counterinsurgency operations become apparent. These operations were in most respects successful, but it was the psychological and political impacts upon the contending groups within the Army, and upon the civilians who either ran, or soon would run, the Department of Defense that is crucial to this case. To assess that impact requires some knowledge of the pattern of Army behavior during the war.

COUNTERINSURGENCY OPERATIONS

The efforts to combat the insurgency that began in the advisory era, 1961-1964, never ended, although they did change somewhat. U.S. Army Special Forces (The Green Berets) had initiated the Civilian Irregular Defense Group (CIDG) program in the early 1960s, in conjunction with the Central Intelligence Agency (CIA). This was a program that aimed to utilize the non-Vietnamese tribes, generally called Montagnards that peopled the highlands of South Vietnam as a combination of border watchers and anti-Viet Cong strike forces. Additionally, the program was aimed at securing some sort of tribal allegiance to the South Vietnamese government, or at the very least reducing Viet Cong access to the tribes. The CIDG program coupled military training with civic action programs designed to improve the lives of tribal members. The CIDG program most closely approximates what the officials of the Kennedy administration probably envisaged counterinsurgency to be. One historian termed the CIDG mission "the most crucial Special Forces task throughout the Vietnam War."[11]

    The CIDG process required a Special Forces "A team" to establish a fortified training camp. Then the team members recruited and trained a "strike force" which then provided defense for nearby villages while a local village militia was trained. Upon completion of training, the "strike force," better trained, better armed, and better led, provided a mobile reaction force to reinforce the village defense forces. As the area was "pacified," the newly trained forces were supposed to be incorporated into the existing South Vietnamese hierarchy of defense forces.[12] On 1 July 1963, the CIA withdrew from the CIDG program, which became the sole responsibility of the Army Special Forces. On that date, Special Forces soldiers in South Vietnam numbered 646, of which 122 were assigned to headquarters units. This small force controlled 14 camps and 50,000 CIDG irregulars.[13] From 1963 until the end of U.S. involvement, though, a shift in the purpose of the CIDG program ensued. Rather than being a program focused on denying the South Vietnamese back country to the Viet Cong, CIDG became a program which also focused on border surveillance, albeit still based upon the general utilization of tribal personnel. By the end of 1965, the number of Special Forces personnel had grown to 1,592. These soldiers controlled 78 camps containing 28,200 CIDG irregulars.[14] By 30 September 1968, there were 3,542 soldiers assigned to the 5th Special Forces Group. The CIDG program then contained 42,000 irregulars in camp strike forces and another 10,000 in mobile strike forces (these latter forces, also known as "Mike Forces," were available for reaction throughout South Vietnam).[15] When General Creighton Abrams assumed command of the Military Assistance Command, Vietnam in 1968, he moved to place the CIDG program totally under the command of the South Vietnamese Special Forces, although the program continued to function in the same manner, but with less effectiveness.[16]

Regular Army soldiers also continued their advisory roles throughout the United States involvement. Many of these soldiers provided advice directly to units of the Army of the Republic of Vietnam (ARVN). This type of advice, which was really a form of security assistance, contributed to counterinsurgency only indirectly through the use of the ARVN to fight the NVA and the Viet Cong. On the other hand, hundreds of advisors were assigned to province and district capitals to advise the Regional and Popular Forces. The latter were militias designed to provide local protection to South Vietnamese villages, and the former were used to respond immediately to local incursions by the NVA and the Viet Cong. These U.S. advisors operated in a hierarchy based at district and province level.[17]

The most dramatic change in the advisory program after the introduction of U.S. ground forces came under the Civilian Operations and Revolutionary Development Support (CORDS) program. The CORDS program was an outgrowth of several years of governmental activity from several agencies in the area of counterinsurgency. By May 1967, President Johnson's key advisors determined that only the military had enough organizational resources to truly carry out an effective pacification program.[18] Consequently, a new office was created in Saigon - Deputy to the Commander, U.S. Military Assistance Command, Vietnam - which was to combine all military and civilian efforts at pacification under one head, and under one integrated program, CORDS. Further, each of the four Corps Tactical Zones comprising South Vietnam would have a civilian deputy devoted to CORDS. All existing province and district advisory staffs, military or civilian, would immediately come under CORDS control. At the province level, there would be only one senior advisor, either civilian or military.

The initial coverage of the program was 250 districts and 12,000 hamlets.[19] At its peak in mid-1969, CORDS employed 6500 U.S. military personnel, mostly Army, and 1100 U.S. civil servants. These Americans supervised over 500,000 South Vietnamese in Regional and Popular Forces, 50,000 Rural Development cadre, and 300,000 South Vietnamese civil servants.[20] CORDS focused not only on defending hamlets and regions, not only on civic action, but also on direct action to root out infiltration by the Viet Cong or the North Vietnamese - what was popularly known as the Viet Cong Infrastructure (VCI). Direct actions included aggressive gathering of intelligence, the arrest of suspected members of the VCI, and even assassination.

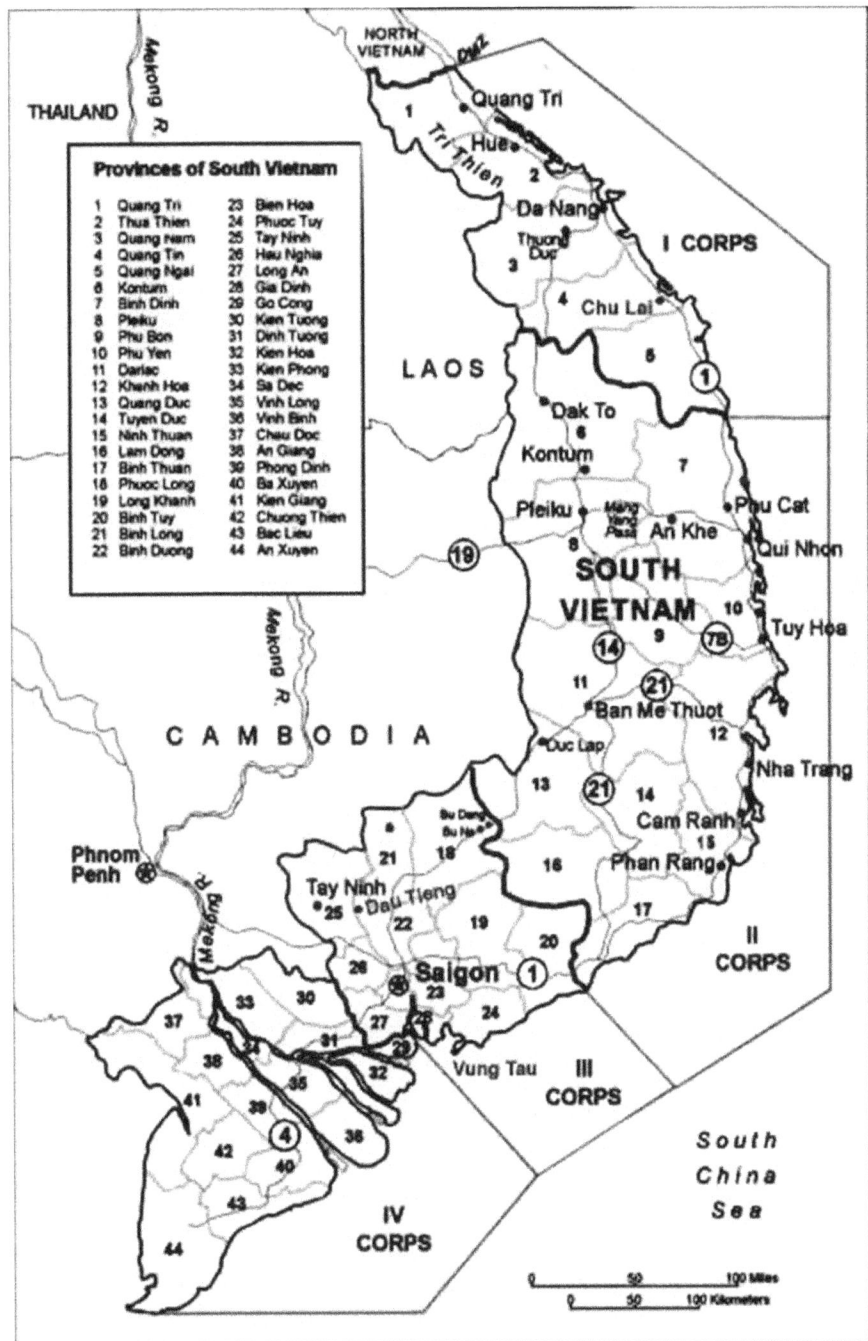

Provinces of South Vietnam

1	Quang Tri	23	Bien Hoa
2	Thua Thien	24	Phuoc Tuy
3	Quang nam	25	Tay Ninh
4	Quang Tin	26	Hau Nghia
5	Quang Ngai	27	Long An
6	Kontum	28	Gia Dinh
7	Binh Dinh	29	Go Cong
8	Pleiku	30	Kien Tuong
9	Phu Bon	31	Dinh Tuong
10	Phu Yen	32	Kien Hoa
11	Darlac	33	Kien Phong
12	Khanh Hoa	34	Sa Dec
13	Quang Duc	35	Vinh Long
14	Tuyen Duc	36	Vinh Binh
15	Ninh Thuan	37	Chau Doc
16	Lam Dong	38	An Giang
17	Binh Thuan	39	Phong Dinh
18	Phuoc Long	40	Ba Xuyen
19	Long Khanh	41	Kien Giang
20	Binh Tuy	42	Chuong Thien
21	Binh Long	43	Bac Lieu
22	Binh Duong	44	An Xuyen

Another program adopted in the post-Tet Offensive years required the stationing of a U.S. Army infantry platoon near a South Vietnamese hamlet. This program mirrored the U.S. Marine successes with Combined Action Platoons. Rather than a small group of advisors, stretched thin by responsibilities across an entire district, this put a sizable unit in place for an extended period, working directly with the Vietnamese. However, this program was not widely used as it appeared just as the U.S commitment to South Vietnam was being curtailed.[21]

COUNTERGUERRILLA OPERATIONS
The other major U.S. efforts in the Vietnam War worthy of investigation in this study were those programs designed to attack directly enemy forces which employed guerrilla tactics. These operations can be dealt with as conceptually distinct from counterinsurgency operations because counterguerrilla operations do not require a focus on the political climate surrounding the insurgency. Counterguerrilla operations are inherently military, and are properly a subset of a comprehensive counterinsurgency program. Counterguerrilla operations are also distinct in that the same methods are available to combat guerrillas operating as adjuncts to conventional operations - partisans. U.S. conventional units conducted the vast majority of counterguerrilla operations in the Vietnam War, although some important operations were conducted by Special Forces.

Operations by guerrillas generally occur best in inaccessible, inhospitable terrain. Guerrillas also blend into the local population, which enhances not only their security but also the collection of information. Guerrilla tactics are much more tactically offensive than defensive, and rely on dispersed small units which combine quickly to create a local numerical superiority. The preferred guerrilla methods are often ambushes or some other small-scale attack, which are most effective against outposts, facilities, or rear areas.

Such tactics require simple weapons and little in the way of logistical support. As one Vietnam veteran and scholar described it,

> "[T]he Viet Cong and NVA relied on dispersion and infiltration, on stealth and deception, on agility and surprise. Only rarely did they stand and fight. Ambush, hit-and-run, attack by fire - those were the traditional tactics. Theirs was a game of slaying the giant by a thousand razor nicks rather than the single blow of a broadax."[22]

How did U.S Army conventional forces counter such operations in the period 1965-1973?

The first division to arrive in Vietnam was the 1st Cavalry Division (Airmobile). This division was the Army's first heliborne division. The purpose behind the testing and fielding of such a unit had been to restore cost-effective mobility to the nuclear battlefield, a concept that was integral to the notions of Flexible Response, the defense doctrine of the Kennedy Administration. However, Defense Department officials felt that the unit could be useful in any kind of war.[23] Such sentiments got a full testing in Vietnam.

The original operations in Vietnam, as represented by the experience of the 1st Cavalry, relied heavily on firepower and aerial movements of large units to cut off suspected lines of enemy retreat. The enemy was an assortment of units, both Viet Cong irregulars, Viet Cong main force battalions, and regiments of the North Vietnamese Army (NVA). All of the enemy units preferred guerrilla tactics.

Heavy bombardments by artillery, helicopter gunships, tactical aircraft, and even B-52 strategic bombers often preceded heliborne assaults in the early years. Some of the firepower "preparations" of landing zones lasted for an hour or more.²⁴ The most common maneuver employed was to land a force near a suspected enemy formation in order to cause the enemy to flee. Simultaneously, another force was dropped into other landing zones to establish blocking positions across the guerrillas' most likely lines of retreat. These tactics were called "hammer and anvil" or "block and sweep."

If successful, the "hammer and anvil" maneuver might be employed repetitively over several days, as occurred during the Ia Drang campaign in 1965. When U.S. intelligence was accurate, this style of counterguerrilla operation could result in heavy casualties for the enemy. In the Ia Drang campaign, the 1st Cavalry killed over 1400 of the enemy. On the other hand, these operations were so huge in terms of the numbers of units and equipment involved, that often U.S. operational security was breached, and the enemy evacuated the landing zones ahead of time. As U.S. operations grew in size until multiple brigades were involved in 1966 and 1967, the enemy began to refuse large scale contacts. In Operation Cedar Falls in January 1967, more than a corps of U.S. and South Vietnamese forces, combining helicopter assaults with the maneuver of armored units, failed to engage any large formation of enemy troops.²⁵ A similar operation several weeks later, Junction City, included an airborne drop as well, with similar results.

Yet, the U.S. Army did change its approach to counterguerrilla warfare while never abandoning the preference for large unit actions. Helicopter mobility made possible "piling on" tactics, whereby air mobile units could quickly reinforce any unit coming into contact with the enemy. To increase the possibility of tactical surprise, units sometimes abandoned initial bombardments.[26] Moving beyond operations that pitted U.S. conventional units against enemy main force units, the U.S. Army also struck at guerrillas in their lairs, or on the move. In a war that had no front lines, these commando-style operations were the closest the Army came to operating "behind enemy lines."

Aside from the use of Special Forces soldiers in the counterinsurgency and advisory efforts, MACV also used them in specially organized teams to conduct reconnaissance and raids. The earliest such unit, finally dubbed Project Delta, was created in May 1964. MACV had the authority to utilize this unit for reconnaissance or raids anywhere within South Vietnam. The Delta unit was a combined effort of U.S. Army Special Forces, South Vietnamese Special Forces, volunteers from tribal CIDG units, and reinforcing elements of the ARVN. Small teams, usually no more than ten soldiers, infiltrated into areas known to contain high concentrations of the enemy. There the team plotted enemy unit locations, supply dumps, and headquarters. They often destroyed or severely damaged these targets by calling in artillery or air strikes. Other teams were built around "roadrunners" - South Vietnamese natives dressed in uniforms of enemy units who travelled down trails in attempts to catch enemy units on the move. Two other "Projects" - Omega and Sigma - were created for the same purposes.[27]

If there was no discernible "front" in the Vietnam War comparable to the front lines which existed in Europe in the First and Second World Wars, the whole of South Vietnam can credibly be seen as the "front." For the North Vietnamese and Viet Cong, consequently, the rear area consisted of their supply bases and supply lines which lay in Cambodia, Laos, and North Vietnam itself. To attack those, the Army created the Military Assistance Command Vietnam Studies and Observation Group (MACVSOG). The name of this staff section, which indicated that it wrote staff reports, was a cover for its real purpose - strategic reconnaissance, strike missions, and interdiction in the areas outside of South Vietnam itself. The mission area included all the countries of Southeast Asia except Thailand.[28] This use of Special Forces soldiers was precisely the mission for which the Army originally created the Special Forces during the Korean War in 1952 - "infiltration deep into enemy territory by land, sea, or air to conduct unconventional warfare - guerrilla warfare, sabotage, and escape and evasion [for downed aviators]."[29]

THE LEGACY OF VIETNAM

What organizational patterns can we discern during the later years of Vietnam that might give us a clue to the Army's behavior in the immediate post-Vietnam era? 1) The Army had a preference for the operations of large units using conventional firepower-oriented tactics. 2) On the other hand, the Army did take part in some dramatic innovation in the prosecution of the war. 3) Even in the realm of counterinsurgency operations, special units and programs often tended to drift away from a focus on the political side of the program and concentrated on the counterguerrilla operations. 4) The effects of the innovations were short-lived.

The Army preference for operations involving large numbers of conventional units is well known.[30] As late as May of 1970, the Army launched Toan Thang 43, a multi-division penetration into Cambodia, involving the heavy use of armored and mechanized forces.[31] The vast bulk of the Army was engaged in such operations. As detailed above, only a pittance was ever involved in true counterinsurgency operations. And as Robert Komer records, this preference for the large war is directly reflected in the Pentagon Papers, which devotes one "slim volume" to the organizational problems of pacification.[32]

Nonetheless, for Robert Komer, who became the chief

pacification advisor as Deputy to the Commander, MACV, the combination of programs eventually lumped together under CORDS, with its official interagency nature, tightly controlled by a hierarchy stretching from the provinces to the command headquarters in Saigon did represent a dramatic innovation. Douglas Blaufarb goes further:

> "The genuine accomplishments of the military in Vietnam...were not the work of the line commanders and their staffs but of military men detached from their units and assigned to CORDS to work as advisers and members of Mobile Training Teams developing the capabilities of Regional and Popular Forces and assisting village chiefs with their security problems."[33]

CORDS "was a unique, hybrid civil-military structure which imposed unified single management on all the diffuse U.S. pacification support programs and provided a single channel of advice at each level to GVN [Government of Vietnam] counterparts."[34] Since the Army had the bulk of the available personnel and material, the Army came to dominate this program. Yet, the pull of the conventional counterguerrilla war was strong indeed. Even the Special Forces, who had been anointed by President Kennedy as his special arm for dealing with "wars of national liberation," found the urge too strong.

Consequently, the Special Forces detachments sent to train Montagnard tribesmen sometimes went to great lengths to change the nature of the program, which had been primarily to develop loyalty to the South Vietnamese government, to use the tribesmen's knowledge of their native terrain to defeat local infiltrations of the NVA and Viet Cong, and to protect the tribal populations from exploitation by the enemy. The Special Forces, however, went far beyond these goals of the CIDG program by forming Mobile Strike Companies (Mike Forces) of CIDG irregulars for use anywhere within the theater. Some of these even received airborne training and conducted combat parachute assaults.[35] Such use of the CIDG soldiers led some critics to dismiss them as "in effect, mercenaries who performed useful service in the remote areas where otherwise the enemy would have had virtually a free hand."[36]

Even the use of the Special Forces to perform strategic reconnaissance and strike missions in the enemy's "rear" was a deviation from the role intended for them originally by the Kennedy administration. The reconnaissance and strike roles were throwbacks to the early days of the Special Forces in the 1950s. However, it was a deviation from the originally intended counterinsurgency mission. In this light, the use of indigenous personnel to augment such unconventional operations reflects the original design of the Special Forces - to support partisan auxiliaries.[37] It was a reflection of the higher profile, more glorious role that the Special Forces would be called to play on any future mid- or high-intensity battle against the Warsaw Pact.[38]

Those soldiers who served as advisors, as adjuncts to CORDS, or in the Special Forces developed a set of experiences and memories drastically different from those who served in the conventional units. But, given that there was innovation by the Army in dealing with the counterinsurgency and counterguerrilla operations, did this experience create a constituency within the service that saw some need to focus Army efforts on non-standard missions such as they encountered in Vietnam? At most, only some 2% of the U.S. forces deployed to Vietnam at the peak of the conflict were involved in the advisory effort.[39] Of these roughly 11,000 soldiers, most were enlisted men or noncommissioned officers. On advisory missions, the percentage of officers to other ranks fluctuated from 20% to 33%, or at most some 3600 officers. Therefore, at the peak of U.S. Army deployment to Vietnam in April 1969, with over 543,000 troops on the ground, of which some 70,000 were officers, about 5% of the officers were involved directly in counterinsurgency.[40] Therefore of the veteran officers who shaped the post-Vietnam Army, the group most involved with the counterinsurgency program was far outnumbered by the veterans who participated in the conventional war. It should not be surprising, based on numerical strength alone, if this former group found it difficult to influence the course of the Army. I will investigate this further below.

THE ARMY RESPONSE: COPING WITH CHANGE

The U.S. security environment had changed significantly by the end of U.S. ground combat involvement in Vietnam in 1972. In 1969, the Nixon administration abandoned the notion of maintaining the military capability to fight two-and-a-half wars simultaneously (that is, wars in Europe and Asia, plus a smaller war somewhere in the developing world). The administration replaced this strategy with the Guam Doctrine, which called for a one-and-half war strategy (a war in Europe and a smaller war elsewhere).[41]

A seminal document describing the origins and process of this internal strategic debate is the "Astarita Report."[42] The report is actually a printed version of a three-hour oral seminar developed in 1973 and 1974 by a small group of specially selected officers. These officers worked directly for the Office of the Deputy Chief of Staff of the Army for Operations and Plans (ODCSOPS). The then Secretary of the Army, Howard Calloway, and the then Chief of Staff of the Army, General Creighton W. Abrams established the mission of the group as nothing less than "to determine if there was a legitimate role for conventional strategy and for the Army in the post-Vietnam world."[43]

The group, formally known as the Strategic Assessment Group, and its subsequent report, came to be named after its leader, Colonel Edward F. Astarita. The group's briefing, however, enjoyed no formal status. Nonetheless, because of its wide dissemination throughout the agencies involved in national defense, the report was decisively influential. The Astarita Group gave the briefing more than 100 times from the Fall of 1973 through the Spring of 1974.[44]

In the introductory pages, one is struck by verbiage quite similar to that used in the early 1990s to describe the post-Cold War world. References were made to the "vexing problems" of economic competition with Japan and West Europe; promising opportunities for "pursuit of parallel interests" with the Soviets and Chinese.[45] The authors at one point quoted a Yugoslav political commentator's opinion that "the United States has won the Cold War."[46] The report paints a picture of a multipolar world of global interdependence that was shrinking ever more rapidly; where the developed world was dependent upon trade; where the shrinking economic world may have "obviated" the usefulness of military force.[47] Much was made of the difficulties and imprecision inherent in trying to chart a course for the future in a rapidly changing world.

The report was also very specific in addressing the changing domestic constraints on U.S. security policy. It noted the end of the bipartisan foreign policy consensus. It also recognized the continuing competition between welfare and defense, with defense having a declining percentage of the federal budget. Perhaps most importantly, the report highlighted the potential policy problems for the military that might arise from an intellectual elite hostile to the military while still, rhetorically at least, committed to idealism abroad. "Ironically," the report noted, "the very persons who decry America's past role as a 'world policeman' are the very same persons who demand that the United States 'do something' about massacres in Burundi, civil war in Chile, and unrest on the Indian subcontinent."[48]

Consequently, the strategic thinkers in the Army concluded that despite a world that might require the upholding of U.S. interests in many regions, "For the foreseeable future this repugnance will tend to limit foreign involvement to those areas where hard tangible United States interests are unequivocally involved."[49] These thinkers further surmised, from the Army perspective, that the only region that sufficiently engaged U.S. interests was Europe.[50] As this report clearly demonstrates, the leadership of the Army in the immediate post-Vietnam era had begun to justify a shift away from the distasteful low intensity conflict missions. The civilian leadership of the nation had forced those missions on the Army in the 1960s; in the absence of such civilian interest, the Army was quickly shedding those missions.

In 1973 the Army also began its conversion from a mixed force of professionals and conscripts to an all-volunteer force. In this climate of rapid organizational change, the Army leadership under Chief of Staff General Creighton W. Abrams, set out to rebuild the Army by putting Vietnam behind it. The leadership intended to accomplish this task through an explicit attempt to focus on the mission that most threatened the US.[51] General Abrams and one of his key deputies, General William E. Depuy, the first commander of the Army's new Training and Doctrine Command (TRADOC) personally led this effort. Abrams grounded his efforts on the assumptions about the international and domestic situations found in the Astarita Report. Abrams was particularly determined that the Army never again live through a politically wrenching experience such as Vietnam. Consequently, "Abrams built into the 16-division structure a reliance on reserves such that the force could not function without them, and hence could not be deployed without calling them up."[52] In this manner, Abrams made it very difficult for the Army to deploy and fight, even in Europe, without first requiring the President to go through the politically difficult task of authorizing the call-up of reserves.[53]

In the late 1970s, Army Chiefs of Staff General Frederick C. Weyand and Bernard H. Rogers and TRADOC Commander Donn Starry continued the processes that Abrams and Depuy initiated.[54] The only significant change was a further emphasis on the need for a heavily armored force capable of delivering high volumes of accurate anti-armor firepower. This emphasis derived from General Starry's experience as commander of V Corps in Germany. General Starry's main concern as a corps commander had been countering the threat posed by a quick Soviet thrust across the Inter-German Border (IGB). Starry referred to this threat as the "Central Battle."[55] The concept of the "Central Battle" of the European theater added a concrete geographical and intellectual "focal point [for] all training and combat developments...."[56] This focal point occupied the vast majority of the Army's intellectual efforts until the very end of the decade.

Given these changes in the U.S. security environment, it is necessary to explore their effects on Army behavior as indicated by changes in Army force structure, doctrine, and training.

FORCE STRUCTURE

The focus on the most essential mission - the defense of Europe - required that the Army become more heavily armed and armored. As a result, the consistent theme in force structuring in this period was the upgrading of anti-armor capability. The major concern was providing enough heavy units to defend or reinforce the European theater. General Abrams felt that 13 divisions were too few to meet all of the Army's mission requirements. Further, he was concerned that those units on active duty consisted of too much "tail" and not enough "teeth;" that is, they did not include enough combat units in comparison to those units devoted to supporting combat, but not actually designed to close with and destroy the enemy. Worse yet, the combat units, in Abrams opinion, did not have adequate tanks, armored personnel carriers, helicopters, or the new wire-guided anti-tank missiles.

Adding emphasis to this perceived need were the lessons the Army took from the 1973 Yom Kippur War. The Army analysts noted the incredible lethality of the newest generations of Soviet tanks, anti-tank missiles, and air defense weapons, especially when used in coordinated combination.[57] The analysts and the Army leaders feared that "Vietnam with its infantry-airmobile emphasis, a war falling outside the 20th century pattern of the combining of arms, might have obscured this general recognition somewhat [of a tactical revolution based on weapons advances]."[58] These fears led the Army to commission a series of force structure studies: the Division Restructuring Study of 1976 and the Division 86 study, begun in 1978. The focus of these studies was determining the equipment and reorganization necessary to allow the Army to win against the Warsaw Pact on a newly dangerous, high-technology, European battlefield.[59]

Abrams, and his successor Weyand, faced two conflicting objectives. Abrams wanted to increase the active-duty divisions from 13 to 16, but simultaneously he had to operate within the existing domestic constraints, which the Astarita Report had correctly foreseen, of the congressionally mandated manpower ceilings. To accomplish these twin goals, Abrams struck a bargain with Secretary of Defense James Schlesinger in which Schlesinger attempted to restrain further cutbacks in the Army if Abrams would cancel "secondary missions."[60] Given this permission, Abrams reorganized the Army so that 70% of its combat service support units (construction engineers, quartermaster, transportation, etc.), and 50% of its combat units were in either the U.S. Army Reserve or National Guard.[61] One can only speculate if "secondary missions" specifically included what we now call low intensity conflict.

By 1975, the strength of the Army had declined from its mid-1968 peak of 1.57 million to 775,000, shrinking from 19 to 13 active duty divisions.[62] By 1980, the figure would fall to 762,000, but organized into 16 divisions.[63] Of those forces most likely to be used for low intensity conflict missions, the Army, in its search for greater anti-armor combat punch, "envisaged mechanizing all of the remaining light infantry divisions exclusive of one airborne and one air assault division."[64] The special operations forces dwindled in importance, and saw their own missions become more focused on supporting the European theater. By the end of this period, SOF funding was only some $400 million.[65] This sum provided for three understrength Special Forces Groups, two Ranger Battalions, and one Civil Affairs Battalion.[66]

THE DOCTRINE

With a change in national strategy as occurred in 1969, one might expect a change in Army doctrine. This was also the aftermath of defeat and the attendant organizational disillusionment and public disaffection with the Army. As one scholar has put it:

> "Racial tensions and drug abuse among soldiers compounded the sense of defeat that, however gilded, attended withdrawal from Southeast Asia. The Army's theoretically highest-priority unit, the

Seventh Army in Europe, was probably at the lowest state of readiness in its history, the victim of a personnel replacement system in Vietnam that used other major commands as replacement pools, resulting in drastic shortages of officers and noncommissioned officers. Public disillusionment with the war in Vietnam became a general sentiment against all war and all military institutions, especially the Army."[67]

DePuy's part in the rebuilding of the Army in the difficult climate after Vietnam centered on doctrine. DePuy had served as a young infantry battalion commander in the 90th Infantry Division which had slogged its way across Europe in a series of attrition battles in World War II. DePuy missed serving in the Korean War, but did command the 1st Infantry Division in Vietnam. His time in Vietnam convinced him that wars of that nature were "an aberration in the historical trend of warfare."[68] He became convinced, instead, that the Yom Kippur War of 1973 was a precursor of future conflicts. This belief, coupled with his view that the Army was in drastic need of reform to purge the experience of Vietnam, formed the basis for the reform of Army doctrine that he led, largely in person.

In 1973 the Army reorganized by creating a special command - the Training and Doctrine Command (TRADOC) – to handle the production of doctrine. The driving motive was intellectual: once a concept of future warfare was defined and detailed, then the Army, in a rational process, could structure forces, conduct training, and buy equipment to provide the capabilities necessary to implement the concept.[69] General Abrams provided the concept for the initial work of TRADOC:

refocus the Army on Europe. He selected Depuy, a like-minded officer, to codify this concept into doctrine.

This new doctrine, which came to be known as the "Active Defense," was contained in the 1976 edition of FM 100-5. The manual proclaimed,

> "This manual sets forth the basic concepts of US Army doctrine. These concepts form the foundation for what is taught in our service schools, and the guide for training and combat developments throughout the Army. Most important, this manual presents principles for accomplishing the Army's primary mission - *winning the land battle.*"[70]

The manual then clarified exactly what would be the focus of the doctrine - "battle in Central Europe against forces of the Warsaw Pact is the most demanding mission the US Army could be assigned."[71] It further asserted that "the U.S. Army is structured primarily for that contingency."[72] The "battle in Central Europe" referred to the expected defensive battle along the Inter-German Border. As NATO forces would be outnumbered, and perhaps outgunned, they were expected to fight a mobile defensive battle that for political reasons could not be seen as trading German territory for time. Rather, the doctrine emphasized identifying the main efforts of Warsaw Pact thrusts, and the lateral shifting of forces to counter those thrusts.

What about the half-war that might have to be fought outside of Europe or north Asia? This edition, and the reforms of Abrams and DePuy in general, largely ignored that possibility. As the Astarita Report shows, both leaders discounted the likelihood that the United States would engage in another light infantry-dominated Vietnam-style operation in the near future. The historical records of TRADOC confirm how little attention the Army's thinkers paid to any issue that did not affect directly the defense of Europe, even operations in the Middle East.

In Fiscal Year 1977, the records show that "Some attention was given...to the unconventional or 'low intensity' area of warfare. Notwithstanding the Army's central concern with the 'mid-intensity' challenge in Europe imposed by the Soviet force buildup.[sic]"[73] When this topic was broached, TRADOC planners admitted that they had given little consideration to such topics. Nonetheless, the planners "found that no need existed for more studies on the tactical lessons learned in Vietnam, but did plan to begin inclusion of specific low-intensity training and doctrine."[74] Despite this promise of concern for such missions, the doctrinal writers continued to plan for the elimination of all of the remaining "straight-leg" infantry divisions, which raises serious doubts about their commitment to "specific low-intensity training and doctrine." [75]

As for wars outside of Europe, FM 100-5 declaimed that:

> "The US Army may find itself at war in any of a variety of places and situations, fighting opponents which could vary from the highly modern mechanized forces of the Warsaw Pact to light, irregular units in a remote part of the less developed world."[76]

Under what set of conceptual guidelines were units to organize, equip, and train for such foes? "The principles set forth in this manual, however, apply also to military operations anywhere in the world."[77] Or, as General Decker put it fifteen years earlier, "Any good soldier can handle guerrillas." The manual also included a chapter titled "Special Environments" which dealt with operations in extreme environmental circumstances - deserts, jungle, cold weather, and urban areas. Even though some of these sections mention that light infantry might be the best force to use - in the mountains and jungles particularly - the manual continually returns to the importance of good air defenses and the incorporation of anti-tank weapons, subjects suitable only for mid- and high intensity conflict.[78] There are no topic headings or listings whatsoever for insurgency, peacekeeping, contingency operations, or counterterrorism.

As early as Fiscal Year 1975, TRADOC planned to write "how to fight manuals" which were derivative of the philosophy of the Active Defense doctrine. Included was a category for "special operations." However, most of the manuals in this category dealt with specialized subjects such as operations at night, in a desert, jungle, or urbanized areas. The only one that would have fallen under a low intensity category was counterguerrilla operations, which if the record is correct, the doctrine writers felt they knew quite enough about already. By Fiscal Year 1979, there were no new derivative "how to right" manuals that dealt specifically with any low intensity warfare topic.[79]

TRAINING

As the Army ignored low intensity conflict at the highest levels, the training programs at all echelons shifted away from low intensity conflict topics. Programs were reoriented to the European battlefield in the case of the main combat arms (armor, infantry, artillery) and on supporting the European battlefield in the other arms. Special Forces training reverted to pre-Vietnam concerns - aid to resistance forces in support of conventional operations and unconventional warfare.[80]

As the Army revamped its doctrine to take account of the perceived Soviet build-up and the lessons of the Yom Kippur War, the means that the planners utilized to translate the new doctrine into training was the formulation of standard scenarios. TRADOC intended the scenarios to focus on the most probable theaters of conflict: the "criteria for selecting a geographical area for a scenario are: clear U.S. interests present; existence of a threat; development of forces conceivable and feasible; presents representative situation; existence of DA [Department of the Army] interests; answers CD (combat development) interest(s)."[81] This kind of thinking set a high standard for inclusion: "All criteria must be satisfied, exm [sic]: U.S. has clear interests in Mexico, but no threat exists; U.S. interests and enemy threat are present in South Vietnam, deployment of forces is no longer conceivable politically."[82] Note again the reflection of the themes contained in the Astarita Report. The doctrinal writers began work on the common training scenarios almost as soon as TRADOC was created in 1973.[83]

Given the events of late 1973, the first scenario developed was, not surprisingly, the Middle East scenario.[84] The idea was to learn as much about the potential for high-technology armored warfare as possible, and then rapidly apply those lessons to training in the European theater. The progress in developing the common scenarios gives clues to the focus of efforts in the six years subsequent to the creation of TRADOC. After the Middle East scenario, next in importance were the European scenarios. However, the planners intended to develop training scenarios also for the Persian Gulf, Panama, Korea, and Thailand. Originally, only the Panama scenario mentioned a low intensity topic - counterinsurgency.[85]

In February 1977, TRADOC published an information booklet on the common scenarios. The booklet contained the completed scenarios and conceptual outlines of the remaining ones.[86] Of 91 pages, the booklet devoted only a half-page to the Panama scenario. However, the booklet did state that "The Panama Scenario is to be developed in CY77 and will address low intensity warfare...."[87] The scenario was based on an assumption of a six month security assistance program applied against an active insurgency which preceded the deployment of combat troops. Another half-page was devoted to the Thailand scenario which was based upon overt aggression by North Vietnam against Thailand, coupled with an insurgent threat.[88]

By June 1978, the Panama scenario was done. The scenario foresaw the Army "involved in Foreign Internal Defense (FID) -- formerly Internal Defense and Development -- Assistance Operations by providing advice, training, combat support and combat service support; and are conducting unilateral/combined combat actions with indigenous forces in...specific land areas threatened by guerrilla warfare, revolution, subversion, or other tactics aimed at internal seizure of power."[89]   The troop list included the infantry brigade permanently assigned to the Panama Canal Zone, the 101st Airborne Division (Air Assault), and several special operations units. "The primary goal of the scenario is to evaluate US Army Special Forces (USASF) and conventional forces in a LIC situation."[90]

Panama clearly fit the TRADOC criteria for a theater that engaged vital national interests and enjoyed popular support for its defense. The development of the scenario also shows the minor concern over low intensity conflict reflected in the doctrinal section above. Additionally, the fact that the scenario was based on several months of inadequate security assistance, followed by deployment of conventional units to conduct combat, and Special Forces to provide training and advice, reflects the sentiment that the Army had already learned all the lessons of the Vietnam War since the Panama scenario envisaged utilizing exactly the same techniques. Even though this scenario was completed by 1978, most of TRADOC's efforts at producing standard training scenarios were directed at the Middle East and Europe. In fact, before completing the Panama scenario, TRADOC had produced the prototype Middle East scenario, an initial European scenario, and then two more European scenarios, one devoted to theater-level conflict, and the other focused on a short-warning conflict. The Panama scenario, and the counterinsurgency mission of low intensity warfare, never occupied more than six pages out of the more than one hundred devoted to scenarios.[91]

How did the TRADOC efforts affect training with respect to low intensity conflict subjects in Army schools and units? In the officer basic and advanced courses for the Armor and Artillery branches, the hours devoted to low intensity conflict topics dropped to zero by 1975. In the Infantry, officer education devoted barely more than 4% of instruction to low intensity conflict. Of this, many of the subjects were technical in nature, differing little from subjects common to any level of conflict, such as issuing an operations order or planning a battalion defensive perimeter. Ignoring low intensity conflict, or teaching common tasks under a low intensity conflict heading, became a pattern that persisted into the mid-1980s for most branches.[92] When TRADOC was established, it was given the mission of translating the Army's missions into doctrine, and then devising training programs to put the doctrine to work. Hence, if most of TRADOC's efforts focused on Europe, it should not be surprising to find that the actual training that the Army conducted reflected this shift, especially given the forceful views of the Army leaders such as Abrams, Depuy, and Starry.

In the 1970s, the Army turned its organizations, doctrine, and training away from low intensity conflict missions. To understand why the Army did so, it is necessary to investigate the possible causes.

EXPLANATION I: CIVILIAN-MILITARY INTEGRATION AND THE SEARCH FOR A MAVERICK

In this period, civilians intervened to promote the all-volunteer military, to further certain sociological ends such as the greater integration of women, and to set post-Vietnam budgetary limits. This was also the era of detente and congressional investigations of abuses by the Central Intelligence Agency. Detente seemed to promise much lowered tensions in the relationship between the United States and the Soviet Union. The investigations of the CIA were reflective of a general unwillingness to intervene actively abroad.[93] The general themes in national security revolved around defense cutbacks after Vietnam and strategic arms control. The Senate even debated amendments to drastically cut U.S. forces overseas in 1973, 1974, and 1975.[94]

On the other hand, civilians did become interested in the strategic implications of the Yom Kippur War in 1973, and in the growing threat of international terrorism.[95]

In President Carter's first year in office, he was concerned that the U.S. should have a hostage rescue capacity similar to that the West Germans demonstrated in the October 1971 freeing of a hijacked Lufthansa plane in Mogadishu, Somalia. As a result of this concern, Army Chief of Staff General Bernard Rogers ordered the creation of the Delta Force as the main U.S. counterterrorist strike force.[96] The idea for such a force had surfaced in the Army in August 1976, and the Army had done preliminary staff work before President Carter became concerned. However, as a result of the president's personal interest, Delta Force immediately received visibility and resources. While Delta Force's creation is a significant departure from the general downgrading of Special Forces in the 1970s, elements within the Army opposed its creation. Additionally, as was demonstrated in the abortive rescue of the U.S. hostages in Iran, although the force existed, it did not have the appropriate means of transportation and interagency liaison and training to succeed.[97]

President Carter also approved the creation of a Rapid Deployment Task Force in August 1977. However, this force was not created until March 1980.[98] Otherwise, the military operated with little civilian interference in this period, particularly in operational matters. As the military slipped in national priority after the Vietnam War, one might argue that the military restructured itself in accordance with the general thrust of policy coming from the three civilian administrations: it oriented itself to the one mission on which all participants in the defense policy making process could agree - the defense of NATO.[99]

The principal constraints on the Army were budgetary and strategic. Budgetary constraints meant that the Army's total strength was limited and it could not acquire the equipment it wanted as rapidly as it wanted to. The strategic constraints allowed the Army to emphasize Europe, but also forced it, in 1976, to adopt a defensive doctrine in keeping with detente and the sensibilities of European allies.[100]

However, civilians in the wider policy community - including those in academia - were not entirely oblivious to the challenge of low intensity missions. A remarkable RAND report from 1977 records the conclusions of a conference held in October 1976. The conference and its report focused on "U.S. Preparation for Future Low-Level Conflict." The attendees included academics, public officials, and high-ranking military officers. What is remarkable about the tone of the report is that it prefigured much of the debate that would still be raging ten and fifteen years later.

The conference discussed the "types and crises and

conflicts...from incidents of terrorism that conceivably could require the employment of military forces to something less than either the Vietnam War or a conventional NATO confrontation."[101] The participants discussed the implications for U.S. forces in a world where "Small groups dedicated to violence can achieve disproportionately large effects in the world."[102] To gauge those implications, the report suggested, "Assume that our military history was composed of such conflicts as Santo Domingo in 1965, Ulster since 1969, Montevideo from 1967 to 1972, Buenos Aires since 1969, Angola in 1974 and 1975, Cyprus in 1974, Lebanon since 1975, and Saigon (not Vietnam, but *Saigon*) in 1975"[103]

The conference concluded that the U.S. needed Special Operations Forces capable of launching quick strikes, light infantry capable of operating in small or large formations over a variety of rough terrain including urban areas, and precision weapons that could be used discriminately. There was also general agreement that the existing Special Forces and airborne units were not sufficient to the task as they were not adequately trained for urban combat or for counterterrorism operations. These units also did not possess necessary logistics, command, control, and planning capabilities for low intensity operations.[104] Further discussion centered on the need for a joint command to "help organize, train, equip, exercise and test elements of existing combat forces for special types of operations...."[105]

One suggestion was that U.S. Readiness Command - the joint command which was responsible for ensuring the war readiness of all U.S. forces - could be utilized for this purpose. However, the report noted that while Readiness Command was prepared for certain contingencies, with respect to low intensity conflict, in no existing command was there "formulation of the needed tasks [or] testing to determine shortfalls."[106] Other attendees noted the institutional problems associated with creating a low intensity capability - no doctrine, small budgets, negative career incentives, and a paucity of instruction in "irregular warfare" at services schools. Another contention was simply that U.S. forces were still inadequately prepared for the European mission, and any efforts to create forces focused on low intensity missions would dilute this main effort. Even so, the argument went, the capabilities needed for low intensity missions were seen as inherent in general purpose forces, which only lacked the appropriate, additional, training for these missions.[107]

The conceptual muddle contained in the conference report is impressive. Attendees differed widely on the missions contained at the lower end of the conflict spectrum, and on whether such conflicts ought to be seen as a special form of warfare. There was further disagreement on who should be responsible for low intensity conflicts - the Department of Defense for all missions, or whether the Department of State should have special responsibility for terrorism.[108] Nonetheless this conference demonstrates that there were a few civilians who were pushing for a response to low intensity conflict, and they had contacts with uniformed personnel, some of whom, such as then-Major General Edward C. Meyer, would shortly rise to prominence.[109] On the other hand, there were too few prominent government officials at the time - civilian or uniformed - who were willing to listen, let alone act, on the ideas presented. With little civilian interference, no maverick would be necessary and none is apparent. The Army leaders astride this era were mainstream officers - Generals Abrams, Depuy, and Starry.

In the absence of civilian demands, the Army proceeded to devise forces, doctrine, and training in accordance with its own perceived needs. Europe, the theater that allowed the Army to remain large and gave it the greatest possible opportunity for autonomy, became the primary focus. Steps were taken to increase force structure, new weapons systems were designed, and the experience of Vietnam was purged. Even though strategically the Army was required to defend, it made its tactical doctrine as offensive as possible, stressing the lateral movement of troops onto the flanks of attacking forces.

EXPLANATION II: INTRAORGANIZATIONAL INTERGROUP CONFLICT

There is little intergroup conflict in this period because the traditionalists, identified in the counterinsurgency period above, maintained an iron control over the Army. The defining collective experience of this group was forged on the battlefields of Europe and Korea. Vietnam was an aberration that they sought to purge from the Army's doctrine and training. Absent any civilian efforts to the contrary, the traditionalists succeeded in turning the Army away from almost any concern for doctrine, forces, or training for low intensity conflict. Instead, they focused the Army on combating what they perceived to be a surging Soviet threat in Central Europe. This was exactly the problem with defeated militaries which Rosen identified: "Defeat by itself does not ensure that significantly new talent will rise to the top of the officer corps, since the postwar officer corps may well be composed of prewar junior officers trained in prewar methods."[110]

However, it is interesting to note that the counterinsurgent group never went away. As stated above, based on their Vietnam experiences, this group could not have been numerous. Peter M. Dawkins' study of the officers who served as advisors demonstrated that about half felt that their advisory service had damaged their careers.[111] While these officers' careers may have been harmed by any of a number of factors during and after Vietnam, their anxiety is certainly a sure sign that many of them felt outside the mainstream of officers who had served in conventional units during the war. Despite the negatives associated with unconventional assignments, or with the whole topic of counterinsurgency, or any other low intensity subject, some officers persisted after Vietnam in trying to bring more attention to the challenge.

One officer, Colonel Donald B. Vought, serving on the faculty of the Army's Command and General Staff College, surveyed the attitudes of his students in the late 1970s. He discovered that over 82% of these officers thought "subconventional" conflict was the "most likely" conflict that the United States would face in the 1980s.[112]

Vought's interest in low intensity conflict had elicited comment at the RAND conference, too. Vought's basic contentions were that the Army and its schooling systems were ignoring the most likely conflicts of the near future. What was taught about the subject was leftover Vietnam-era instruction on internal defense and development.[113] Aside from Vought, there is very little evidence of the counterinsurgent group's continued existence. TRADOC's Fiscal Year 1977 records show that "TRADOC planners felt that training and doctrine for the unconventional arena should go into the training programs. Late in the period, the headquarters was reviewing recommendations to this end submitted by the Institute of Military Assistance and the Combined Arms Center."[114]

The Institute for Military Assistance was the official name of Ft. Bragg's special warfare center in the mid- to late-1970s. The name change reflected the reduction in the importance of the center with the decline in emphasis on counterinsurgency and other special missions in the aftermath of Vietnam. The name change might also reflect the contentious relations between Abrams and the Special Forces community that began when Abrams took over the command of MACV. Abrams had ordered the Special Forces to turn the CIDG program over completely to the South Vietnamese. He also brought murder charges against the Special Forces commander for the summary execution of a Vietnamese double agent. Finally, Abram's handpicked successor as commander of Special Forces in Vietnam had absolutely no Special Forces training or background, an act that the Special Forces soldiers greatly resented.[115] Whatever the motive, "special warfare" was reduced to mere "military assistance" when Abrams began to restructure the Army.

These actions indicate the degree of dominance the traditional group had over its rivals. If there was a natural place for the counterinsurgent group to congregate, the Institute would have been it. This is probably why the Institute occasionally appears in the records as requesting consideration for training programs in the area of low intensity conflict.[116]

The Combined Arms Center is the official name of Ft. Leavenworth, KS, which contains, as a subordinate entity, the Command and General Staff College. As Vought was a high-ranking officer on the staff and faculty of the college in 1977, it is reasonable to assume that he was probably the driving force behind the request from that quarter that TRADOC consider low intensity conflict as a subject for training programs. The bulk of the evidence, though, demonstrates that though this group existed, it had little influence, and less power to affect the path the Army was on.

CONCLUSION

The leadership of the Army emerged from the Vietnam conflict convinced that such wars would be the anomaly. The leadership was generally disenchanted with the counterinsurgency experience, becoming convinced that only "real" wars were worthy of the Army's attention - the idea that war is a war is a war, but only as long as it is a war, involving lots of high-firepower combat, and not some other use of the military for missions such as nation-building. To the extent that the Army had to worry about missions outside of either Europe or Korea, it would just declare, as it did in the 1976 doctrinal manual, that forces prepared for these major conflicts could handle any other that might arise - low intensity conflict as a lesser included case - or such missions could simply be assigned to the disfavored Special Forces, as was the case with hostage rescue and the creation of Delta Force. How well do the competing models explain such occurrences?

After the establishment of the All-Volunteer Army, civilians essentially left the Army alone. Nonetheless, the Army's actions were in general accord with national policy. In Posen's words, civilian and military policies were "integrated." Since neither civilian nor military leaders wanted anything more to do with messy little conflicts of the Vietnam variety in this period, we are left with saying that there was no cause for the civilians to intervene and no need for the civilians to find and elevate a maverick. Left to its own devices, according to Posen's approach, the military will seek to reinforce what it already knows best. This era certainly supports this contention. On the other hand, Posen's approach does not seek to illuminate the internal dynamics of military organizations. If we seek to explain the full flavor of the Army's actions, and the manner in which those actions occurred, we have to look elsewhere.

Rosen's focus on intergroup conflict permits us to explain the Army's change away from low intensity conflict in terms of the dominance of the traditionalists. This group was able to rebound from the civilian interventions of the 1960s, reversing most of the changes and accommodations they had made with civilian reformers in that earlier era. By directing the researcher to look for intergroup conflict, Rosen's approach does illuminate the manner in which the traditionalists, absent outside interference from civilians, reasserted their dominance. It is interesting to note that the only deviation from the traditional focus on a European-style conflict was when President Carter personally expressed an interest in a non-standard mission - hostage rescue. Even then, the traditionalists succeeded in keeping the resources devoted to that particular mission to a bare minimum. Additionally, whereas Posen's view of organizations, aside from the rare maverick, is monolithic, Rosen's approach leads one to look for groups that "lose," in this case, the counterinsurgent visionaries, who, while not powerful, were still present and agitating.

The evidence of this case offers substantial support for Posen's model. The Army refashioned itself zealously to wage war in Europe. While domestic and international political factors made the basic Army doctrine defensive at the strategic level, the Army made its tactics as offensive as possible. On the other hand, Rosen's focus better explains the process of change within the Army. Hence, once again, the evidence suggests that a synthesis of the two models is best.

The two approaches may be used best to complement each other. Both Posen and Rosen rely on the "environment" which surrounds the military. That environment is described in the Astarita Report, which noted that civilian and military leaders perceived that the main international threat came from the Warsaw Pact, and that domestic opinion prevented involvement in any conflict remotely similar to Vietnam. Since civilian and military leaders were in agreement, civilians allowed the military to prepare for the commonly acknowledged threat as the military saw fit, within the parameters set by domestic opinion.

The military proceeded by almost completely reversing the course the Army had taken in the Vietnam era - counterinsurgency subjects were drastically reduced in schools and unit training, and all but ignored in new doctrine, and light infantry was to be completely mechanized. Special Forces groups were cut from seven to three. This process was more than a mere reflection of an organization reinforcing what it knew best - after all, it knew best at that moment how to wage a war like Vietnam. Rather, the process reflects the dominance of a group which had one specific view of war - an upgraded version of the war waged in Europe thirty years previously, reinforced by the ground war waged in Korea.

The synthesis of the strong points of the two models suggests the following pathway: changes in the security environment, combined with a lack of civilian activism, allowed group conflict within the Army to decide the path that the Army of the 1970s would take. Because the defeat in Vietnam put into disfavor the "counterinsurgency group," the traditionalist group decisively won the internal debate, and enshrined its view of warfare.

Chapter 4 Endnotes

[1] Douglas S. Blaufarb, *The Counterinsurgency Era: U.S. Doctrine and Performance, 1950 to the Present* (New York: Free Press, 1977) 311.

[2] Robert M. Komer, *Bureaucracy at War: U.S. Performance in the Vietnam Conflict* (Boulder, CO. : Westview, 1986) 111. This work is an updated version of Komer's original report on pacification, *Bureaucracy Does Its Thing; Institutional Constraints on U.S./GVN Performance in Vietnam* (Santa Monica, CA.: Rand, 1972).

[3] Harry Summers, *On Strategy: A Critical Analysis of the Vietnam War* (New York: Dell, 1984) 113.

[4] Stephen Peter Rosen, *Winning the Next War: Innovation and the Modern Military* (Ithaca: Cornell University Press, 1992) 8.

[5] For his discussion on the characteristics of wartime innovations see Rosen 22-24.

[6] Rosen 9.

[7] See Barry R. Posen, *The Sources of Military Doctrine* (Ithaca: Cornell University Press, 1984) 501.

[8] Rosen 5.

[9] The classic statement of this comes from Summers' personal experience. See Summers 21. One of the key general officers in the post-Vietnam Army reforms, General (retired) Richard Cavazos, put it succinctly, "They never whipped nothing bigger than a platoon." Telephone interview with General Cavazos, 20 August 1993.

[10] The most forceful argument from this school is Summers, particularly 107-118 and 130-131. It is also interesting to note that Summers' book was an effort officially sanctioned by the Army to learn the lessons of Vietnam. Telephone interview with General (retired) Edward C. Meyer, 9 August 1993. Hereafter cited as "Meyer interview." Summers' conclusions were also corroborated by several of the other general officers interviewed for this book.

[11] Shelby L. Stanton, *Green Berets at War: U.S. Army Special Forces in Southeast Asia, 1956-1975* (Novato, CA: Presidio, 1985) 39.

[12] Colonel Francis J. Kelly, *U.S. Army Special Forces, 1961-1971* (Washington, D.C.: Department of the Army, 1973) 33-35.

[13] Kelly 35-36. Stanton 51-52, 58.

[14] Stanton 112.

[15] Stanton 176.

[16] Charles M. Simpson, *Inside the Green Berets: The First Thirty Years* (Novato, CA: Presidio, 1983) 200-202.

[17] *The Pentagon Papers*, Senator Gravel ed., vol. II (Boston: Deacon Press, 1972) 411-413, 451. ARVN infantry battalions received five U.S. advisors. Artillery battalions got three. Each district originally got 3 advisors.

[18] Blaufarb 240. See also *Pentagon Papers*, vol. II, 480- 493.

[19] Blaufarb covers the founding of CORDS on 240-241. Stanton also notes that it was not uncommon to require A- teams from the CIDG program to

function as district advisors as well. Stanton 106. For some of the key decisions leading to the expansion of the advisory program, see also *The Pentagon Papers*, vol II, 411-413. 450-451, 466.

[20] These figures come from Summers 235. District advisors were generally a small force of U.S soldiers headed by one or two officers at the rank of lieutenant or captain. They generally lived in a fortified compound, often co-located with the Regional Forces platoon. See *The Pentagon Papers*, vol II, 451. See David Donovan, *Once a Warrior King* (New York: Ballantine, 1985), for a vivid first-person narrative of the actions of one young lieutenant who became the senior adviser for a Mekong Delta district in the early 1970s.

[21] For an excellent account of such a platoon in the 173d Airborne Brigade, see James R. McDonough, *Platoon Leader* (New York: Bantam, 1985). The U.S. Army's 1st and 25th Infantry Divisions also experimented on a small scale with such programs. See *Pentagon Papers*, vol. II, 494.

[22] Dave R. Palmer, *Summons of the Trumpet: U.S.-Vietnam in Perspective* (Novato, CA: Presidio, 1976) 250.

[23] See Andrew Krepinevich, *The Army and Vietnam* (Baltimore: Johns Hopkins, 1986) Chapter 2, and Russell F. Weigley, *History of the United States Army*, rev. ed. (Bloomington, IN: Indiana University Press, 1984) chapter 23.

[24] Kenneth D. Mertel, *Year of the Horse: Vietnam* (New York: Bantam, 1968) 170-171. Mertel commanded one of the 1st Cavalry's battalions in the Ia Drang battles.

[25] See Palmer 137-139.

[26] Shelby L. Stanton, *The Rise and Fall of an American Army: U.S. Ground Forces in Vietnam, 1965-1973* (Novato, CA: Presidio, 1985) 137, 145.

[27] On the origins of unconventional warfare activities dating back to the CIA-sponsored Vietnamese Army 1st Observation Group in 1956, see Simpson 144-152. For Projects Delta, Omega, and Sigma, see Simpson 153, and Kelly Chapter 6.

[28] Stanton, *Green Berets at War*, 205; Simpson 146-147, 149.

[29] George C. Morton in the "Foreword" to Stanton, *Green Berets at War*. Morton was the first commander of U.S. Army Special Forces Vietnam (Provisional), a command formed in September 1962.

[30] Andrew J. Krepinevich called this preference the "Army Concept." See Krepinevich Chapters 1 and 2.

[31] Palmer 233-236. Stanton, *The Rise and Fall of an American Army*, 145-147, 337-340.

[32] Komer 115.

[33] Blaufarb 288.

[34] Komer 118. Komer points out that even though the military dominated CORDS by virtue of control over resources, the creation of the unified command structure, and the high ranking placement of civilians such as Komer within the military hierarchy, "resulted in greater U.S. civilian

influence over pacification than had ever existed before." Komer 110. Interestingly, "unity of command" is one of the principles of war.

[35] For the CIDG parachute operations, see Kelly 140-141, and Simpson 123-134. As Deputy Commander of the 5th Special Forces Group, it was Simpson's responsibility to train and qualify the Mike Forces in airborne operations. Kelly was his commander.

[36] Blaufarb 259. Mercenaries are soldiers who serve merely because of the pay they receive and to a lesser extent, because of the personal bonds they form with their group or leaders. Many observers describe the CIDG tribesmen as more loyal to the Army Special Forces than they were to the South Vietnamese government.

[37] Harry Summers' writings on the Vietnam War were on the required reading lists of most Army schools by the late 1980s. He viewed activities such as CORDS as "a valuable adjunct to our military operations against North Vietnam." See Summers 234. In his efforts to downplay the significance of the insurgency in Vietnam to the ultimate outcome - and in so doing deemphasize the importance of the whole counterinsurgency movement - Summers cited Sir Robert Thompson on the difference between guerrilla war and revolutionary war: "Revolutionary war is most confused with guerrilla or partisan warfare. Here the main difference is that guerrilla warfare is designed merely to harass and distract the enemy so that the regular forces can reach a decision in conventional battles....Revolutionary war on the other hand is designed to reach a decisive result on its own." The implication that runs through this work of Summers is simply that the use of guerrillas by either side in Vietnam was merely as adjuncts or auxiliaries, just as had been expected when Army originally created the Special Forces. See Summers 234.

[38] See Blaufarb 260 where the author makes a similar point. See also John R. Galvin, "Special Forces at the Crossroads," *Army*, December 1973, 21-24. General Galvin's impression of the Special Forces in Vietnam was exactly that they preferred the "derring-do" missions over the less-heroic politico-military tasks of counterinsurgency. Interview with General (retired) John R. Galvin, 27 July 1993, West Point, NY.

[39] The reported statistics on advisers differ. The official Army history is Jeffrey J. Clarke, *Advice and Support, the Final Years: The U.S. Army in Vietnam* (Washington, D.C.: U.S. Army Center of Military History, 1988). Clarke gives the figures for 1969 as 5683 advisers assigned directly to CORDS and another 2305 advisers in Mobile Training Teams (MTTs) operating under CORDS control, for a total of 7988. Many of the differences in counting come from the various categories to which an adviser might be assigned. Not all were directly involved in the counterinsurgency effort. Some were logistics advisers to conventional ARVN forces, for example. The total of 7988, however, is the official number assigned to CORDS, and hence specifically to counterinsurgency activities. Compare these numbers to those cited above from Blaufarb 240-241, and Summers 235. See also Peter M. Dawkins, "The United States Army and the Other War in Vietnam: A Study of the Complexity

of Implementing Organizational Change," Ph.D. dissertation, Princeton University, 1979, 54-55, 131. Dawkins reports that never more than 750 officers and 1500 enlisted men were serving as district and province advisors at any point in time. Furthermore, the figures in the Army's official history of the Special Forces in Vietnam show roughly one officer to every 5 enlisted soldiers serving in A teams. Peak strength of the Special Forces was roughly 2700. See Kelly 67, 82.

[40] The total deployment numbers come from Office of the Secretary of Defense, *Department of Defense Selected Manpower Statistics, Fiscal Year 1991* (Washington, D.C.: USGPO, 1991) 112. The number of officers is derived from the percentage of officers to total strength - 13.08% - given in Richard A. Gabriel and Paul L. Savage, *Crisis in Command: Mismanagement in the Army* (New York: Hill and Wang, 1978) 185.

[41] Amos A. Jordan and William J. Taylor, ed., *American National Security: Policy and Process*, rev. ed. (Baltimore: The Johns Hopkins University Press, 1984) 73-76. 43 See also Charles E. Kirkpatrick, "Building the Army for Desert Storm," *The Land Warfare Papers*, No. 9 (Arlington, VA: The Institute of Land Warfare, 1991) 1.

[42] I drew the following information from "The Astarita Report: A Military Strategy for the Multipolar World," ed. Harry G. Summers (Carlisle, PA.: U.S. Army War College, 1981). This copy was published in 1981 based on the original 1974 report. Hereafter referred to as "Astarita Report."

[43] Astarita Report v.

[44] Astarita Report v.

[45] Astarita Report 1.

[46] Astarita Report 2.

[47] Astarita Report 6.

[48] The trends are described in Astarita Report 3-10. The quote comes from page 20.

[49] Astarita Report 20.

[50] Astarita Report 21.

[51] Lewis Sorley, "Creighton Abrams and Active-Reserve Integration in Wartime," *Parameters*, Summer 1991, 42-46; Paul H. Herbert, *Deciding What Has to Be Done: General William E. DePuy and the 1976 Edition of FM 100-5, Operations* (Ft. Leavenworth: U.S. Army Command and Staff College, July 1988) 37; Herbert I. London, *Military Doctrine and the American Character: Reflections on Airland Battle* (New Brunswick: Transaction Books, 1984) 11.

[52] Sorley, 45.

[53] Some believe that this action on the part of Abrams was a direct result of his job as Vice Chief of Staff of the Army in the mid-1960s, where he was responsible for increasing the Army to fight in Vietnam without being able to use the trained manpower in the reserve structures. This belief is now a legend within the Army. See Sorley 45.

[54] General Weyand was the Chief of Staff from October 1974 until the end of September 1976. General Rogers held the post from October 1976 until June 1979. Both adhered to the plans that Abrams originally set in motion. General Starry commanded TRADOC from 1977 until 1981.

[55] John L. Romjue, *A History of Army 86, Volume I: Division 86: The Development of the Heavy Division, September 1978-October 1979* (Ft. Monroe, VA: TRADOC, 1982) 12.

[56] Brooks E. Kleiber, Richard P. Weinert, John L. Romjue, *U.S. Army Training and Doctrine Command Annual Historical Review, 1 October 1976 to 30 September 1977* (Ft. Monroe, VA: TRADOC, 29 August 1978) 11.

[57] Brooks E. Kleiber, Richard F. Weinert, John L. Romjue, *TRADOC Annual Report of Major Activities, FY 1975* (Ft. Monroe, VA: TRADOC, 20 Sept 1976) The first chapter of this historical summary is "The 1973 Arab-Israeli War and Its Impact on TRADOC." From the first page of the summary: "the implications of the October war for U.S. Army training and doctrine were so great that the historical record of TRADOC for Fiscal Year 1975 can best be illuminated by beginning with this subject." The TRADOC annual historical summaries until the end of Fiscal Year 1977 point to the impact of the 1973 war on all of TRADOC's force structuring and doctrinal endeavors. This summary was corroborated by letters to the author from General (retired) Donn A. Starry, 6 August 1993, and from General (retired) John H. Foss, 1 August 1993.

[58] Romjue, *Division 86*, 1.

[59] Romjue, *Division 86*, vi, 1.

[60] Lewis Sorley, *Thunderbolt: From the Battle of the Bulge to Vietnam and Beyond: General Creighton Abrams and the Army of His Times* (New York: Simon and Schuster, 1992) 363.

[61] The general relationship of the reserve and active components of the Army remained unchanged until after the Persian Gulf War. As Abrams had intended, the U.S. government had to call up tens of thousands of reservists to adequately support the Desert Shield and Desert Storm operations, thus engaging the American people directly in the war effort.

[62] Weigley 568-569; Sorley, "Creighton Abrams," 43.

[63] *Department of Defense Selected Manpower Statistics* 51.

[64] John L. Romjue, *A History of Army 86, Volume II: The Development of the Light Division, the Corps, and Echelons Above Corps, November 1979-December 1980* (Ft. Monroe, VA: TRADOC, 1982) 25.

[65] Caspar W. Weinberger, *Annual Report to the Congress*, FY 1988 (Washington: USGPO, 1 Feb 1988) 294.

[66] Weinberger 295.

[67] Herbert 5.

[68] Herbert 19.

[69] This process came to be known as the Concepts Based Requirements System.

[70] FM 100-5 *Operations* (Washington, D.C.: Headquarters, Department of the Army, 1976) i. Emphasis in original.

[71] FM 100-5 1-2.

[72] FM 100-5 1-2.

[73] Kleiber, 1978, 181-182. This and the following quotation appear under a heading of "Low Intensity Capabilities." This was the first such heading in the TRADOC files.

[74] Kleiber, 1978, 131-182. General Foss was one of the officers who drew up the initial TRADOC scenarios. In retrospect, General Foss stated that TRADOC had every intention of eventually addressing counterguerrilla contingencies in Panama and Thailand, but "we just never got to it." Telephone interview with General (retired) John W. Foss, 5 August 1993. Hereafter cited as "Foss interview." In the late 1970s, TRADOC did address, barely, the Panama scenario.

[75] See Kleiber, 1976, 92, and Richard P. Weinert, John L. Romjue, *U.S. Army Training and Doctrine Command Annual Historical Review, 1 October 1978 to 30 September 1979* (Ft. Monroe, VA: TRADOC, January 1981) 204.

[76] FM 100-5 1-2.

[77] FM 100-5 1-2.

[78] FM 100-5 chapter 14.

[79] See Kleiber, 1976, 92, and Richard P. Weinert 204. As General Foss later recalled, "We had gone through the low-intensity conflict and the escalation into the mid-intensity war of '65-'71.... The Army knew a lot about it, taught it extensively in schools and knew it was a difficult task." General (retired) John M. Foss, letter to the author, 1 August 1993. Hereafter cited as "Foss letter."

[80] Donald B. Vought, "Preparing for the Wrong War?" *Military Review*, May 1977, 30. Although Vought used the term "low-intensity conflict," the Army training programs he addressed focused on Internal Defense and Development (IDAD), the heart of a counterinsurgency program, but only a part of what came to be called low intensity conflict.

[81] John L. Romjue, MEMORANDUM FOR RECORD, SUBJECT: Combat Developments Scenarios Briefing to the TRADOC Advisory Group, 12 November 1974. This document is in file 870-5D "Combat Development Scenarios" in the TRADOC archives.

[82] Romjue, MEMORANDUM FOR RECORD.

[83] Romjue, MEMORANDUM FOR RECORD. One of the officers who developed the first scenarios recalled that the initial briefings occurred the day before the Yom Kippur War began. Naturally, the war and its results caused a complete revamping of their work. Foss interview.

[84] Brooks E. Kleiber, Richard P. Weinert, John L. Romjue, *Annual Report of Major Activities, FY 1974: A History of TRADOC's First Year* (Ft. Monroe, VA: TRADOC, 1975) 246-7, 250.

[85] Kleiber, 1975, 248.

[86] *Information Booklet, TRADOC Standard Scenarios for Combat*

Developments (Ft. Monroe, VA: TRADOC, February 1977) . TRADOC File 870-5D.

[87] *Information Booklet* 34.

[88] *Information Booklet* 34, 38. Including maps, the booklet devoted a total of four pages to these two scenarios.

[89] *Change 1 to TRADOC Pamphlet 71-11* (Ft. Monroe, VA: TRADOC, 9 June 1976) 2-16. TRADOC File 870-5D.

[90] *Change 1* 4-55. Testing the command and control, doctrine, and organization of the Special Forces was one intention of the Panama scenario. Another was the testing of air mobile forces in foreign internal defense and counterinsurgency situations. See *Change 1* 4-56.

[91] Most of the material in TRADOC File 870-5D deals with the development and testing of the European scenarios, with some emphasis on the Korean scenario. TRADOC historian John Romjue, who had been at TRADOC since its inception, remembered discussing the topic of why Vietnam-style contingencies were not included in the initial TRADOC efforts with then-Lieutenant Colonel John Foss. Foss replied that such scenarios just did not have a very high priority. The weight of the evidence confirms this. Telephonic interview with John Romjue, 18 February 1993. Confirmed by Foss letter.

[92] These figures come from Vought 30. Krepinevich found the same occurrence in his study of Army training for counterinsurgency in the early 1960s. See Andrew Krepinevich, *The Army and Vietnam* (Baltimore: Johns Hopkins, 1986) 46-47, 51.

[93] That unwillingness manifested itself strongly in the case of U.S. covert involvement in Angola in 1975. Congress eventually banned such action. The congressional records are full of references to "another Vietnam." See, for example, Senate Committee on Foreign Relations, *U.S. Involvement in Civil War in Angola, Hearings before the Subcommittee on African Affairs*, 94th Cong., 2d sess. (Washington, D.C.: USGPO, 1976) 6-50.

[94] See Phil Williams, *The Senate and U.S. Troops in Europe* (New York: St. Martin's Press, 1965) chapters 7-8.

[95] Congress was interested in international and domestic terrorism, and any possible links between the two. See House Committee on Internal Security, *Terrorism, Hearings before the Committee on Internal Security*, parts 3-4, 93d Cong., 2d sess. (Washington, D.C.: USGPO, 1976), and Senate Committee on the Judiciary, *Terroristic Activity: Hostage Defense Measures, Hearings before the Subcommittee to Investigate the Administration of the Internal Security Act and Other Internal Security Laws*, part 5, 94th Cong., 1st sess. (Washington, D.C.: USGPO, 1976).

[96] Colonel William G. Boykin, "Special Operations and Low Intensity Conflict Legislation: Why Was It Passed and Have the Voids Been Filled?" U.S. Army War College student paper, 12 April 1991, unpublished 4. See also Charlie A. Beckwith and Donald Knox, *Delta Force* (New York: Harcourt Brace Jovanovich, 1983) chapter 16.

[97] It is interesting to note that the capability for hostage rescue was not given to the CIA. Hostage rescue required a small force which could operate clandestinely. However, one can only surmise that in the climate of the times, particularly given the congressional distaste for the CIA-led operations in Angola in 1975, the CIA was in retreat and not likely to be given any new, sensitive missions.

[98] John F. Reichart and Steven R. Sturm, "A Summary of Developments Since 1975," *American Defense Policy*, 5th ed., ed. John F. Reichart and Steven R. Sturm (Baltimore: Johns Hopkins University Press, 1982) 140.

[99] The Yom Kippur War and the events in Angola shook those who had faith in detente. See Williams chapter 8, and House Committee on International Relations, *U.S.-U.S.S.R. Relations and Strategic Balance, Hearings Before the Subcommittee on International Political and Military Affairs*, 94th Cong., 2d sess. (Washington, D.C.: USGPO, 1976).

[100] On the European constraints, see Herbert chapter 6.

[101] Brian Jenkins, George Tanham, Eleanor Wainstein, and Gerald Sullivan, *U.S. Preparation for Future Low-Level Conflict* (Santa Monica: RAND, July 1977) iii. This was a report of a conference held October 15-20, 1976, at the RAND Corporation, Washington, D.C.

[102] Jenkins 3.

[103] Jenkins 3. Emphasis in original.

[104] Jenkins 8.

[105] Jenkins 6.

[106] Jenkins 8.

[107] Jenkins 9.

[108] Jenkins 4.

[109] Meyer was a behind-the-scenes force pushing for the creation of a counterterrorist unit in 1976. See Beckwith 103, 108. Meyer later confirmed that he made presentations at the RAND conference which focused on the U.S. need to cope with low intensity missions. Meyer interview.

[110] Rosen 9.

[111] Dawkins 54-55, 68, 73, 131. Rosen cites this same information, 102-105. On the other hand, Dawkins, an adviser himself, rose to the rank of Brigadier General. Two other advisers, Colin Powell and Norman Schwarzkopf, rose to become Chairman of the Joint Chiefs and Commander-in-Chief of Central Command (CENTCOM) during Desert Shield and Desert Storm. Hence, advisory duty did not necessarily signal either the end of one's career, or a truncated career.

[112] Vought 22-23. The Command and General Staff College was the school attended by mid-career officers, mostly majors. In 1977 those attending were likely to have served as junior officers in Vietnam.

[113] Along with Vought's *Military Review* article, he had attended the International Studies Association Conference, 28-30 October, 1976, at Ohio State, and delivered a paper entitled "Speak Stickly and Carry a Big Soft: The

U.S. Army Prepares for Future Low Intensity Conflict." See the footnote in Jenkins 8.

[114] Kleiber, 1978, 181-182.

[115] See Stanton, *Green Berets at War*, Chapter 10. For a much more pro-Abrams view, see Sorley, *Thunderbolt*, Chapter 20.

[116] The request appears in the records under a heading "Low Intensity Capabilities." Kleiber, 1981, 181.

CHAPTER 5

ACCEPTING THE PERIPHERAL MISSION II, 1979-1989

"...in default of knowing what should be done, they do what they know."

— Marshall Maurice Comte De Saxe

This chapter investigates the Army response to changes in U.S. national strategy in the period 1979-1989. This case begins with a series of crises in 1979 and ends with even more dramatic events - the fall of the Berlin Wall and the imminent dissolution of the Warsaw Pact in 1989.

As in the other cases, undergirding this period are the continuing effects of misconceptions about low intensity conflict. In this period, most of the leaders and officials involved exhibited an understanding that low intensity conflict was more than simply limited war of the Korean style. Yet, the idea that any war is the same remained strong among the traditionalists, as did the related concept that no matter how important low intensity missions might be, they could be handled as a "lesser included case" of the training received by soldiers who focused almost exclusively on combat. As for the misconceptions that low intensity conflict is synonymous with special operations or that low intensity conflict is just some manifestation of revolutionary insurgency, this case indicates that some still strongly held to these views, while others, equally important and powerful, rejected them. In any case, the muddle over the parameters and meaning of low intensity conflict was still evident, and contributed much to the outcomes observed.

In the 1980s, civilians once again sought to exert direct influence over the operational matters of the Department of Defense. Therefore, this case provides a good test for Posen's structural model of military change. As in the other chapters, the Posen model would lead one to expect heated resistance from military leaders to such "meddling" by civilians. If the civilians were successful in their intervention, the history of this period ought to exhibit changes in Army's behavior with respect to the challenge of low intensity conflict. As indicators of changed behavior, the Army would be structuring forces whose primary mission would be low intensity conflict. Further, those forces would be rationally trained within doctrinal concepts that differed from forces designed for firepower-intensive mid- and high-intensity battlefields. Given the political ambiguities inherent in low intensity conflict, and given the political strictures placed on the use of force in most low intensity missions, the forces would be more lightly armed and would be trained in the restrained use of firepower.

Since the period that this chapter covers is one where civilians actively intervened in the operational matters of the military, it provides a difficult test for the Rosen model, which is generally depreciative of civilian influence. To support the Rosen model, the evidence of this period would have to show that the changes in the Army's behavior were due primarily to conflict between groups of visionary and traditionalist officers, and not due to any civilian influence. Or, the evidence could show that the changes would have happened anyway even if the civilians had not acted.

What the evidence from this period does show is that, for some civilian critics and for some Army officers, low intensity conflict became serious business in the 1980s. Civilian advocates came from both the executive and legislative branches. At least two of the Army officers were Chiefs of Staff, Generals Meyer and Wickham. Consequently, in the first seven years of this period, these visionary military leaders initiated broad changes in the Army to confront the challenges of low intensity conflict, and were supported by vigorous civilian reformers. The Army began to respond to the challenges of low intensity conflict by structuring forces, writing doctrine, and instituting training programs that were focused on the various facets of the phenomenon.

However, the efforts of Meyer, Wickham, and their civilian allies met resistance from traditional officers who sought to retain the focus on future conflict in Central Europe. Moreover, the tenure of these Chiefs was too short to fully overcome the resistance and set in motion fundamental change. By the end of the period, the traditional officers were still firmly in power.

Both civilians and officers who were advocates for

responding to low intensity conflict were further divided by degrees of commitment. Some civilian advocates wanted a general response to the challenge. Others wanted specific responses to specific low intensity missions, such as counterterrorism. Within the Army, officers like General Meyer thought that Special Operations Forces (SOF) were the only answer needed for low intensity conflict. General Wickham, on the other hand, felt that SOF were too narrowly tailored, and hence advocated giving low intensity missions to conventional units - light infantry divisions - as well.

The period once again demonstrates that Posen's model is too dependent upon a military maverick as an agent of change. Nonetheless, civilian reformers did have an effect on the Army, but that effect is only fully illuminated through an appreciation for the internal group dynamics of the organization. Based on this case, a synthesis of the emphasis on civilian reformers in the Posen model and the emphasis on internal group conflict in the Rosen model suggests the following pathways to change. When visionary military leaders are in power, and act in concert with activist civilian authorities, fundamental change in organizational repertoires becomes possible. On the other hand, when civilians try to enact reform in the absence of military visionaries, or without taking advantage of existing visionaries, traditionalists are able to thwart much of the reform. The result is only small, grudging change - peripheral change - in the standard repertoires of the organization. As was the case in the 1960s, such peripheral changes can be further negated or reversed by traditionalists when the reformers are gone.

THE SECURITY ENVIRONMENT

There is no comprehensive document, such as the Astarita Report, that succinctly summarizes the strategic vision of the Army at the outset of this period. However, there are several items of evidence available from Army and political leaders that, cumulatively over the whole period, provide the necessary historical background into the development of the Army's changing strategic vision. There were two significant changes in the security environment that affected the Army in this period: 1) a perception that the Soviet challenge now extended globally, not only in the indirect fashion of "wars of national liberation" as in the early 1960s, but also directly; and 2) the American public became more supportive of an active foreign policy and a strengthened military.

In July 1979, the Sandinista movement overthrew the Somoza regime in Nicaragua, and quickly adopted an anti-American attitude. On 15 October 1979, reformists overthrew the El Salvadoran government, precipitating widespread fighting between left-wing guerrilla groups, government forces, and anti-leftist militias.

Additionally, in one incredible 53-day period beginning on 4 November, the entire focus and credibility of U.S. security policy was put into question. On 4 November, Iranian Shiite militants seized the U.S. embassy in Tehran, taking hostage 52 Americans. On 20 November, Sunni radicals seized the Grand Mosque in Mecca. Many Muslims speculated that such a brazen assault had to have U.S. involvement or Israeli involvement, or both. Early on 21 November, the Iranian Supreme Leader, Ayatollah Khomeini, issued a statement that said, "It is not far-fetched to assume that this act has been perpetrated by the criminal American imperialism....It would not be far-fetched to assume that, as it has often indicated, Zionism intends to make the House of God vulnerable."[1] Later on 21 November, the U.S. embassy in Pakistan was burned and two Americans killed as the crowds chanted "Death to the American dogs!" and "Avenge the sacrilege in Mecca!"[2] Anti-American demonstrations also broke out in Turkey, India, Kuwait, and eastern Saudi Arabia.[3]

On 2 December, mobs sacked the U.S. embassy in Libya. Finally, on 27 December, Soviet airborne forces invaded Afghanistan.

The events in the Middle East and Southwest Asia led President Carter to proclaim in his State of the Union Address, 23 January 1980: "Any attempt by an outside force to gain control of the Persian Gulf Region will be regarded as an assault on the vital interests of the United States, and such an assault will be repelled by any means necessary, including military force."[4]

Unfortunately, the military services had capabilities focused on European scenarios. The crises that began in 1979 pointed up the weakness of the U.S. military in general, and of the Army in particular, to respond to crises on the peripheries of the US-Soviet competition. The seeming inability of the Carter administration to respond adequately reinforced the critics of the administration who had argued for a more vigorous defense establishment.[5] While not disagreeing that the perceived Soviet build-up in Europe posed serious threats, these critics called for the means to combat other Soviet threats on the periphery of the Cold War, whether those threats came from regional conflict in the Persian Gulf, terrorism, or a new spate of Soviet- and Cuban-backed insurgencies. The criticism of U.S. defense capabilities aided the defeat of President Carter in 1980.[6] The Reagan administration, not unlike the Kennedy administration twenty years before, came to power in 1981 committed to building up the military capabilities of the United States for all forms of conflict.

By February 1980, the Army officially had changed its focus from that of the late 1970s. General Meyer, the Army's Chief of Staff declared that "the most demanding challenge confronting the U.S. military in the decade of the 1980s is to develop and demonstrate the capability to successfully meet threats to vital U.S. interests outside of Europe - without compromising the decisive theater in Central Europe."[7] This was to be a tall order - not only must the European theater retain primacy, not only must the defense of South Korea be maintained, but new capabilities must be found for intervention, once again, in the so-called peripheries. General Meyer also gained public attention when he began describing the Army as "hollow." He went so far as to say that the United States Army had become "a prudent risk force."[8] This phrase meant that the Army could still perform its missions of defense of Europe and South Korea, but at an uncomfortable level of risk.

The events of 1979 also affected the domestic factors of the security environment. William Schneider recorded that the "two traumatic events" of 1979 - the Iranian hostage seizure and the Soviet invasion of Afghanistan - and the dramatic failure of the attempted rescue of the American hostages in April 1980, led to a 65% approval rating for increased defense spending by January 1981.[9] Support for increased levels of defense spending remained high throughout the 1980s.[10]

During the 1980s, the concern for the strategic threat of regional instability remained steady in the Reagan and Bush administrations. Although this concern was always linked to the potential for Soviet meddling and expansionism, it was also focused on the increased importance of the Third World as a source of markets and strategic minerals.[11] Furthermore, instability in the Third World raised the possibility of unmanageable refugee flows and threatened U.S. basing and transit agreements.[12] Secretary of Defense Caspar Weinberger summed up the threat: "For [our adversaries], low-intensity warfare represents a cost-effective means of aggression for advancing their interests, while minimizing the prospect of a forceful response by the United States and our allies."[13]

However, it would take several years before the United States had forces large enough, with the right equipment, and the necessary sealift and airlift to make credible interventions in the Middle East, or elsewhere. The new emphasis on a non-European contingency, though, prompted serious reform efforts aimed at doctrine, organizations, and equipment that could enhance deployability. From late 1979 until 1987, low intensity conflict, as a reason for organizing forces, requesting budget dollars, and for driving the development of doctrine, picked up amazing speed.

THE ARMY RESPONSE

In the 1970s, the Army had turned away from conflicts that might lead to a Vietnam-style involvement. It focused, rather, on the one mission upon which there was wide agreement within the service and among policy makers - the defense of Western Europe. There were those within the Army, though, who continued to point out that the most likely conflicts of the future might very well be the ones the service was adamantly ignoring (see Chapter 4). Events in 1979 and 1980 seemed to bear out this criticism.

The Army began the decade as part of the failure of the Iranian rescue attempt at Desert One. It would be sent into combat in Grenada, earning once again less than high marks for performance. However, in the last days of the decade, the Army performed quite well in the invasion of Panama.

Additionally, the Army received more non-mainstream missions in the areas of counterterrorism, counternarcotics, and both pro- and counterinsurgency. The area of largest growth was in Latin America, where Army troops operated continually in Honduras from 1983 and in Bolivia, Ecuador, Peru, Belize, and Costa Rica at various times. Most of these were "nation assistance" missions that fell under the internal development portion of Internal Defense and Development (IDAD) programs. Significantly, though, the Army supported anti-drug missions in

Bolivia beginning in 1986. While the operations in Bolivia involved nation assistance, they focused primarily on aiding drug interdiction.[14] Additionally, by 1988, the Army had begun similar internal development activities in Africa.

To cope with the new security environment and the resulting new missions, the Army began a series of changes in force structure, doctrine, and training that lasted the entire decade.

FORCE STRUCTURE

The Army began the process of building forces and doctrine to answer the demands of the Carter Doctrine, and the new assertiveness of the Reagan Administration.

Ultimately it was the composition rather than the size of the Army that changed in this period.

In 1978, General Donn A. Starry, the commander of TRADOC, who was concerned about the utilization of emerging technology to fight what he called the "Central Battle" in Europe, initiated a study to develop the appropriate force structure for the late 1980s, or the "Army 86 Study" as it came to be known.[15] The study eventually called for 11 heavy divisions and set into motion plans, which "as late as 1979 envisaged mechanizing all of the remaining light infantry divisions exclusive of one airborne and one air assault division."[16]

The move to mechanize the Army came to a stop with the ascendancy of General Meyer who had advocated enhancing light forces with higher technology even prior to the events of late 1979.[17] By 1980, creating light, deployable forces was a national priority. The new light forces would have the "double missions of independent use in contingencies and reinforcement of forces already deployed."[18]

On 1 March 1980, the Headquarters, Rapid Deployment Force, was established at MacDill Air Force Base, Tampa, FL, under the auspices of U.S. Readiness Command.

This increased the pressure on the Army to provide forces that were rapidly deployable and, given the turmoil in the Middle East, capable of fighting armored forces. Consequently, in May of 1980, the Army designated the 9th Infantry Division at Ft. Lewis, WA, as its "test bed" for a new deployable division armed with high-technology anti-armor weaponry, which, Army planners hoped, could handle deployment to, and combat in, the Middle East, or a reinforcement mission to Europe.[19]

Unfortunately, the necessary high technology made the 9th Division too heavy for truly rapid deployment, was not lethal enough to defeat armored forces, and finally was not funded by Congress.[20] The demise of the high-technology light division did not end the search for rapid deployment forces. Meyer's successor, General John Wickham, became the advocate of a "fighter-heavy, more deployable force that could be delivered with minimum resources, and would represent a credible force on the future's most likely battlefield."[21] Moreover, Wickham's new light infantry divisions (LIDs) would "be optimized for employment at the lower end of the conflict spectrum in a contingency mission, yet [would] retain utility for employment at higher conflict levels (NATO)."[22]

The goal was a light division of 10,000 men capable of deploying in 500 or fewer air sorties "oriented primarily to contingencies in the Pacific, Latin America, and Africa."[23] The LIDs would have secondary missions in NATO, the Middle East, and Southwest Asia depending on the terrain and proper augmentation.[24] Eventually, the Army formed four of these divisions. In view of their creation as crisis response forces, Wickham gave the LIDs the highest priority possible for equipment and personnel within the Army - Authorized Level of Organization (ALO) 1.[25]

The Army also strengthened the Special Operations

Forces (SOF) community. In September 1987, the Army created a personnel management branch for Special Forces officers, who hitherto had been detailed from other branches, often hurting their chances for promotion in their primary fields. The number of Special Forces Groups rose from three to five. A third Ranger battalion and a fourth Psychological Operations battalion were added.[26] The Army also created the U.S. Army Special Operations Command, an overarching headquarters to control all Army SOF activities, and specialized subordinate headquarters as well.[27]

Faced with a changed security environment that required it to find forces for rapid deployment into low intensity scenarios, the Army created such forces by realigning its existing force structure. Divisions which had existed to support the European and Korean scenarios, while not stripped of that mission, were restructured to fight low intensity conflicts. Funding for both the active and reserve SOF communities also rose much more rapidly than for the Army as a whole.[28]

By the end of this period, some 55,000 Army troops had low intensity conflict as one of their primary missions. While this was still less than 8% of the total Army, it represented a significant increase in Army capabilities to deal with low intensity missions.

DOCTRINE

After a slow start, the Army made dramatic progress by the mid-1980s in the production of new doctrine to cope with the challenge of low intensity conflict. These manuals, pamphlets, and circulars, in fact, are some of the best evidence that the Army did respond, at least intellectually, to the new challenges. The years 1985 and 1986 are good parallels to 1962 and 1963 in this respect. Yet, by the late 1980s, the progress slowed for reasons that will be discussed below.

In 1979, none of the so-called "How-to-Fight" manuals considered current by TRADOC had anything to do, specifically, with low intensity conflict.[29] However, in January 1981, the Army issued its first manual dedicated to low intensity conflict.[30] This effort was no doubt the outcome of the concern expressed by some members of the TRADOC community in the late 1970s over the lack of intellectual effort put into contingencies outside of Europe or Korea (see Chapter 4). The manual, though, exhibited very little in the way of new thought on the subject of low intensity conflict. In a remarkable display of the confusion of low intensity conflict with counterinsurgency, the manual begins by interchanging the phrase "internal defense and development" (IDAD) with the phrase "low intensity conflict":

> "this manual provides...concepts and doctrine concerning the conduct of INTERNAL DEFENSE AND DEVELOPMENT (IDAD) assistance operations which occur in a LOW INTENSITY CONFLICT (LIC) environment categorized as Type A or Type B...."[31]

A "Type A LIC" involved direct combat action by U.S. forces "to establish, regain, or maintain control of specific land areas threatened by guerrilla warfare, revolution, subversion or other tactics aimed at internal seizure of power." A "Type B LIC" involved advice and support to foreign government forces engaged in the same kind of conflict.[32]

What about other operations? The 1981 manual mentions four other operations only in passing: internal conflict, peacekeeping, unilateral operations, and evacuation of U.S. nationals. The first category, "internal conflict," dealt with U.S. support to the UN or other treaty organization to restore order in a country. "Unilateral operations" dealt with operations involving vital U.S. interests when the UN or other organizations were unwilling to act.[33] The manual spent less than a page on these operations, summing up that "Although this manual provides guidance for operations involving... [IDAD], many of the principles may be applied in other efforts to restore order and establish peace."[34]

The manual then presented theoretical chapters on "The Environment of Developing Nations" and "Insurgency." After the theory, the manual proceeded to address specifically the employment of most major Army units and weapons systems against guerrillas, including the use of armor, armored cavalry, and antitank platoons, finding a mission for each one.

This first attempt at a manual devoted to low intensity conflict, was, in essence, a counterguerrilla operations manual. Almost no space was devoted to the military's role in the development end of IDAD beyond simply making such statements as "The brigade also will conduct military civic action in conjunction with civil affairs programs."[35] The manual does not at all address the subtle nuances of fire control, avoidance of collateral damage and civilian casualties, or the focus on promoting the legitimacy of the host government.

As another example of how slow the Army was to face the doctrinal implications of the changes in the security environment, in 1982 the Airland Battle edition of FM 100-5 appeared. A contentious debate within the Army and between the Army and the academic community had spawned the new manual.[36] Overturning Active Defense, the 1982 edition focused on offensive maneuver operations, even in the defense, to maintain the initiative. As in 1976, the manual was focused primarily on armored combat in Europe to the detriment of other theaters and conflicts at the lower end of the spectrum.

The manual made only a general reference to any non-European scenario. It stated that the Army had to be ready to fight in two environments - a sophisticated battlefield, and an unsophisticated battlefield populated by "light, well-equipped forces such as Soviet-supported insurgents or sophisticated terrorist groups."[37] Beyond this the manual contained a three page chapter titled "Contingency Operations" which was a reaction to the Carter Doctrine and the recognized need to deploy and fight rapidly in the Middle East.[38] The manual also addressed "unconventional warfare", but as totally ancillary to conventional operations. The notion that Army forces might be involved in fostering insurgencies unconnected to conventional operations, or might engage in counterinsurgency, or might have to conduct peacekeeping or counterterrorist operations was not to be found.

Beginning early in this period, the Department of Defense came under greater criticism from scholars and soldiers for a perceived lack of capabilities for dealing with low intensity conflict. This criticism was partly a manifestation of interest that some had maintained throughout the 1970s, but was mainly a result of the events of 1979.[39] Additional criticism and studies exploded in the early 1980s, especially after the Army began its Army of Excellence reorganization study in 1983.[40]

Certain offices and officers within the Army also turned their attention to the Army's doctrinal shortcomings in dealing with low intensity conflict. In early 1983, the Army commissioned a study of low intensity conflict by Kupperman and Associates, Inc.[41] In August 1983, TRADOC concluded that Army Special Forces had inadequate doctrine and force structure for its likely missions.[42] In December 1983, Lieutenant General Carl Vuono, the commander of the Combined Arms Center at Ft. Leavenworth, sent a message to the commander of TRADOC stating that the JFK Special Warfare Center found the definition of low intensity conflict to be incomplete. Vuono suggested initiating efforts to redefine the phenomenon and incorporate it into a new FM 100-20.[43]

Shortly thereafter, TRADOC documents acknowledged that the "LIC issue [is] unclear..." and that "Army doctrine [is] fragmented...."[44] However, TRADOC did consider that General Wickham's initiatives on behalf of the light infantry divisions were having an impact on how the Army handled low intensity conflict. Another internal TRADOC document pointed out that the principal weakness of the recent FM 100-20 was its focus on IDAD. The document called for the filling of "doctrinal voids" on peacekeeping, civil affairs, and heavily emphasized dealing with the topic of the use of "military capabilities" in low intensity conflict, rather than just the use of military force.[45]

In June 1984, the Special Warfare Center produced a new draft of FM 100-20, which TRADOC quickly rejected because it still insufficiently dealt with the full range of missions within low intensity conflict in favor, yet again, of counterguerrilla operations.[46] In the subsequent two years, TRADOC refashioned the working concept for low intensity conflict and the AirLand Battle Doctrine. In the publications proceeding from this effort, the Army finally began to incorporate mission categories beyond the counterguerrilla portions of IDAD.

In TRADOC Pamphlet 525-44 *U.S. Army Operational Concept for Low Intensity Conflict*, of February 1986, TRADOC established four "general categories" of "emerging" low intensity conflict doctrine: foreign internal defense, peacekeeping, peacetime contingency operations, and "terrorism counteraction."[47] The pamphlet required the usage of the low intensity conflict concepts in all TRADOC training institutions and scenarios.[48]

Despite promises that the new edition of FM 100-5 would include low intensity conflict, and that a new edition of FM 100-20 was in the offing, the actual changes were slower to come.[49] AirLand Battle doctrine was revised, and in 1986, a new edition emerged. The revised edition hewed to the same principal subjects of armored warfare in central Europe, but did at least mention low intensity conflict. Seven paragraphs addressed counterinsurgency, peacetime contingency operations, peacekeeping and counterterrorism.[50] The manual later devoted a four-page chapter to contingency operations, defining them as "military actions requiring rapid deployment to perform military tasks in support of national policy."[51] While these minor changes were movement in the direction predicted by TRADOC, they hardly represented inclusion of low intensity conflict in mainstream doctrine.[52]

However, doctrinal progress was made within the subject of low intensity conflict itself. In May 1986, TRADOC issued Field Circular 100-20 *Low Intensity Conflict*.[53] In this circular, only four chapters covered IDAD, and none was devoted exclusively to counterguerrilla operations. Counteracting terrorism received two chapters; peacekeeping and contingency operations received one chapter each.[54] However, six of eight annexes were still devoted to IDAD. The circular also placed much greater emphasis than any preceding document on the political and often non-military nature of low intensity operations.

The Army's progress in producing low intensity conflict doctrine slowed markedly in the late 1980s. As the decade closed, the Army had still not issued a new low intensity field manual. The delay was partly a reflection of the absorption of the entire issue of low intensity conflict into the joint arena.[55] Having reached an acceptable internal definition of the phenomenon and the likely mission categories, the Army was now forced to refight the definitional battle with other services and agencies that had low intensity missions. Army doctrine now had to be coordinated across service and agency lines.

In January 1986, the Army and the Air Force established

the Center for Low Intensity Conflict at Langley Air Force Base, VA.[56] In October 1986, as a result of the Nunn-Cohen Amendment to the Goldwater-Nichols Act, U.S. Special Operations Command (USSOCOM) was created with the legislatively-mandated mission to develop doctrine for all Special Operations Forces, regardless of service.[57] With this proliferation of agencies, centers, and commands involved in low intensity conflict, Army doctrinal progress slowed.

The Army definition for low intensity conflict in 1986 had been:

> "A limited politico-military struggle to achieve political, social, economic, or psychological objectives. It is often protracted and ranges from diplomatic, economic, and psychological pressures through terrorism and insurgency. Low intensity conflict is generally confined to a geographic area and is often characterized by constraints on the weaponry, tactics, and the level of violence."[58]

However, the Center for Low Intensity Conflict records that one of the reasons why a new definition was needed was that the existing Army definition tended to make policymakers confuse low intensity conflict with special operations. The new interagency definition of low intensity conflict consumed two years of governmental effort. One of the Army generals involved in the process recalled that single biggest problem was "defining what it [low intensity conflict] was and what the Army was supposed to do."[59] He also remembered the difficulty of "explain[ing] to laymen that special operations [were] not synonymous with low intensity conflict." One of the civilian leaders in the process recalled simply that the Army definition was "inherently inaccurate," and that the entire concept of low intensity conflict was "misleading."[60] Compared to low intensity conflict, special operations seemed conceptually clear.

In 1988 a National Security Council-led effort produced a new definition of low intensity conflict, which was still in effect in 1993:

> Political-military confrontation between contending states or groups below conventional war and above the routine, peaceful competition among states. It frequently involves protracted struggles of competing principles and ideologies. Low-intensity conflict ranges from subversion to the use of armed force. It is waged by a combination of means employing political, economic, informational, and military instruments. Low-intensity conflicts are often localized, generally in the Third World, but contain regional and global security implications. Also called LIC.[61]

The 1986 and 1988 definitions are not radically different. The principal change, resulting from increased civilian input, is the emphasis placed on the combination of means which downgrades the importance of military force. Nonetheless the controversy over the appropriate definition continued. It was not before 1990 that the Army, Air Force, and USSOCOM could agree on a field manual.

Additionally, the Army continued to have problems getting low intensity doctrine accepted internally, and this, too, contributed to the slowing of progress in the late 1980s. The

Army, focused as it still was, on the combat requirements necessary to win a mid- to high intensity war, was having difficulty with the concept of "indirect application of power," which was seen as fundamental to low intensity conflict. Consequently, by the end of the decade the Army had not yet moved low intensity conflict into the mainstream channel for the production of forces, equipment, and training - the Concepts Based Requirements System (CBRS).[62] As then-Major General Gordon R. Sullivan put it in March 1988,

> The Concepts Based Requirements System (CBRS)...does not treat the indirect application of power, which we are directed to employ by national policy. (*The National Security Strategy of the United States*, The White House, January 1988).... Until we deal with these capabilities requirements systematically, development of doctrine, training, force structure, and material will continue to be an ad hoc arrangement.[63]

TRAINING

In the 1980s, the Army structured forces to engage in low intensity conflict, and then provided them with updated doctrine. In comparison, the Army's focus on training for low intensity missions remained somewhat underdeveloped, even though it did make some progress.

By the end of this period, the Army had beefed up officer training programs at all echelons by creating common scenarios for low intensity conflict exercises. Similar to the counterinsurgency period, low intensity training programs exploded across Army schools. By the late 1980s, most officer schools in the various branches contained at least one course or instructional period devoted to low intensity conflict. By May 1988, the Army's Command and General Staff College offered six different course or instructional periods devoted to low intensity topics. By December 1990, this number had grown to ten.[64] Unlike the 1960s, though, these courses also addressed the other mission categories of low intensity conflict, although counterinsurgency remained the most studied subject.

The Army also led in the effort to create the Joint Readiness Training Center (JRTC) at Ft. Chaffee, AR. The JRTC was modeled after the National Training Center, but was devoted largely to training for raids, rescues, and insurgency operations.[65] The revamped Army SOF and the new light infantry divisions staged regular exercises at this facility. The nation-building deployments to Central America and Africa were also billed as "training." Finally, those infantry battalions tabbed to serve as part of the Multi-National Force and Observer unit in the Sinai pursuant to the Camp David Accord undertook training focused on peacekeeping operations.[66]

In the 1981 FM 100-20, most of the tasks suggested for training were common tasks such as marksmanship, arm and hand signals, patrolling and map reading. These tasks would have been fundamental to combat at any intensity of war.[67] By 1986, the focus was much better. In the 1986 Pamphlet 525-44, the Army declared that "forces must be educated or trained in the importance of low intensity conflict and what roles the Army will be expected to play."[68] The pamphlet also required that conventional forces - the bulk of those expected to participate in a low intensity conflict - have "habitual association and training with augmentation units" such as Civil Affairs units, Psychological Operations units, and other SOF.[69] The manual also identified such needs as an understanding of international law, laws of the nations within which the Army might operate, the creation of regional experts, and for peacekeeping, the need for mediation , fairness, firmness, and friendliness.[70]

Despite this flurry of training activity, not all of it was directed specifically at low intensity conflict topics. Misconceptions confusing low intensity conflict with special operations, and confusion about the full capabilities of light infantry divisions, hampered efforts to focus on high quality training for low intensity missions. As late as 1988, officers from the Center for Low Intensity Conflict (CLIC) made the following observations about a workshop on Army light forces held at the Army Command and General Staff College. In the workshop's study, there were no references to:

> "'tasks necessary for operations in a noncombatant low intensity role.' In fact, the study group's documents connected the LIC environment entirely with the special operations forces (SOF) and did [not] even otherwise mention LIC anywhere in the contents."[71]

Similarly, in a review of the training conducted at the JRTC, CLIC officers observed that much of it was focused on "peacetime contingency operations," which, as noted above in Chapter 2, is the low intensity mission category most closely resembling standard combat operations in mid- or high intensity warfare. Moreover,

> "noncombatant tasks took on the cast [only] of possible future parts of the concept of low intensity [training]. Also, too much emphasis fell on COIN [counterinsurgency] tasks as suitable only for SOF and completely outside the competence of conventional forces. Even

more alarming was the discovery that no attention went into the training of leaders and units about the inherent 'political restrictions in a low intensity environment.' Moreover, the [JRTC] shunned the business of instructing leaders and units how to operate effectively under the inevitable LIC 'constraints on the use of force.'"[72]

Hence, as in doctrine, the Army made progress in training to confront the challenge of low intensity conflict, while not quite giving it the attention it truly deserved as the most likely form of conflict that the Army would face. Now the analysis must turn to the factors that motivated the Army in the 1980s to make the changes in force structure, doctrine, and training in the manner that it did.

EXPLANATION I : CIVILIAN-MILITARY INTEGRATION AND THE SEARCH FOR A MAVERICK

This period contains evidence that supports Posen's view of military change. At the start of the decade, civilian officials perceived the need for a credible response to low intensity conflict. Reform proceeded along two lines as civilian legislators and civilian administrators of the executive branch took direct action to effect change in military organizations, particularly in the Army.

From the executive branch, the Reagan administration came to power convinced of the need to revitalize SOF. Funding was immediately increased and the Secretary of Defense, Caspar Weinberger, acted personally to influence the Joint Chiefs of Staff. On 1 January 1984, the Department of Defense created the Joint Special Operations Agency to provide command and control for the services' SOF.[73] In 1985, President Reagan established the President's Blue Ribbon Commission On Defense Management, also known as the Packard Commission. This commission recommended giving regional commanders-in-chief enhanced responsibility to deal with low intensity situations. The President did this by executive order in April 1986. In 1988, the President established the Commission on Integrated Long Term Strategy which once again highlighted the low intensity threat and U.S. inadequacy in facing it.[74]

The Packard Commission report also undergirded the legislative defense reform movement. Despite increased funding and heightened executive and legislative branch interest in using U.S. forces for low intensity conflict, Loren B. Thompson observed that:

> "Critics claimed that the service bureaucracies were resisting efforts to upgrade special operations forces and that senior Pentagon political appointees were blocking plans to establish an organization capable of meeting the challenges of low-intensity conflict."[75]

Consequently, the debate surrounding the Goldwater-Nichols Defense Reorganization Act of 1986 was filled with legislative expressions of dismay at the military inadequacies for engaging in low intensity conflict. In the debates leading to the act, at least one congressman, Dan Daniel of Virginia, and one Senator, William S. Cohen of Maine, went so far as to call for the creation of a new military service.[76] On June 26, 1986, Daniel and a number of colleagues introduced House Resolution 5109 to create a National Special Operations Agency outside of military control to focus exclusively on the problem of low intensity conflict. The agency would have had a status similar to that of the

Central Intelligence Agency or Defense Intelligence Agency. The agency would have reported directly to the Secretary of Defense and the President.⁷⁷ The Senate proposed a similar bill that would have created a Defense Special Operations Agency within the existing structure of the Department of Defense.⁷⁸

No understanding of the full measure of civilian interest in the strategic challenge of low intensity conflict can be had without realizing that the military was responding to two separate branches of the government. The executive branch pressure came directly from the Secretary of Defense, but also from lower-level Defense officials such as Noel C. Koch, Principal Deputy Assistant Secretary of Defense for International Security Affairs. The legislative pressure was bipartisan and powerful, including Senator Sam Nunn, who would come to chair the Senate Armed Services Committee (SASC) in 1987. According to two of the chief Senate legislative assistants working on these issues - Chris Mellon and James Locher - the civilian reformers were concerned that the military, still focused on Europe, would not adequately address the needs of low intensity conflict, despite the efforts of the Secretary of Defense Weinberger and others like Koch. Hence, the initial legislative attempts by Daniel and Cohen were used to goad the military into action. The military response was inadequate.⁷⁹

In Posen's structural view of military organizations, effective change resulted from the actions of determined civilians who overcame resistance from hidebound military traditionalists. There is much in this case to suggest this process. In reaction to the perceived unwillingness of the military to change itself, or of the executive branch to force more radical changes on the military, Congress passed the Goldwater-Nichols Department of Defense Reorganization Act and the Nunn-Cohen Amendment to the Defense Authorization Act for FY 1987 (also known as the Nunn-Cohen Amendment to the Goldwater-

Nichols Act).[80] The second act specifically directed the creation of an Assistant Secretary of Defense for Special Operations and Low Intensity Conflict, the creation of a new unified command - the U.S. Special Operations Command - and the creation within the National Security Council of a special board to coordinate all low intensity activities across all executive branch agencies and departments.[81] What would be the logical result of such scrutiny and action? According to one observer of the reform process, "No one could mistake the assumption underpinning this aspect of the law: LIC now rivaled -- at least distantly -- conventional warfare as an area of DOD activity and concern."[82]

Despite this high level of outside civilian interest in the military's response to low intensity conflict, that response was not what was hoped for by the reformers. The mere creation of structures, as Posen himself would have predicted, did not end the institutional resistance to change. Some of the resistance came from the civilian bureaucracy in the Defense Department, but much of it came from military officers. When the Daniel and Cohen legislation was introduced, the military responded by offering to create a Joint Special Operations Command under a three-star general. While this would have represented a step forward from the Joint Special Operations Agency, which was led by a two-star, the legislators felt that the response would still mean that the Defense Department would pay inadequate attention to funding, equipping, training, and structuring forces for low intensity conflict.[83] Hence, the civilians enacted the Nunn-Cohen amendment.

The military continued to resist by closing Readiness Command and establishing the new unified Special Operations Command (SOCOM). Readiness Command had been located at MacDill Air Force Base in Tampa, FL, which meant that the new SOCOM would be far from its civilian protectors in Washington. The initial staff officers of SOCOM were holdovers from

Readiness Command, and the military was slow to augment the new command with officers who had special operations backgrounds. Finally, the military delayed turning over budget authority to the new command as specified in the Nunn-Cohen legislation.[84]

As Posen's model would have predicted, the debate also turned acrimonious over the question of expertise. Senior Army leaders felt that the civilian reformers were operating outside their area of expertise. In retrospect, some of the key Army generals of the period spoke of the civilians as single-minded "zealots," or, in the case of Daniel and Cohen, as men who did not have the security of the United States truly at the core of their actions. The closing of the European-focused Readiness Command was also seen as a mistake. Most scathing, however, was the comment by one general that Locher's involvement represented "personal aggrandizement by the fellow who wrote the [Nunn-Cohen] legislation, then got himself appointed to the job. It was, and yet is, a shabby piece of business by a West Point graduate who apparently lost his bearings somehow. . . [and never] served on active duty."[85]

As Noel Koch later recollected, one general summed up the prevailing attitude of the military about the civilian attempts at reform: "You guys think you can tell people what to do, but if they don't want to do it, they're not going to do it."[86] As the Center for Low Intensity Conflict described the situation as late as 1989, even given the public support of the new Secretary of Defense, Dick Cheney, some "officers remained determined just 'to sit back and have it [low intensity policy and strategy] shoved down their throats.'"[87]

Despite the resistance, the civilian reformers remained steadfast in their determination. In the first days of the Bush administration, Senators Nunn, Warner, Kennedy, and Cohen sent a letter to Lieutenant General (retired) Brent Scowcroft, who was appointed the Assistant to the President for National Security Affairs. The purpose of the letter was to draw Scowcroft's attention "to a long-neglected, but critical, issue: deficiencies in U.S. capabilities to engage effectively in low intensity conflict."[88] The Senators were concerned that the Reagan administration Defense Department had not faithfully adhered to the intent of the provisions of the 1986 legislation. Similarly, in December 1989, Rep. Ike Skelton of the House Armed Services Committee, who was then conducting a study of education and training within the military, felt that the Pentagon's civilian officials responsible for low intensity conflict were butting up against a "mind-set and an historical and a national focus on the threat from the Soviet Union."[89]

Posen's model places heavy emphasis on a military maverick that the civilian reformers could use to overcome the institutional resistance such as that alluded to in the preceding paragraphs. As in the counterinsurgency case, though, the civilian reformers did not find or use a maverick. The potential candidates were, like Maxwell Taylor of the early 1960s, too successful in the mainstream to be considered mavericks. Among active duty officers, Generals Edward C. Meyer, John A. Wickham, Jr., John Galvin, and Wallace E. Nutting were the officers most closely identified with attempting to make the Army face the challenge of low intensity conflict. However, none of these general officers remotely fit the maverick description.

Neither legislators nor executive branch officials found active-duty mavericks to aid their causes. Since none of the senior leaders of the Army at the time had an extensive background in low intensity operations, the civilians would have had to force the services to reach down into the ranks.[90] As in the early 1960s, the civilians were unwilling to do so.

The closest thing to a "maverick" in this case is the Special Operations Policy Advisory Group (SOPAG). This group was composed of retired general officers of high stature, each personally selected by the secretary of defense. SOPAG's role was to provide high quality advice to the Secretary of Defense in his program to revamp SOF, but advice that was divorced from the daily interservice wrangling of the Pentagon.[91]

One of the SOPAG members was Lieutenant General (retired) Samuel V. Wilson. Wilson had an impeccable record of special operations service - Office of Strategic Services behind Japanese lines in World War II, foreign area service in the Soviet Union, interagency duty with the Central Intelligence Agency, Defense Intelligence Agency, the State Department, and the command of special forces units at all levels. Wilson was also a close associate of General Meyer and significantly influenced Rep. Dan Daniel.[92] In this respect, Wilson performed the service Posen foresaw for mavericks - that of providing needed military understanding and expertise to civilian reformers - from outside the military. Wilson's own view of his and his colleagues' service on SOPAG was that they performed the role of the "responsible maverick." They were not "bulls in the china shop" trying to embarrass their former services by making bold public statements.[93] Had the reformers in the executive or legislative branch brought Wilson back to active duty, they might have been far more effective. As it was, Wilson played a role similar to that of Brigadier General William P. Yarborough, commander of the Special Warfare Center in the counter insurgency era - available for advice, but underutilized.[94]

The Army generally opposed the elevating of SOF whether the pressure came from the administration, from Congress, or even from key Army leaders. No doubt the advice of Wilson and the other members of SOPAG was good, but their influence within the ranks was minimal given their retired status. That no true mavericks were found or used might explain why the services resisted change as much as they did, and to a large degree why they did so successfully. By the end of the decade, much of the Army's approach to low intensity conflict was still, as General Sullivan put it, ad hoc.

EXPLANATION II: INTRAORGANIZATIONAL INTERGROUP CONFLICT

As presented above, ample evidence exists to suggest that some military leaders believed that the security environment had changed in the 1980s. The conflict between groups in the Army revolved around the issue of the appropriate response to those changes.

The group of traditionalists that stymied President Kennedy and set the tune for the reorganization of the post-Vietnam Army disappeared in the 1980s. That group had been forged primarily on the battlefields of Europe in World War II. Replacing them, a new set of traditionalists arose, trained in the requirements of defending the Fulda Gap or the Korean Demilitarized Zone. The new group was rather like the favored sons of the older group. Following the iron law of oligarchy, the traditionalists had perpetuated themselves.[95] This is the same group of traditionalists that any use of the rival Posen model would also identify as the opponents to change.

The traditionalists, old and new, were willing to accommodate interest in low intensity conflict, but only to a degree. Ensconced at the level of service chief, regional commander-in-chief, or major command, they fought the establishment of the Joint Special Operations Agency by the executive and the reforms of Goldwater-Nichols by Congress. When they lost such battles, they delayed implementing the directives, pleading lack of funds or specific guidance.[96] Consequently, their views held sway in Army schools far after civilian or uniformed reformers required changes. The traditionalists were also vocal in their opposition. A criticism often heard was that "'LIC' may be many things, but what it is not is conflict that is low in intensity."[97] Or, the whole notion of low intensity conflict was derisively dismissed as "a curious new view of the universe."[98] To the soldier in a firefight or in a minefield, echoing the enduring misconception, war is war.[99]

While the traditionalists emerge from this decade still in control of the Army, they did lose a substantial amount of power in the first seven years of the decade. A contending group - "visionaries" - rose to hold important offices in these years which they used to move the Army to face the challenge of low intensity conflict. Rather than acting as mavericks, Generals Meyer and Wickham as Chiefs of Staff, Gorman and Galvin at Southern Command and General Nutting at Readiness Command all provided the necessary mainstream intellectual and institutional support to force the Army to deal with low intensity conflict through most of the 1980s.

General Meyer was considered a proponent for enhancing light forces in general and special operations forces in particular.[100] As Chief of Staff of the Army General Meyer stopped the mechanization of the Army's remaining infantry divisions upon assuming office in 1979 several months before the unsettling events of late 1979, to which he also responded very rapidly. As noted in the preceding chapter, as a Major General, Meyer had attended the RAND conference in 1976 which was devoted to U.S. weakness with respect to low intensity missions. One recommendation of that conference had been to strengthen U.S. special operations capabilities, particularly with respect to counterterrorism and hostage rescue.[101] Hence, Meyer came to office with a good appreciation for the job to be done, and he remained a consistent advocate of upgrading Army light and special forces.

Meyer was succeeded by General Wickham, who also earned a reputation as a Chief bent on enhancing the Army's capabilities to respond to low intensity missions. Wickham's efforts were even more vigorous than those of Meyer. He became the driving force behind the light infantry divisions, the revamping of Army low intensity conflict doctrine in the mid-1980s, the creation of the Joint Readiness Training Center, and the key role the Army played in the 1986 Joint Low Intensity Conflict Project.[102]

General Wallace E. Nutting assumed command of Southern Command in the Autumn of 1979 just as the United States was once again confronted with the problem of counterinsurgency. Even though Nutting was a career armor officer, he moved, as he later put it, "from the most conventional assignment – command of an armored division in the Fulda Gap of West Germany - to the most unconventional assignment - Commander of SOUTHCOM."[103] Nutting moved quickly to utilize what he considered the best of the Vietnam lessons. He had his staff obtain and study old manuals from the Civil Operations and Revolutionary Development Support (CORDS) program. He brought in medical and engineering units to conduct civic action and established Mobile Training Teams for the region's armed forces. He also sought to keep all of these activities overt. In this he was unsuccessful as the Department of State and the Central Intelligence Agency wanted many of the programs to remain covert, particularly any program that was devoted to "strikes" - raids, retaliations, or unconventional warfare missions. According to Nutting, the CIA, under the control of the old OSS officer William Casey, "got the [strike] missions and predictably flubbed it."[104]

Nutting's experience as Commander of SOUTHCOM led him to call low intensity conflict "very likely the most important challenge facing the Army and the nation during the coming generation...."[105] In 1983 Nutting became commander of U.S. Readiness Command, and prompted a massive, Army-led interagency study of low intensity conflict in 1986.[106] This study was extremely influential not only within the service, but also among the civilian reformers.[107]

General Paul Gorman succeeded Nutting at Southern Command. In charge of all the military activities in Central and South America in the mid-1980s, Gorman surmised that low intensity conflict had turned war upside down.[108] General Gorman was willing to consider the impact that low intensity missions would have on his unified command, and argued for a "bayonets last" doctrine in dealing with counterinsurgency. Moreover, he was willing to express his thoughts bluntly and openly and demanded that Army institutions respond to his concerns.[109] Gorman's successor at SOUTHCOM, General John Galvin, became the Army's most articulate as well as prolific advocate for responding to low intensity conflict.

As SOUTHCOM commander, Galvin spoke and wrote extensively on the subject, noting the threat it posed and the military's inadequacies in facing it. Echoing Rosen's notions of conflicting communities with differing visions of war, Galvin wrote:

> "When we think about the possibilities of conflict we tend to invent for ourselves a comfortable vision of war, a theater with battlefields we know, conflict that fits our understanding of strategy and tactics, a combat environment that is consistent and predictable, fightable with the resources that we have, one that fits our plans, our assumptions, our hopes, and our preconceived ideas."[110]

Significantly, Galvin pointed toward the training of young

officers not only in "our vision of modern warfare," but also to be able to "understand the changing environment of conflict."[111] When asked about the impact of a military maverick in effecting fundamental change, Galvin was skeptical. He believed that innovation required the concentration of power over time, hence "a single maverick, a Billy Mitchell, cannot do much...."[112] Moreover, "If you want change, you have to form a team....Then that team has to last over time. That means you need new recruits, because you don't...spend a lifetime in one position of influence."[113]   Galvin became Supreme Allied Commander, Europe in 1987. Although he became responsible for the key strategic area - Europe - Galvin expanded the European Command's operations by continuing to use resources as he had in Latin America. He sent small teams of U.S. forces throughout Africa to perform a variety of engineering, medical, and military training tasks.

There is also some evidence about younger visionaries. Some of the senior officers interviewed for this study spoke of the "Special Operations Mafia" that worked covertly with civilian reformers to advance their cause. On General Wickham's staff, there was also a small group of officers known as "Project 14" who were instrumental in Wickham's focus on rapidly deployable light infantry divisions.[114]

In the late 1980s, all the leading visionaries but Galvin had retired, and Galvin could no longer devote himself to low intensity issues given the problems in Europe in the late 1980s. While the visionaries were able to effect much change in force structure, training, and doctrine by the mid-1980s, they were not allowed a free hand, despite their powerful positions. They were able to initiate broad changes, but their efforts were often modified in style or substance by the traditionalists.

For example, while General Meyer was pushing to enhance light, deployable forces, the commander of TRADOC,

General Starry, sought to ensure "the operational concept of the light division [dovetailed] with that of its heavy counterpart."[115] Indeed, planners working on the concept for light forces were ordered to use one of TRADOC's standard European scenarios.

Additionally, General Richard E. Cavazos, commander of Forces Command (FORSCOM), complained to Wickham that the,

> "seemingly boundless consumption of flying hours and other aviation resources in support of unprogrammed training exercises in Central America is a significant and growing concern....The political ramifications of a further "readiness" drop prior to the elections are self-evident.... The very great importance of the Central American exercises is unquestioned, and some limited Army aviation training benefit is recognized."[116]

This message only makes sense in the context of "readiness" for some other deployment and use of Army troops, most likely for Europe, given 1) that only limited training benefit was seen as coming from operations in a low intensity environment, and 2) that FORSCOM's mission was heavily focused on preparing units in the continental United States for the reinforcing of Europe.

In a later message, Cavazos complained about the use of Army Ranger units in joint exercises:

> "I'll run one more time at the windmill. The basic issue is the control by the Army of its conventional forces and conventional

operations versus the JCS relegating the Army to a subsumed role in special operations. I challenge those that say that JSOC [Joint Special Operations Command] is the way to plan missions above battalion level....Rangers are a conventional force of great skill. It was not SOC that trained this force.... I regard the new SOC as another stove pipe to be resourced. The belief that SOC would deploy and be accepted by CINC's has not proved out.... We've enough splinter groups in the Army."[117]

It is also crucial to note that after Wickham's retirement in 1987, much of the emphasis on the light infantry division and on doctrine for low intensity conflict changed. The balance of institutional power was swinging back to traditionalist leaders. Planning for the use of light infantry divisions shifted to their use in conjunction with heavy forces. Rather than focusing on low intensity missions, the light forces found themselves sent to the National Training Center in the desert at Ft. Irwin, CA, or to the Return of Forces to Germany (REFORGER) exercises in Europe to practice close coordination with armored forces in defensive and offensive schemes against an armored opponent. By using light forces to guard rear areas in these scenarios, heavy forces were free to act as mobile reserves. Light forces also proved helpful in target acquisition and as forces to breach complex Soviet obstacle systems.[118] Also, as noted in the section on training above, much of the training of light forces at the JRTC had shifted to the one mission area that traditionalists easily understood - short duration operations involving combat. In the absence of the visionary leaders, the traditionalists returned to emphasize the utility of light forces on the margin of the traditional mission.[119]

The power of the traditionalists can also be traced to the feeble mention of low intensity conflict in the 1986 edition of FM 100-5, despite the obvious interest of the Army's Chief of Staff.[120] The fact that so little doctrine was produced for low intensity conflict after 1986 might not only have been the result of interagency definitional squabbles, but also of the disdain the traditionalists held for the subject.

To underscore the success of the traditionalists in watering-down the reforms of the visionary leaders, consider the 1988 report of a panel led by General Gorman, who had by then retired. The report stated that, despite the efforts of the 1980s, "neither the U.S. Army nor any other of the U.S. armed services have considered such [low intensity] operations sufficiently in developing doctrine, training programs, force structure, or materiel." Furthermore, "U.S. force structure, equipment, and doctrine, designed for accustomed combatant missions, are not well-suited to pursuing non-combat roles...." The report also stated that even SOF commanders often complained that low intensity missions "compromised their readiness" for higher intensity missions. Finally, the report noted that such criticisms, and their solutions which would depreciate the value of fire support and maneuver, "frequently strike U.S. military officers, doctrinally conditioned to believe in the primacy of the combat function, as startlingly novel."[121]

Given the strength of the Rosen approach in providing a tool to describe the conflict between the traditionalists and the visionaries, what is not evident is the process of transformation that Rosen's approach would predict. Despite having very strong advocates for change in key leadership positions, the Army finished the 1980s with no regular process by which officers schooled in the requirements of low intensity conflict could rise to positions of higher rank and influence. Despite the increases in training, there was no established path of education and training for Army low intensity specialists. Officers still could not get repetitive assignments in units or jobs which were focused on low intensity requirements.

It might be argued that Special Forces, which finally obtained official status as an Army branch for officer personnel management in the mid-1980s, had such paths, and that the Army came to have general officers with Special Forces backgrounds who could aspire to command at least the unified U.S. Special Operations Command.

However, it has always been a mistake to confuse low intensity conflict with special operations. If the visionaries wanted to create General Galvin's team of new recruits, then the new Special Forces branch and U.S. SOCOM were only steps in the right direction.

CONCLUSION

Much as in the 1960s, civilians forced change on the Army in this period, but the quality of that change was determined by the receptiveness of the Army. Again as in the 1960s, ultimately, the civilians did not achieve the success they desired. The civilians could force structural changes in terms of new offices within the Department of Defense and a new military command, but they could not force conceptual changes onto soldiers within the Army. The general's comment to Noel Koch was quite correct: if soldiers "don't want to do it, they're not going to do it."

Some of the difficulty in achieving conceptual change derived from misconceptions about low intensity conflict that contributed to confusion and rancor, even among the visionaries in the Army and the civilian reformers. Perhaps the crowning achievement of the civilian reformers in this era was the creation of U.S. SOCOM and the ASD SO/LIC. But, in a prime example of the power of the "LIC equals special operations" misconception, note that the unified Special Operations Command is endowed with great power to deal with special operations, which by no means are focused solely on low intensity conflict. The new assistant secretariat within the Department of Defense necessarily focused much of its effort on liaison with the new command.

Similarly, the traditionalists remained adamant in their focus on heavy combat, or warfighting, with the belief that low intensity conflict could be handled at the margin of traditional missions. Hence, for many traditionalists the only low intensity missions worthy of consideration were "guerrilla hunting" or combat-related contingency operations, and here, force was to be used liberally. As one traditionalist put it, "If they [civilians] want to use force, tell them that the grass won't grow again where it's used."[122]

Even in the visionary camp, the often subtle distinctions between the various mission categories caused conceptual problems. Because the concept and definitions of low intensity conflict are so ambiguous, the phrase takes on different meanings for different people. General Meyer thought that most low intensity problems could be handled by SOF, but much of his focus, outside of possible deployments to the Middle East, was on counterterrorism and hostage rescue.[123] General Wickham expanded on this concept to include organizing and training conventional forces for counterinsurgency in Latin America.[124]

As in the two cases in Chapters 3 and 4, no mavericks are apparent. However, Posen's view that perceptive civilian officials have to intervene to force change on a hidebound military certainly is confirmed, once again, in this period. Civilian officials in both the executive and legislative branches vigorously sought changes in the Army's behavior. Perhaps because no mavericks were found, or were used, helps to explain why the changes of the 1980s, like the changes of the 1960s, encountered so much resistance from within the Army. The evidence from the 1960s and the 1980s suggests that Posen placed too much reliance on mavericks as agents of change in his model. As the synthesis below argues, if civilians act to influence the military, they will prompt some change. The effectiveness of their actions, though, depends on the group(s) within the military with whom the civilian reformers choose to work.

As stated in the introduction to this chapter, for the evidence of this period to confirm Rosen's approach, it would have had to show that a group of visionaries within the Army would have reformed the Army even without civilian intervention. While Generals Meyer, Nutting, and Wickham began to work on the problem of low intensity conflict before civilian scrutiny became intense in the mid-1980s, the evidence does not lead one to conclude that the Army would have moved to face the challenge adequately without the prodding by civilians. The traditionalists simply remained too strong.

On the other hand, as in the 1970s, Rosen's model remains useful for what it tells us about the dynamics internal to the Army. Rosen tells us that true change generally takes a generation - a time sufficient for the recruitment, education, training, and promotion of adherents to some new way of war. In this period, a new group of traditionalists, too young to have experienced World War II or Korea, but knowing very well the distasteful experience of Vietnam, found their purpose in the continued defense of Europe. Some of their contemporaries, the visionaries, did not deny the need to defend Europe, but did seek to force the Army to face other challenges as well. This period suggests that the conflict over the future of the Army began among the groups that inherited the Army from the World War II generation, and that the struggle was not complete at the end of the period.

The analysis of this case suggests that neither of the competing explanations gives an entirely accurate view of the change process within the Army. Both models rely on some change in the security environment as a trigger for action. Civilians, traditionalists, and visionaries within the Army, perceived such changes in this period. They differed, however, on how to respond to the changes. Posen's model seems to depreciate the possibility that leaders of military organizations might willingly act in concert with civilian reformers to promote innovation, while Rosen's model seems to depreciate the possible impact of civilian pressure. The strengths of both models lead to the following synthesis.

When visionary military leaders are in power, and act in concert with activist civilian reformers, fundamental change becomes possible. On the other hand, when civilians try to enact reform in the absence of military visionaries, or without taking advantage of existing visionaries, traditionalists are able to thwart much of the reform. The result is only small, grudging change - peripheral change - in the standard repertoires of the organization. Such peripheral changes can be negated or reversed by traditionalists when the civilian reformers are gone.

The preceding analysis suggests a final point about the effect of time. Political science models can be excessively static, looking at an organization at one point in time, and then at another, with the intention of measuring the difference. Rosen points out that most peacetime military innovations require a generation to institutionalize. Given that in this period, power oscillated between the visionaries at the beginning of the decade and the traditionalists at the end of the decade, it is necessary to remember that what we are observing might be change that is yet incomplete. Neither the traditionalists who would discount the importance of Low Intensity Conflict, nor the visionaries who would elevate its importance, had won a clear victory by the end of this period. By the time of the invasion of Panama in late December 1989, the pendulum had swung once again to the traditionalists who preferred to focus on the major mission of confronting a Soviet threat in Europe (albeit reduced). Whether the Army would retain, in the 1990s, the low intensity-oriented structures, doctrine, and training that were strengthened in the 1980s was still not clear.

Chapter 5 Endnotes

---

[1] Yaroslav Trofimov, *The Siege of Mecca: the Forgotten Uprising in Islam's Holiest Shrine and the Birth of Al Qaeda* (New York: Doubleday, 2007) 108.

[2] Trofimov 109.

[3] Trofimov 202.

[4] Quoted in Amos A. Jordan and William J. Taylor, ed., *American National Security: Policy and Process*, rev. ed. (Baltimore: The Johns Hopkins University Press, 1984) 414.

[5] William Schneider, "Conservatism, Not Interventionism: Trends in Foreign Policy Opinion, 1974-1982," *Eagle Defiant: United States Foreign Policy in the 1980s*, ed. Kenneth A Oye, Robert J. Lieber, Donald Rothchild (Boston: Little, Brown, 1983) 35.

[6] See Schneider 33, and Kenneth A Oye, Robert J. Lieber, Donald Rothchild, "Preface," *Eagle Defiant: United States Foreign Policy in the 1980s*, ed. Kenneth A Oye, Robert J. Lieber, Donald Rothchild (Boston: Little, Brown, 1983) v.

[7] General Edward C. Meyer, *E.C. Meyer, General, United States Army Chief of Staff, June 1979-June 1983* (Washington, D.C.: USGPO, 1984) 52. This is a collection of Meyer's public papers and speeches. Hereafter cited as "Meyer papers."

[8] "Hearing Before the Senate Armed Services Committee on the FY81 DOD Appropriation: Army Programs," Meyer papers 65. Meyer's concerns for the manning of the Army with high quality personnel were aired in his first press conference on 17 September 1979. His concerns were a consistent theme of much of his testimony before Congress and in subsequent press conferences.

[9] Schneider 35.

[10] Schneider found a 61% level of support in 1986, and a 53% level as late as 1990. Support for defense spending was coupled with support for an active, but reasonable, foreign policy. See William Schneider, "The Old Politics and the New World Order," *Eagle in a New World: American Grand Strategy in the Post-Cold War Era*, ed. Kenneth A Oye, Robert J. Lieber, Donald Rothchild (New York: Harper Collins, 1992) 40, 41, 56.

[11] Caspar W. Weinberger, *Annual Report to the Congress, FY 1985* (Washington: USGPO, 1 February 1984) 13. The subject of low intensity conflict is not included in this report under a separate title. Rather, the information on regional instability and the importance of the Third World falls under the chapters "The Challenges We Face: Protecting U.S. Interests in a Changing World," and "Meeting the Challenge." It is also interesting to note that "low-level conflict" is addressed in the subsection "Special Operations Forces." These forces are said to be "uniquely suited" to this style of conflict which the Reagan administration believed would "pose the threat we are most likely to encounter throughout the end of this century." Note that the "low

intensity conflict equals special operations" misconception is still operating strongly.

[12] See, for example, Caspar W. Weinberger, *Annual Report to the Congress, FY 1988* (Washington, D.C.: USGPO, 1 January 1987) 57; Frank C. Carlucci, *Annual Report to the Congress, FY1990* (Washington, D.C.: USGPO, 17 January 1989) 43; Fred C. Ikle and Albert Wohlstetter, et al, *Discriminate Deterrence: Report of the Commission on Integrated Long-Term Strategy* (Washington, D.C.: USGPO, January 1988) 11. By 1987, low intensity conflict appears under the title "Conventional Deterrence and Low Intensity Conflict" in the chapter "Pillars of U.S. Defense Policy." In the Bush administration Defense Department report in 1989, the topic appears as a separate entry, "Low Intensity Conflict," in the chapter "U.S. Defense Policy and Strategy." Hence, the topic goes from obscurity in 1979, to a standard topic of strategic and policy concern in a few short years.

[13] Weinberger, *Annual Report, FY 1988*, 57.

[14] Sewall H. Menzel, "Operation Blast Furnace," *Army*, November 1989, 26.

[15] John L. Romjue, *A History of Army 86, Volume I: Division 86: The Development of the Heavy Division, September 1978-October 1979* (Ft. Monroe, VA: TRADOC, 1982) vi, 12.

[16] John L. Romjue, *A History of Army 86, Volume II: The Development of the Light Division, the Corps, and Echelons Above Corps, November 1979-December 1980* (Ft. Monroe, VA: TRADOC, 1982) 25.

[17] John L. Romjue, *A History of Army 86, Volume II*, 25.

[18] Romjue, *A History of Army 86, Volume I*, 124. See also Romjue, *A History of Army 86, Volume II*, 2 on the 28 September 1979 meeting between Starry and Meyer, reference studying the need for light forces: "They agreed to a statement that spelled out a clear dual mission. The light division should be able to deploy rapidly to reinforce forward forces in NATO. It would also conduct worldwide contingency operations to destroy enemy forces and to control land areas, including population and resources."

[19] Romjue, *A History of Army 86, Volume II*, 41.

[20] John L. Romjue, *The Army of Excellence: The Development of the 1980s Army*, unpublished draft (Ft. Monroe: TRADOC, 1992) 37.

[21] Field Circular 100-1 *The Army of Excellence* (Ft. Leavenworth, KS: US Army Combined Arms Combat Development Activity Force Design Directorate, 1 September 1984) 1-3. Wickham assumed duties as the Army Chief of Staff in June 1983 and served until mid-1987. As one of his first duties, he replaced the Army 86 studies with a new series of studies titled "Army of Excellence," which were to build upon the success of the Army 86 series and the influx of new weaponry and new missions. 18 See Romjue, *The Army of Excellence*, 47-48.

[22] Field Circular 100-1 2-1.

[23] Romjue, *The Army of Excellence*, 73. The primary combat mission of the Light Infantry Divisions (LIDs) would be to defeat other light infantry in low

to mid-intensity conflicts. William J. Olson, from the Office of the Assistant Secretary of Defense for Special Operations and Low Intensity Conflict, was emphatic on the purpose of the light infantry division: "the LID is designed for LIC." See his "The Light Force Initiative," *Military Review*, June 1985 8. See also U.S. Senate, *The Army's Light Division, Hearings before the Committee on Armed Services*, 99th cong., 1st sess. (Washington, D.C.: USGPO, 1985) 3, 37.

[24] Army planners judged light infantry to be the most capable at operating in "close terrain" - terrain where vehicles and aircraft were constrained - such as urban areas, jungle, mountains, and heavily forested regions. For the sake of deployability, the LIDs would carry only minimal logistical support, and would thus need to be resupplied rapidly by follow-on forces.

[25] Romjue, *The Army of Excellence*, 115. As General Abrams had done in the 1970s, the Army of the 1980s created these new divisions without a corresponding increase in the absolute size of the Army.

[26] Weinberger, Annual Report, 1988, 295.

[27] These included the U.S. Army Special Forces Command, the 75th Ranger Regiment headquarters, the U.S. Army Civil Affairs and Psychological Operations Command, and the 160th Special Operations Aviation Regiment headquarters. See "Special Operations Forces: A Primer," *AUSA Background Brief*, no.42, April 1992. The U.S. Army Special Operations Command had previously been the 1st Special Operations Command, which had had control of Army SOF assets since 1982. See Romjue, *The Army of Excellence*, 175.

[28] Across the Department of Defense, SOF were slated to grow in active duty manpower by 80%, from 11,600 in FY 1981 to 20,300 by FY 1990. See R. Lynn Rylander, "Tools of War/Skills of Peace: The U.S. Response to Low Intensity Conflict," *Key LIC Speeches, 1984-1989*, ed. William F. Furr and Ronald L. Zelms (Langley Air Force Base, VA: Center for Low Intensity Conflict, September 1989) 22.

[29] Richard P. Weinert, John L. Romjue, *U.S. Army Training and Doctrine Command Annual Historical Review, 1 October 1978 to 30 September 1979* (Ft. Monroe, VA: TRADOC, January 1981) 204. This page contains a table of all current field manuals for that fiscal year.

[30] Department of the Army, Field Manual 100-20 *Low Intensity Conflict* (Washington, D.C.: Headquarters, Department of the Army, 1981).

[31] FM 100-20, 1981, 13.

[32] FM 100-20. 1981, 14.

[33] FM 100-20, 1981, 15. See chapter two above for fuller definitions of the current official categories of low intensity conflict.

[34] FM 100-20, 1981, 15.

[35] FM 100-20, 1981, 207.

[36] Edward Luttwak, Steven Canby, and William Lind were the key civilian academic critics. Lind also headed the self- styled "Military Reform Caucus" allied with Senator Gary Hart. See the brief discussion in Herbert I. London,

Military Doctrine and the American Character: Reflections on Airland Battle (New Brunswick: Transaction Books, 1984) 4-6. A good summary of the entire debate can be found in John L. Romjue, *From the Active Defense to Airland Battle: The Development of Army Doctrine from 1973-1982* (Ft. Monroe, VA: TRADOC, June 1984) and Asa A. Clark, IV, et al, ed., *The Defense Reform Debate* (Baltimore: Johns Hopkins University Press, 1984).

[37] Field Manual 100-5 *Operations* (Washington, D.C.: Department of the Army, 1982) 1-1.

[38] FM 100-5 chapter 16.

[39] One of the earliest scholarly efforts was Sam Sarkesian and William Scully, ed., *U.S. Policy and Low Intensity Conflict* (New Brunswick, NJ: Transaction Books, 1981).

[40] As an example of this explosion, the Air University Library Index to Military Periodicals contains only a few sporadic listings for counterinsurgency, and none for the topic of low intensity conflict, from 1976 through 1983. Beginning in 1984, counterinsurgency topics appeared under the heading "Low Intensity Conflict" for the first time. There were four that year, 18 in 1985, and increasing totals until a maximum of 42 appeared in 1990. The topics get so specific, if not arcane, as to treat the palletizing of cargo for low intensity conflict, the use of submarines, and the role of the public affairs officer.

[41] Kupperman and Associates. Inc., *Low Intensity Conflict* (Washington, D.C.: Department of the Army, 30 June 1983). The first volume of this report is unclassified and available on microfilm from the Defense Technical Information Center.

[42] Romjue, *Army of Excellence*, 69.

[43] Lieutenant General Carl E. Vuono, Commander of Combined Arms Center and Ft. Leavenworth, Letter to Commander, TRADOC, SUBJECT: Definitions, 14 December 1983. Contained in Joint Low Intensity Conflict Project Files, Book 1, TRADOC Archives. Hereafter cited as "JLIC Files." General William R. Richardson was then TRADOC Commander.

[44] FACT SHEET for Deputy Chief of Staff for Doctrine for roundtable discussion with CG TRADOC reference LIC, TOPIC: "Low Intensity Article, Concept & Dissemination," April 1984. JLIC Files, Book 1. This was an internal TRADOC staffing document. The unknown author also proposed that TRADOC publish a concepts manual, known as a "525 series," on the topic of low intensity conflict. Within two years, TRADOC did.

[45] Talking Paper, SUBJECT: Low Intensity Conflict (LIC), 14 May 1984. JLIC Files, Book 1. See the following passage: "Low intensity conflict is characterized by the employment of military capabilities -- rather than military force -- in concert with other aspects of national power to achieve political, economic and social goals."

[46] Colonel Thomas P. Leavitt, Director, Combat, DISPOSITION FORM to Deputy Chief of Staff for Doctrine [TRADOC], SUBJECT: Low Intensity

Conflict Concept, 21 Dec 1984. JLIC Files. Book 1.

[47] TRADOC Pamphlet 525-44 *U.S. Army Operational Concept for Low Intensity Conflict* (Washington, D.C.: Department of the Army, 10 February 1986) 2. Hereafter cited as "Pamphlet 525-44."

[48] See General William R. Richardson, "Foreword," Pamphlet 525-44.

[49] See Pamphlet 525-44 C-l.

[50] Field Manual 100-5 *Operations* (Washington D.C.: Department of the Army, 5 May 1986) 4-5.

[51] FM 100-5, 1986, 169.

[52] Often, Army leaders ask recently retired general officers to comment on doctrine. The TRADOC Commander, General Richardson, asked General(retired) Meyer to comment on a draft of the 1986 edition of FM 100-5. With respect to the manual's contention that its contents applied worldwide to any level of conflict, Meyer's response in September of 1985 was, "Very simply, I'm not sure! As the contents of the draft relate to low-intensity operations, it leaves me with more questions than answers." Letter, General (Retired) Meyer to General Richardson, 17 September 1985. JLIC Files, Book 3.

[53] The Army used "field circulars" as embryonic doctrine - they fill the gap between some new concept (often represented in a TRADOC 525 series pamphlet) and a fully-staffed and critiqued field manual. The circulars gave enough doctrinal guidance to commanders to enable them to put into action TRADOC' s latest thinking on a subject. TRADOC did issue a concepts document, Pamphlet 525-44 *U.S. Army Operational Concept for Low-Intensity Conflict*, in early 1986. TRADOC had rejected two earlier drafts in June 1984 and June 1985 as still being too focused on IDAD.

[54] In this edition, contingency operations included the "strike, raid, rescue, recovery, demonstrations, show of force, unconventional warfare, and intelligence operations...." See Field Circular 100-20 *Low Intensity Conflict* (Ft. Leavenworth, KS: U.S. Army Command and General Staff College, 30 May 1986) 9-1.

[55] One observer and participant in these debates recalled that much of the impetus for reform with respect to low intensity conflict was over by 1987 because the advocates for Special Operations Forces became "sated" after the Nunn- Cohen Amendment. Interview with Colonel Joe Collins, former Special Assistant to the Army Chief of Staff, 1987-1989, 9 August 1993, West Point, NY.

[56] Thomas Crouch, *Semi-Annual Historical Report (1 April - 31 December 1986) for the Army-Air Force Center for Low Intensity Conflict (A-AF CLIC)* (Langley Air Force Base, VA: CLIC Reference Collection). Subsequent semi-annual historical reports cited as "A-AF CLIC" followed by the inclusive dates. One might look at the establishment of the CLIC in the midst of the jointness debate then ongoing in Congress as a preemptive strike by the Army and the Air Force. As it was, the Navy and the Marine Corps chose not to participate in

the CLIC, perhaps fueling that debate further.

[57] "Special Operations Forces: A Primer," *AUSA Background Brief*, no. 42, April 1992.

[58] Field Circular 100-20, v.

[59] Telephone interview with General (retired) Carl E. Vuono, 16 Aug 1993. His sentiment was echoed by two other generals interviewed. General Vuono commanded TRADOC 1986-1987, and then served as Army Chief of Staff, 1987-1991.

[60] Telephone interview with Chris Mellon, 6 August 1993. Mellon was the Legislative Assistant who worked on special operations and low intensity conflict issues for Senator William Cohen in this period.

[61] A-AF CLIC, 1 January - 30 June 1988, 12.

[62] A-AF CLIC, 1 January - 30 June 1988, 14.

[63] MG Gordon R. Sullivan, Deputy Commandant, U.S. Army Command and General Staff College, MEMORANDUM FOR: Commander, U.S. Army TRADOC, SUBJECT: Low intensity Conflict Capabilities Requirements Study, 8 March 1988. This document is contained in A-AF CLIC, 1 January - 30 June 1988.

[64] See *Low Intensity Conflict Education and Training Within the DOD: A Compilation of Course and Instructional Periods*, Vol I (Langley Air Force Base, VA: Center for Low Intensity Conflict, May 1988) and Vol II (Langley Air Force Base, VA: Center for Low Intensity Conflict, December 1990).

[65] A-AF CLIC, 1 April - 31 December 1986. The CLIC helped design the scenarios for use at the JRTC.

[66] Conversation with CPT Brian Lacey, 28 June 1993, West Point, NY. Lacey served a peacekeeping tour in the Sinai as a member of the 82d Airborne Division in the mid-1980s. According to Lacey, the 82d trained on handling civil disturbances every 90 days, as it was one of the Army units assigned such duties for the United States itself. Hence, peacekeeping training was not really added to his unit's Mission Essential Task List. Rather, existing crowd control training was changed to encompass peacekeeping tasks overseas. The training also expanded to include an orientation of the region and the Arab-Israeli conflict, and the judicious use of force under restrictive rules of engagement. Another officer who served in the 101st Airborne Division (Air Assault) in the same period, CPT Curt Masiello, reported that additional training in crowd control and civil disturbances was added to his unit's tasks in preparation for the Sinai mission. Conversation with CPT Curt Masieilo, 28 June 1993, West Point, NY.

[67] FM 100-20, 1981, 270-271.

[68] Pamphlet 525-44, E-l.

[69] Pamphlet 525-44, D-l.

[70] Pamphlet 525-44, E-l.

[71] A-AF CLIC, 1 January 1988 - 30 June 1988, 13.

[72] A-AF CLIC, 1 January 1988 - 30 June 1988, 13. My own personal

experience highlights the changing face of LIC training in the 1980s, both the good and the bad. At my Officer Basic Course in late 1984, the subject of low intensity conflict never came up. By early 1987, my Officer Advanced Course devoted two weeks to the topic, but the instruction revolved around supporting a pro-western Iranian revolt against a radical Iranian regime which was supported by Soviet regulars. The scenario was decidedly mid-intensity as it envisaged a mechanized U.S. task force operating against a mechanized Iranian-Soviet task force.

[73] Noel C. Koch, testimony before the House Appropriations Committee, 10 April 1984, U.S. House of Representatives, *Department of Defense Appropriations for 1985, Hearings before a Subcommittee of the Committee on Appropriations*, 98th cong., 2d sess., pt. B (Washington, D.C.: USGPO 1984) 789.

[74] William J. Crowe, "Implications of Low-Intensity Conflict for U.S. Policy and Strategy," *Low-Intensity Conflicts: Old Threats in a New World*, ed. Edwin G. Corr and Stephen Sloan (Boulder: Westview, 1992) 296. Admiral Crowe also points out that this commission also estimated that an adequate LIC response would only cost on average $12 billion.

[75] Loren E. Thompson. "Low-Intensity Conflict: An Overview," *Low-Intensity Conflict: The Pattern of Conflict in the Modern World*, ed. Loren C. Thompson (Lexington, MA: Lexington, 1989) 12.

[76] See Rep. Dan Daniel, "The Case for a Sixth Service," *Armed Forces Journal International*, August 1985, 70-75. Daniel (D-Va.) was chair of the House Armed Services Readiness Subcommittee which had oversight for special operations. See also Noel Koch, "Objecting to Reality: The Struggle to Restore U.S. Special Operations Forces," *Low-Intensity Conflict: The Pattern of Conflict in the Modern World*, ed. Loren B. Thompson (Lexington, MA: Lexington, 1989) 67, 69.

[77] See James Adams, *Secret Armies* (New York: Atlantic Monthly, 1981) 281. See also the text of H.R. 5109. According to the text, all forces, budget authority, training, doctrine, and control of missions would have come under the control of the new agency. I obtained the text in a personal file from an anonymous source. Hereafter cited as "Personal file."

[78] This was S. 2453. Adams 261.

[79] Mellon interview; Telephone interview with James Locher, 30 August 1993. From 1983 to 1985, Locher was the SASC study director for the effort that produced "Defense Organization: The Need for Change." This October 1985 staff study became the blueprint for Goldwater-Nichols. Locher would eventually become the Assistant Secretary of Defense for Special Operations and Low Intensity Conflict (ASD SO/LIC). For more on the interactions between Koch and Locher, see Colonel William G. Boykin, "Special Operations and Low-Intensity Conflict Legislation: Why Was it Passed and Have the Voids Been Filled?" Individual Study Project, U.S. Army War College, unpublished 8-11, 17.

[80] For a good summary of the process and the nature of these changes, see Vince Davis, "Organization and Management," *American Defense Annual, 1987-1988*, ed. Joseph Kruzel (Lexington, MA: Lexington, 1988) 171-199.

[81] Thompson, "Low-Intensity Conflict," 12-13.

[82] Colonel Albert N. Barnes, "Commander's Preface." A-AF CLIC, 1 January 1987-30 June 1987, 1.

[83] Mellon interview; Locher interview.

[84] I have used the term "military" in a general sense. Since the bulk of SOCOM's assets came from the Army, and since Readiness Command had been primarily an Army-dominated joint command, the Army bears much of the responsibility for these actions. This resistance is detailed in the following: Letter from Rep. Earl Kutto, Rep. Dan Daniel, and Rep. John R. Kasich to Secretary of Defense Caspar W. Weinberger, 11 March 1987; and Letter from Sen. William S. Cohen and Sen. Edward M. Kennedy to Secretary of Defense Caspar M. Weinberger, 19 May 1987. Contained in Personal File.

[85] Remarks from four retired four-star generals personally involved in the events of this period.

[86] Letter from Noel C. Koch to Sen. William S. Cohen, undated. Personal file.

[87] A-AF CLIC, 1 January 1989-30 June 1989 24.

[88] Sam Nunn, John Warner, Edward M. Kennedy, William S. Cohen, Letter to Brent Scowcroft, Assistant to the President for National Security Affairs (Designate), January 25, 1989. Contained in A-AF CLIC, 1 January 1989-30 June 1989.

[89] A-AF CLIC, 1 July 1989-31 December 1989 17.

[90] On the background of the senior leaders in this period, see Chris Mellon, "The Low Frontier: Congress and Unconventional Warfare," remarks at the National Defense University, unpublished, 11 January 1988, 36-37. Copy provided by Chris Mellon. The lack of career prospects for officers with special operations or low intensity backgrounds, and the possibility of elevating junior officers, was also noted and discussed in Noel C. Koch, 10 April 1984 testimony, 790-795.

[91] Koch, "Objecting to Reality," 57. Koch noted "that once ranking generals and admirals retired, they were capable of astonishing public departures from the established orthodoxy of their parent services."

[92] Locher interview.

[93] Telephone interview with Lieutenant General (retired) Samuel V. Wilson, 1 September 1993.

[94] Yarborough was a member of SOPAG as well until 1992. He resigned because too many members without sufficient background had been brought into the group, forcing the older members to spend an inordinate amount of time getting the new members "up to speed." Telephone interview with Lieutenant General (retired) William P. Yarborough, 5 August 1993. This does suggest that civilians made at least some use of SOPAG to directly influence the service chiefs through the prestige of the appointees, and not necessarily

to provide needed expertise.
[95] According to Robert Michels, the iron law is that "Organization implies the tendency to oligarchy." The oligarchy then tends to self-perpetuation. See the discussion of Michels' views in James A. Bill and Robert L. Hardgrave, *Comparative Politics: The Quest for Theory* (Lanham, MD: University Press, 1981) 154-156.
[96] Most of Koch, "Objecting to Reality," is devoted to these delaying tactics.
[97] Colonel D. Dennison Lane and Lieutenant Colonel Mark Weisenbloom, "Low-intensity Conflict: In Search of a Paradigm," *International Defense Review*, no. 1, 1990, 37.
[98] In the words of two critics who were high-ranking officers writing under false names, "The change in Army leadership in June 1983 brought a curious new view of the universe. The Army's global responsibilities had somehow changed overnight and now required that significant, new, rapidly deployable light forces be created whose focus was low-intensity conflict." Major General Sam Damon and Brigadier General Ben Krisler, "'Army of Excellence'? A Time to Take Stock," *Armed Forces Journal International*, May 1985, 66.
[99] See the criticism in Damon and Krisler above. Also see Harry Summers, "A War Is A War Is A War Is A War," *Low- Intensity Conflict: The Pattern of Conflict in the Modern World*, ed. Loren B. Thompson (Lexington, MA: Lexington, 1989) 27-49.
[100] Boykin 17.
[101] Brian Jenkins, George Tanham, Eleanor Wainstein, and Gerald Sullivan, *U.S. Preparation for Future Low-Level Conflict* (Santa Monica: RAND, July 1977) 8. This was a report of a conference held October 19-20, 1976, at the RAND Corporation, Washington, D.C.
[102] Telephone interview with General (retired) John A. Wickham, 5 August 1993.
[103] Telephone interview with General (retired) Wallace E. Nutting, 11 August 1993.
[104] Nutting interview.
[105] Letter from General Wallace A. Nutting to General William R. Richardson, Commander of TRADOC, 15 November 1984. JLIC Files, Book 1.
[106] Nutting set forth the need for such a study in two letters to General William R. Richardson in August and November 1984. The letters are contained in JLIC Files, Book 1. The final report of the study was the *Joint Low-intensity Conflict Project, Final Report* (Ft. Monroe, VA: U.S. Army Training and Doctrine Command, 1 August 1986). The report contained two volumes. The first volume dealt with the issue and nature of low intensity conflict. The second, which was classified, gave the project's specific recommendations.
[107] Locher interview.
[108] This view of Gorman's thought comes from Colonel Huba Was De Czege, Director, School of Advanced Military Studies, Ft. Leavenworth, KS, Letter to

General Richardson, Commander of TRADOC, 13 May 1985. JLIC Files, Book 1.

[109] General Gorman would also go on to chair a working group that focused on low intensity conflict for Fred C. Ikle and Albert Wohlstetter, et al, *Discriminate Deterrence: Report of the Commission on Integrated Long-Term Strategy* (Washington, D.C.: USGPO, January 1988). In retrospect, Gorman said, approvingly, that the Army's response to low intensity conflict in the 1980s was no different than it had been in the 1970s. And, contrary to the "bayonets last" doctrine of his time as SOUTHCOM commander, Gorman contended that "The whole purpose of the Army is to fight, not to build bridges or to give shots to children." Nor did he look favorably upon the use of the Army as "an humanitarian agency." Telephone interview with General (retired) Paul F. Gorman. The bulk of the documentary evidence, however, shows that Gorman acted, and spoke, differently about low intensity conflict in his last years of service, and immediately thereafter. In another interview, one of Gorman's contemporaries explained that Gorman would have been just as strong an advocate for heavy armored forces if he had been a commander in Europe. As it was, SOUTHCOM and low intensity conflict were his responsibilities, and he became an advocate for responding to the challenges at hand.

[110] John R. Galvin, "Uncomfortable Wars: Toward a New Paradigm," *Key LIC Speeches, 1984-1989*, ed. William F. Furr and Ronald L. Zelms (Langley Air Force Base, VA: Center for Low Intensity Conflict, September 1989) 26.

[111] Galvin 33.

[112] Interview with General John R. Galvin, 18 December 1992, West Point, NY.

[113] Galvin interview.

[114] Wickham interview. The leader of Project 14 was then- Brigadier General Colin Powell. Powell figured prominently in the Army's and the Defense Department's shift in strategic vision in the early 1990s.

[115] Romjue, *Army 86*, vol II 27. Meyer himself called those who opposed him the "Depuy and Starry faction." Meyer interview.

[116] Message from Commander, Forces Command [General Cavazos] to Chief of Staff of the Army, 151700Z March 1984, SUBJECT: Flying Hour Bankruptcy, Wickham Papers, Front Channel Messages, January 1983-February 1985. The Wickham Papers are stored at the U.S. Army Military History Institute, Carlisle Barracks, PA. Forces Command was responsible for all continental U.S. Army forces, subordinate to U.S. Readiness Command, at the time of the message.

[117] Message from General Cavazos, Commander of FORSCOM, 172135Z February 1984, SUBJECT: Rangers as part of SOC, Wickham Papers, Backchannel Messages, June 1983-March 1985, Subfile: Incoming, February 1984.

[118] For a discussion of this change in emphasis in the late 1980s, see Romjue,

Army of Excellence, 256-258.

[119] Wickham's successor as Chief of Staff, General Carl E. Vuono, spoke of "striking a balance" between heavy and light forces after the years when "zealots" for lighter forces had dominated the debate over force structures and future conflict. Vuono interview.

[120] See the Was de Czege letter, JLIC Files, Book 1. Was de Czege, a principal author of the 1982 edition of FM 100-5 and deeply involved in the revision, talks about "guerrilla hunting" in the letter, and the need for good doctrine for this sort of conflict as well as good doctrine for advisory duty. He does not talk about the need for low intensity conflict doctrine. As it was, even guerrilla hunting got short shrift in the 1986 edition.

[121] All quotes in this paragraph come from Paul F. Gorman, et al, *Supporting U.S. Strategy for Third World Conflict: Report by the Regional Conflict Working Group Submitted to the Commission on Integrated Long-Term Strategy* (Washington, D.C.: Department of Defense, June 1988) 26.

[122] Note above the observations of the JRTC by officers from the CLIC: too much of the JRTC was focused on peacetime contingency operations and counterinsurgency. The latter mission was also too readily seen as the special province of SOF. A-AF CLIC, 2 January 1988 - 30 June 1988 13. The quote comes from a telephone interview with General (retired) Richard E. Cavazos, 20 August 1993.

[123] Meyer interview.

[124] See, for example. A-AF CLIC, 1 July 1968-31 December 1988 16. The CLIC stressed that SOF had an important, but not a dominant role, in low intensity conflict. Indeed all forces had a role to play. In the supporting documents attached to this report, see Colonel Albert M. Barnes, Commander CLIC, Letter to United States Special Operations Command, SUBJECT: Review of USSOCOM LIC Umbrella Concept, 5 December 1988: "In the LIC, as well as MIC and HIC environments, SOF assets play an important supporting role...but by no means the major role.... It must be kept in mind that the interagency nature of LIC operations and their inherently politically directed nature *forces* a supporting role on *all* military operations in this environment." Emphasis in original.

CHAPTER 6

AFTER THE COLD WAR:
OLD CHALLENGES, NEW FREEDOM

"The United States is not likely, over the next 20 years, to undertake a major, protracted, conventional war against any Third World adversary."

— General Paul F. Gorman, 1988[1]

"We must have a force of broad capabilities - able to rescue societies caught in the pre-industrial revolution, while still able to fight 21st century wars."

— General Gordon R. Sullivan, 1993[2]

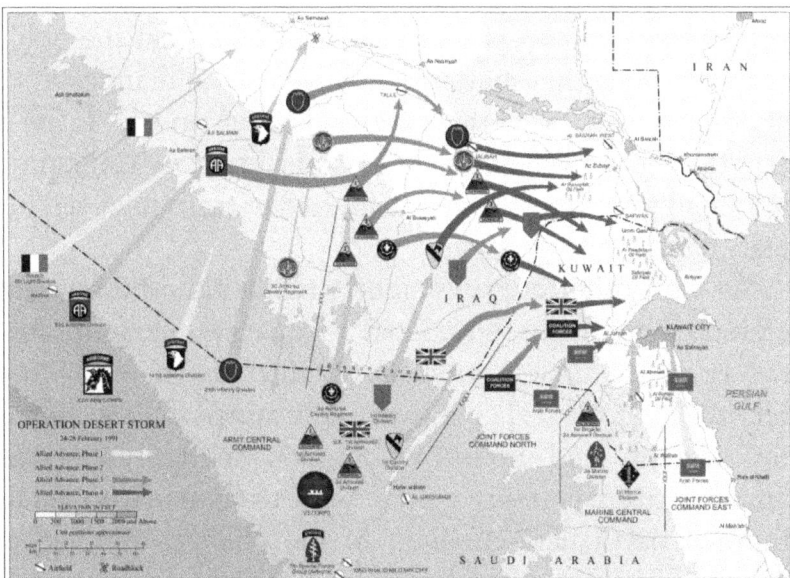

Operation Desert Storm

This period begins with the ending of the Cold War, followed by the successful defense of Saudi Arabia and the liberation of Kuwait - a regional crisis, or a "half-war" of the type that military planners generally gave lip service to in the preceding two decades. By the end of 1991, the adversary of the Cold War, the USSR, ceased to exist.

Even before the demise of the USSR and the advent of the Iraqi crisis, the Army was planning to significantly reorganize itself along smaller lines. The disappearance of the threat in Europe merely hastened this process and deepened the force and budget cuts. While the USSR was gone, the challenge of low intensity conflict and of regional crises remained. Much of the debate in this period was focused on how to confront these remaining threats, and at what level of priority. With the Soviet focus gone, there was intellectual latitude to reconsider old beliefs. The belief that low intensity missions were the near-exclusive province of special operations forces (SOF) suffered a serious blow, particularly from the humanitarian intervention in Somalia. This was true, similarly, of the belief that the only low intensity missions that mattered involved some manifestation of revolutionary war. Still, the toughest belief proved to be that soldiers trained for the exigencies of mid-intensity combat could easily extend that expertise to the myriad of tasks involved in low intensity conflict.

As with other chapters above, neither the Posen nor the Rosen model, by themselves, is an adequate explanation for the Army's response to low intensity conflict in the early 1990s. Rather, the Army's response was determined by the nexus of civilian pressure and intergroup conflict. Civilian policymakers continued to exert pressure on the Army to change from its focus on Europe, particularly in light of the changes in the Soviet Union, and ultimately, its demise.

In the Bush administration, executive branch civilians did

not push the Army as hard as did civilian legislators in Congress. Consequently, the Army leadership was able initially to exploit these differences to remain focused on any possible resurgent threat from the Soviet Union. After Desert Storm, new Army leadership was more willing to meet civilian demands for changes in force structure, doctrine, and training.

In the Clinton administration, the Secretary of Defense had been one of the persistent congressional critics of earlier defense policies. Thus, after 1993, the combination of similar executive and legislative pressures for change met a more willing Army leadership. As a result, the Army seemed poised for fundamental organizational change which would elevate low intensity conflict missions to equal status with mid- and high-intensity missions.

This chapter confirms the synthesis developed at the end of chapter 5: civilian intervention into the operational doctrine of the Army can provoke change. However, the character of the change depends on whether the civilians act through "traditionalists" or through "visionaries." If the civilians work through the traditionalists, much of the impetus for reform will be thwarted, and any changes will be easily reversed peripheral changes. If the civilians work through visionaries, fundamental organizational change is possible, although it may begin as incremental, or peripheral, change.

SECURITY ENVIRONMENT

As early as October 1989, General Colin Powell, the new Chairman of the Joint Chiefs of Staff, had come to the conclusion that the reforms initiated by Soviet Premier Mikhail Gorbachev would usher in a new security era for the United States.[3] Consequently, Powell immediately set to work defining the new environment that the United States would face in the decade of the 1990s.

With the demise of the Soviet Union in late 1991, and the success of Operations Desert Shield and Desert Storm, other leaders, uniformed and civilian, also weighed in. The result was a greater focus on regional threats to U.S. interests. Chief among these threats was the ill-defined "instability," and the well-understood threat of proliferation of advanced weaponry to regional powers.

The Bush administration's views changed more slowly at first than did Powell's. While viewing favorably the events in Europe in late 1989, the administration initially cautioned that "No one can predict the ultimate resolution of these events...."[4] Low intensity conflict was, according to Secretary of Defense Dick Cheney, still the most likely form of conflict.[5] Yet, in keeping with the one of the misconceptions, Cheney's first report to Congress dealt with low intensity conflict totally within the context of special operations forces.[6] Under the influence of the Iraqi operations, Cheney's next report was much more focused on regional conflict, while still remaining cautious on the Soviet Union.[7] The new strategic focus was now what President Bush had termed "peacetime engagement" - the shifting of "defense planning from countering the global challenge posed by the Soviet Union to responding to threats in major regions...."[8]

Despite Powell's broad vision of the potential for change, and the Bush administration's slower approach to change, much of the thrust of the new strategy remained focused on the mid-intensity dangers of future Iraqi-style wars brought on by the proliferation of high-technology weapons and weapons of mass destruction.[9] Widespread agreement among the various leaders in the services and the legislature was not achieved. None of the service chiefs immediately agreed with Powell. All of them argued for a future more like the past.[10] The Army's initial plan envisioned reducing the force only down to 625,000, mostly in response to the anticipated results of the Conventional Forces in

Europe (CFE) Treaty.[11]

Domestic factors in the security environment also argued for a different approach to defense. Desert Shield and Desert Storm occurred during an economic recession, the savings and loan bailout, and the rancor over large annual budget deficits, and the requirements of the Gramm-Rudman law, which could have required automatic cuts as large as 25% in the defense budget. Partisans of all political persuasions agreed that the United States had entered a period of fiscal difficulty and constrained budgets, a sentiment similar to those expressed in the Astarita Report of 18 years earlier. Even though President Bush's 2 August 1990 speech in Aspen, Colorado, announced huge cuts in defense, there were several legislative leaders who sought more, particularly given the changes in central Europe.[12]

In particular, Representative Les Aspin, who as the leader of the House Armed Services Committee found fault with both the pace of change and the ultimate strategy. Often using Congressional Budget Office figures on adequate defense spending in the post-Cold War era, Aspin asked for larger cuts than the Bush administration was willing to make as early as June 1991.[13] Furthermore, Aspin disagreed with the fundamental basis of the new strategy, which was to restructure U.S. forces based on multiple capabilities. Aspin wanted the strategy to be based on perceived future threats.[14] Interestingly, though, Aspin defined such threats as regional instability. Whereas General Powell emphasized the decisive commitment of force for only the clearest of objectives, Aspin seemed willing to structure forces for murkier missions such as peacekeeping and peace enforcing.[15] Aspin objected to Powell's formulations in that they implied that forces would be used only in extreme cases.

The result of the strategic debate within the Bush administration was the new National Military Strategy of 1992. The new strategy was "built upon the four key foundations of the

National Defense Strategy: Strategic Deterrence and Defense, Forward Presence, Crisis Response, and Reconstitution." Proclaiming success in the Cold War, Powell's strategy foresaw future threats arising from "the uncertainty and instability of a rapidly changing world."[16] The threat was defined as simply "the unknown, the uncertain," but did reflect the national strategy's shift to regional rather than global threats.[17] This new military strategy was coupled with the Bush administration plan to reduce defense spending by roughly 25% known as the "Base Force Plan." The plan would reduce the Army by close to one-third, including six of the eighteen active duty divisions. The plan would also greatly reduce U.S. deployments overseas (forward presence), forcing greater reliance on U.S.-based rapidly deployable forces (crisis response). Forward presence, though, was not to be just the stationing of troops in Europe or Korea. It also included many low intensity missions such as security and humanitarian assistance which required soldiers to operate overseas temporarily from home bases in the United States.[18]

The initial modifications of the Clinton administration appeared to be along the lines that Secretary of Defense Les Aspin advocated while leader of the House Armed Services Committee. The administration planned to reduce the Army further, but also to use it more frequently, particularly in situations which were not as clear and unambiguous as the previous administration sought. Rather than seeking an early end to the U.S. humanitarian mission in Somalia, as the Bush administration intended, the Clinton administration extended it, placing the U.S. troops, most coming from the Army's 10th Mountain Division (Light), under UN authority. The Clinton administration also sent 300 Army soldiers to police the Macedonian border with Serbia. In its early days, the Clinton administration also offered thousands of troops for a UN peacekeeping effort in Bosnia, and another brigade-sized force for nation-assistance in Haiti.

These events reflected a change in emphasis and willingness to use force short of war. Aspin reorganized the Defense Department by creating two new assistant secretary positions to reflect the new strategic views that emphasized the fear of regional instability and fear of "the unknown, the uncertain:" the Assistant Secretary of Defense for Democracy and Human Rights and the Assistant Secretary for Nuclear Security and Counter Proliferation.[19]

THE ARMY RESPONSE

The result of this tumult in the strategic view of the security environment was that low intensity conflict entered the mainstream for all of the services. The Navy and Marine Corps even adopted a "littoral" strategy, or as some called it, a "brown water" strategy, that foresaw the future in terms of force projection from the sea and not maritime dominance, which was taken as a given.[20]

The Army also reconfigured its thinking. As Army Chief of Staff Gordon Sullivan put it, "America needs a different model by which to raise, equip, organize, educate, train, fight, coordinate, and sustain her armed forces."[21] Sullivan also suggested two ways of viewing the use of force: "war," and "operations other than war."[22] The latter became low intensity conflict by its latest name. Sullivan maintained that this new view of warfare was necessary in order to replace the negative aim of containment - stopping the spread of Soviet power - with a positive aim - "to promote democracy, regional stability, and economic prosperity."[23] Additionally, this shift in views would allow the Army to get smaller, yet more active at home in all manner of civic undertakings from disaster relief to the vaccinating of inner city children, thus contributing to "the challenges of domestic regeneration."[24]

The consequence of Sullivan's views, which were very different from those of his predecessor, was that the Army would be much more active at home and abroad, despite reducing its size by at least 33%. In 1993 the Army had 590,000 soldiers on active duty. Under the new policies, about 25,000 were engaged in deployments to more than sixty countries on any given day.[25] This was double the amount of 1992, and was slated to rise, while the Army's end strength was slated to fall. Almost all of these deployments would fall into the categories of low intensity conflict.

To respond to these changes in the security environment and in the national strategy, the Army completed, or planned, major changes in force structure, doctrine and training.

FORCE STRUCTURE

The size and final composition of the Army in this period were not settled issues. The Army's size under the Base Force plan included 12 active divisions, of which at least four were in the light category.[26] Other plans had the Army variously at ten, nine, eight, or six, with the light-heavy mix unknown.[27]

In recognition of the changes in the security environment, with the increased emphasis on regional and non-traditional threats, one community which fared well was the SOF community. Not only had Army Special Forces avoided budget cuts, but a new Special Forces Group, and five Theater Area Special Forces Support Commands were added to the active force structure.[28]

In fact, some of the force structure gains for the SOF resulted directly from concerns for low intensity missions. This represented a departure from the past. One of the enduring misconceptions is that low intensity missions such as counterinsurgency can be handled easily by troops trained for mid- or high intensity conflict - the modern manifestation of

General Decker's famous "Any good soldier can handle guerrillas" quote. As a consequence, units were created for a war fighting mission, even in the SOF, and then were assigned low intensity missions as secondary concerns. Or, as one SOF leader put it, "Whatever is needed in LIC, or a peacetime contingency operation, is already present [in the Special Operations Forces] due to [planning for] war."[29] However, in the 1990s, the SOF structure was enlarged because of its applicability to low intensity conflict.[30] These changes give some indication that civilian administrators and legislators continued to place value on the multifaceted capabilities of SOF, and that the Army translated that support into action.

DOCTRINE

In late 1990, the Army issued a new edition of FM 100-20, now titled *Military Operations in Low Intensity Conflict*. As was Army policy, the new doctrinal manual was supposed to drive the development of derivative "how to fight" manuals as well as requirements for unit organizations, training, and equipment.[31] However, as will be noted below, the new manual was almost dead upon arrival. This edition represented, however, a significant improvement over both the 1981 edition and the interim field circular of 1986.

The 1990 edition maintained the four broad categories from the mid-1980s: insurgency, terrorism, peacekeeping, and peacetime contingency operations. The manual devoted chapters to each category. The writers addressed in detail the political environment of each of the different categories, emphasizing the often highly charged political nature of low intensity conflict, and the ever present ethical, moral, and legal dilemmas.[32] Another significant change was the inclusion, as an "imperative," of the notion of "legitimacy, " defined as "the willing acceptance of the right of a government to govern or of a group or agency to make and enforce decisions."[33]

In another change, in the section on "U.S. Military Support to Insurgency," the manual stated that since "support for insurgency is often covert, many of the operations connected with it are special activities."[34] Consequently, Army Special Forces, with their training in unconventional warfare, were the primary means, supported by conventional units with technical capabilities such as communications or intelligence analysis. The manual went on to say that within areas under insurgent control, the task for U.S. forces essentially becomes one of Internal Defense and Development (IDAD).[35] In essence, supporting insurgency became a combination of two other missions - unconventional warfare and IDAD. Success in all low intensity operations, according to the manual, depended upon encouraging and sustaining legitimacy.[36]

With this manual, the Army moved low intensity conflict much beyond the near total counterinsurgency focus of the earlier doctrinal publications. Yet, because the topic of low intensity conflict was treated so lightly in the main doctrinal manual then in existence - the 1986 edition of FM 100-5 *Operations* - the new FM 100-20 was not taken seriously. Moreover, the new FM 100-20 was put into revision almost upon being issued.

The Chief of Staff, General Carl Vuono, and his doctrine writers at TRADOC, determined that having two doctrines - one for war fighting and another for low intensity conflict - no longer made sense.[37] The chief doctrine writer for the 1993 edition of FM 100-5, Colonel James McDonough, maintained that all Army operations deserved treatment in the new manual.[38] Moreover, McDonough thought that low intensity conflict should be seen "as part of a wider, general theory of war."[39] To encompass this wider theory, "Doctrine should address nonconventional operations in operations short of war, during limited hostile action and in conditions of war and its aftermath."[40] Also, "Future doctrine should be expanded to incorporate our evolving missions in areas such as stability operations, nation assistance and contraband flow."[41]

Working on these views, strengthened by the changes in the security environment, the Army went so far as to close down the Army Proponent Office for Low Intensity Conflict, and absorbed the functions of that office into the standard doctrine offices of the Command and General Staff College at Ft. Leavenworth. If low intensity conflict was to be treated as a part of standard Army operations, then a separate office seemed unnecessary. On the other hand, the possibility exists that the issue had once again become so contentious that no office wanted the responsibility.[42] Contentiousness also arose over the definition and scope of low intensity conflict with President Bush's 2 August 1990 speech at Aspen, Colorado. Bush spoke of "peacetime engagement," which observers took to mean, variously, a new security strategy for the United States, a component of a new strategy, or a new name for low intensity conflict. Where the Bush speech seemed to refer to the whole breadth of American foreign policy, Secretary of Defense Cheney in his 1991 annual report called peacetime engagement "a strategy that seeks to counteract violence and to promote nation-building."[43] Among the crafters of the U.S. statements on national strategy and military strategy, "peacetime engagement" was in competition with "active presence" and "forward presence" as names for U.S. activities abroad.[44] For the Office of the Assistant Secretary of Defense for Special Operations and Low Intensity Conflict (ASD SO/LIC), peacetime engagement was "the multipolar aspect, less major regional wars, of our evolving security policy."[45] That is, for ASD SO/LIC, peacetime engagement was everything normally associated with low intensity conflict.

The resulting interagency confusion made the writing of Army doctrine very difficult. Officers from the Center for Low Intensity Conflict (CLIC) who worked with the team that developed the new edition of FM 100-5 found it necessary to remind the other members in attendance that "Congress had directed DOD to address LIC and [also] by reminding the body that a large and useful amount of LIC doctrine and concepts already existed."[46] These officers also "were troubled to meet participants who had 'an aversion to the term "LIC"' and were so ready to ignore 'all excellent concepts and useful [extant low intensity conflict] doctrine in the process'."[47] The CLIC officers also recorded the unresolved disagreements among the Army and ASD SO/LIC representatives over peacetime engagement. Reminiscent of the long-standing disagreement over war fighting versus low intensity conflict, the Army argued for a narrow interpretation that encompassed only activities not involving combat. ASD SO/LIC wanted the expansive definition that included all activities short of a Desert Storm.[48] Ultimately, the Army adopted a new name for low intensity conflict - "operations other than war."

Perhaps as a result of the confusion, the 1993 edition of FM 100-5 exhibits certain discontinuities. As promised by McDonough, the manual propounded a unified vision of Army operations that fully incorporated what had been known as low intensity conflict. The process of rewriting FM 100-5 *Operations* had begun before Desert Shield and Desert Storm.[49] In the aftermath of the Gulf War, the rewriting began anew to incorporate lessons learned and the new military strategy. Consequently, the opening statement is a direct reflection of the changed strategy: "[This manual] addresses fundamentals of a force-projection army with forward-deployed forces."[50] Furthermore, the manual "is the authoritative guide to how the Army forces fight wars and conduct operations other than war."[51]

Yet, the manual quickly assured the reader that:

> "Winning wars is the primary purpose of the doctrine in this manual....The manual also addresses the related fields of joint and combined operations, logistics, the environment of combat, and operations other than war. But, its primary focus is war fighting and how commanders put all the elements together to achieve victory at least cost to American soldiers."[52]

With these statements, it becomes clear that low intensity conflict, now called operations other than war, had made it into the mainstream of Army thinking. But, unlike joint and combined operations - respectively operations with sister U.S. services and with allied foreign militaries - or logistics, the vast majority of operations other than war are not directly linked to war fighting. The manual's writers seem uncomfortable with the difference, proclaiming in one instance, that "the spirit of the offense...characterizes the American soldier."[53] This directly conflicts with some of requirements for low intensity missions as will be noted below.

The writers wrestled with the notion of how to handle anything less than war fighting. In a subsection titled "The Range of Military Operations," the manual states,

> "The Army classifies its activities during peacetime and conflict as *operations other than war*. During *peacetime*, the US attempts to influence world events through these actions that routinely occur between nations. *Conflict* is characterized by

> hostilities to secure strategic objectives.
> The last environment - that of *war* -
> involves the use of force in combat
> operations against an armed enemy."[54]

Clearly there is confusion here between conflict, combat, hostilities, and war. The confusion, which the manual never resolves, stems, perhaps from changeover in leadership at TRADOC. After the Gulf War, General Frederick Franks, the commander of VIIth Corps in Desert Storm, replaced General John Foss at TRADOC. According to Foss, before Desert Storm the initial writing of the manual was to have focused even more heavily on low intensity conflict. However, after the Gulf War, Desert Storm became "the model for the future."[55]

The remaining ambiguities no doubt reflect the lack of agreement among the writers and reviewers of the manual. One clue to the dividing line between these terms comes from the views of General Sullivan, who became Chief of Staff in mid-1991:

> "The concept of 'war' is usually understood
> in terms of conventional combat: the
> armies of one nation-state or alliances of
> nation-states fighting those of another.
> Every other act of violence, use of force, or
> form of hostility is characterized as
> 'operations other than war.'"[56]

Sullivan's distinction between these terms is very close to the definitions established for this book in chapter 2 above. However, his distinctions would allow any interstate combat to be called war, no matter the level of violence or casualties, thus allowing the definitional problem of the "small war" to creep back in. Finally, the manual's definitions also lump low intensity conflict missions, which all involve at least some chance of combat, into the same category as domestic civic missions involving almost no chance of combat whatsoever. While the 1993 edition of *Operations* continues, and even expands, the conceptual fuzziness of low intensity conflict, it does break new ground by bringing low intensity missions into the mainstream and giving them near-equal billing with war fighting. The manual notes that a regional commander-in-chief may be conducting peacetime and conflict operations in one part of his region simultaneously with a war in another part.[57] The manual then devotes an entire chapter to the topic of operations other than war, heavy with highlighted, inset references to "operations other than war" which had been conducted at home and abroad since 1990 - such as support to civil authorities in the aftermath of Hurricane Andrew in Florida, a nation-assistance mission involving immunizations in Cameroon, and Operation Provide Comfort in Northern Iraq.

Note that the missions in Florida and Cameroon involved practically no threat of combat, while the humanitarian mission in Northern Iraq did. One officer interviewed for this book stated that missions such as the one in Florida, officially dubbed "support to civil authorities," would occupy much more of the Army's time in the future in reflection of the Clinton administration's policies.[58] Absent a potential conflict situation, vaccinations in Cameroon would differ little from vaccinations in American cities or rural areas. The Army lumped these operations together with those that involved the potential of combat, and those that involved small-scale combat.[59] Another officer suggested that the Clinton administration officials on the National Security Council were uncomfortable with the very notion of "war" and "conflict," preferring to call all operations, absent a declaration of war, "peace operations."[60] Hence, one can perhaps surmise the reason for the shift away from low intensity conflict to "operations other than war." This category had now officially grown, incredibly, broader and more diffuse.[61]

The manual notes the necessity of including this category of operations in the capstone doctrine because "Army forces have participated in operations other than war in support of national interests throughout its history."[62] And, in an even grander sense, "The entire Army... is involved daily in operations other than war."[63]

What does the manual say of the conduct of these operations? Continuing the progress begun in the 1990 edition of FM 100-20, the chapter highlights the importance of legitimacy, restraint, and perseverance: "In operations other than war, victory comes more subtly than in war. Disciplined forces, measured responses, and patience are essential to successful outcomes."[64] In further contrast with the FM 100-5 manuals of the 1970s and 1980s, with their concentration on speedy victory by massed maneuvering of armored units, in operations other than war "the activities of relatively small units can have operational - and even strategic - impact."[65]

The concern for perseverance and restraint in the chapter on operations other than war comes across strange in comparison to the focus in the rest of the manual on speed, maneuver, and firepower. In a manual that proclaims that the American soldier is imbued with an offensive spirit, notions such as patience, subtlety, and measured response are an odd fit. The aggressiveness and lack of hesitation inherent in an offensive spirit clearly conflict with the reticence and judiciousness inherent in the idea that "the use of overwhelming force may complicate the process toward the Army's stated objectives." Certainly the training required of the soldier faced with an operation other than war would be more similar to that of a police officer than of a combat soldier. Yet, the manual, reflecting the "Any good soldier..." mindset, simply states, "In preparing to fight the nation's wars, the Army develops the leadership, organizations, equipment, discipline, and skills for a variety of operations other than war."[66]

This edition of FM 100-5 broke new ground in its treatment of low intensity missions. The nagging discontinuities in its treatment of the primary purpose of the Army - war - and its treatment of the activities in which the Army engages daily are no doubt a reflection of the debate mentioned above over the scope and definition of low intensity conflict. That the topic had been brought into the capstone manual is also a direct reflection of the perceived changes in the security environment and the missions that the Army was required to perform as the manual was being written. Any changes in FM 100-5 *Operations* also directed future force structuring efforts, and provided the foundation for changes in training programs.[67] With the new capstone doctrine in place, the Army began work on FM 100-23 *Peace Operations*, which was to be the replacement for the 1990 edition of FM 100-20. In keeping with the categories of activities set forth in FM 100-5, this new manual would address all activities not included in "war," and would significantly expand the treatment of peacekeeping and peace enforcement in light of operations that had been recently conducted in Somalia and Macedonia.[68]

While the effect on Army force structure was not yet apparent by the end of 1993, the new doctrine had an immediate impact on training as will be discussed in the following section.

TRAINING

The content of Army training reflects what the Army itself expects to do. The Army's new doctrine may have been "the authoritative guide to how the Army forces fight wars and conduct operations other than war."[69] The Army may have officially elevated low intensity conflict to a daily concern for the Army. For these changes to have impact, though, required Army leaders to translate them into concrete programs for force structure and training. As noted above, force structure was still fluid and would be ultimately governed by budgetary pressures. Only a few units were programmed to be structured primarily for low intensity operations. Rather, existing units were to be assigned low intensity missions as secondary concerns. However, the changes in the manner of Army training after 1990 was a strong indication of perhaps fundamental change in the basic organizational behavior of the Army. The changes in training directly reflected 1) civilian guidance from the executive branch, and 2) experience with the missions the Army received in the early 1990s.

The immediate impact of Desert Storm on training seems to have been to validate the armored warfare training conducted in view of the European threat, and to underscore the necessity of maintaining the ability to fight an armored conflict in any future regional contingency. However, the increase in the number of non-traditional uses of the Army in the period immediately following Desert Storm forced the Army to focus on these missions in a specific manner that had not been seen previously in the entire period that this study covers. Moreover, in 1992, the Secretary of Defense ordered unified commanders to incorporate low intensity missions into their planning and coordination.[70] To operate effectively in the changed environment, the unified commanders had to have trained troops. The Army, with the mission of supplying the bulk of the troops likely to engage in low intensity missions, moved to change training to confront the post-Cold War world and inculcate the regional focus of the new national military strategy.

The effort to change training for low intensity missions ran up against the enduring notion, given continued credence even in the new FM 100-5 that training for war fighting was so good that low intensity missions could be handled with ease.[71] However, such wishful thinking was not borne out by events.

Artillery officers deployed to Somalia in early 1993 had prepared traditionally for the mission by studying the order of battle and weaponry available to the Somali warlords.[72] Since fire support turned out not to be crucial to the humanitarian mission, despite the danger from heavily-armed clans, the artillerymen were assigned as civil affairs staff officers in the Army battalions and brigades which composed the relief force. Normally, units of this size were not authorized this staffing unless specially augmented by reserves.[73] Similarly, the 10th Division's engineer battalion was deployed to Somalia. Like all divisional engineer battalions, this one had been configured to support offensive operations. They found in Somalia that they needed construction skills that they had not been practicing.[74]

The 10th Division's infantry trained prior to deployment on basic tasks such as patrolling, establishing and manning check points, and general information on Somali society and culture. Since the division had been one of the primary units sent to aid in the Hurricane Andrew relief operation in 1992, the division took their Florida experience and added to it the possible ingredient of hostilities. What they found upon arrival is that they had had insufficient time to train on controlling riotous crowds that their knowledge of the underlying culture and its current problems was superficial, that they were unprepared for the lack of basic infrastructure, and were unskilled in operating as part of an international force. In short, they had trained on basic war fighting tasks and found themselves unprepared for the reality of a low intensity mission.[75]

In June and July 1993, several hundred Army troops deployed to Macedonia as part of a UN peacekeeping force patrolling the Yugoslav-Macedonian border. However, the commander of the UN force would not allow the U.S. forces to assume patrolling duty until after they had extensive training in how to operate under very restrictive rules of engagement. The UN commander feared that the U.S. soldiers had been trained to be too aggressive to handle the job of peacekeeper, which sometimes requires soldiers to surrender rather than provoke, and only to fire after having been fired upon.[76]

With such examples as these, and under pressure from civilian authorities, Army officials began to change their view on training. As one Army official put it, units "can take many of the same skills, particularly individual skills, and transfer them to low intensity missions. Where it gets difficult is at higher ranks...."[77] Officers and senior noncommissioned officers on humanitarian or peacekeeping missions had to deal directly with media, representatives of nongovernmental organizations, and noncombatants in huge numbers. "Hence, there are a multitude of supplemental training tasks that we need to focus on."[78] In the view of the commander of the Army Engineer school, the unit deficiencies like the ones noted above had to be addressed through changes in the tasks on which the units practiced, known as the Mission Essential Task List. Those tasks were then exercised in training scenarios and exercises.[79]

The highest quality training exercises available to the Army occurred at the Combat Training Centers (CTCs). These were the Joint Readiness Training Center (JRTC), the National Training Center at Ft. Irwin, CA, and the Combat Maneuver Training Center at Hohenfels, Germany. Established in the 1980s, the latter two CTCs focused almost exclusively on preparing for war in Europe. By 1993, the Army changed the content of training at the CTCs to reflect the most likely employment of soldiers. The training became much more sophisticated than just guerrilla-hunting and border defense. The scenarios included media, often true journalists invited to observe and interview, and a variety of "civilian" players who acted as terrorists, snipers, friendlies, and neutrals. The Chief of Staff, General Sullivan, described the purpose of this training: "The ability of a commander to deal with civilians of unknown loyalty or political persuasion is crucial and is one [in] which we were often found lacking in Vietnam."[80]

While the National Training Center incorporated noncombatant and other civil-military scenarios into its training, the focus of this CTC, however, remained on waging armored warfare, but against potential, heavily-armed Third World adversaries.[81] The European CTC, which used to focus exclusively on training units to combat Soviet armored formations in Central Europe, changed to focus on operations across the conflict spectrum. In particular, it began training Army units for possible peacekeeping or peace enforcement missions in the Balkans. The units trained according to a variety of scenarios which included irregular and regular forces armed with an array of weaponry. As at the other two CTCs, dealing with noncombatants was heavily emphasized.[82]

The only paradoxical element to these changes is the stationing of a light armored cavalry regiment at the JRTC. A superficial analysis would suggest that this was an intelligent move given the armored remnants that were available to potential adversaries in Yugoslavia and Somalia. However, the decision was made to station the armored force at the JRTC before those contingencies became likely, however fortuitous it may have turned out.[83] The decision was likely influenced more by the desire to retain a light armored force capable of early reinforcement of XVIIIth Airborne Corps forces in a future crisis similar to Desert Storm.

The changes in the manner of Army training after 1990 is a strong indication of perhaps fundamental change in the basic organizational behavior of the Army. Unlike changes in training in the early 1960s or in the 1980s, which were often more cosmetic than real, most of the changes by 1993 appeared to be largely in the direction desired by civilian authorities. The question now becomes which of the two competing models - the structural model of Posen or the human resources model of Rosen - is the better explanation for the change.

EXPLANATION I: CIVILIAN-MILITARY INTEGRATION AND THE SEARCH FOR A MAVERICK

Like the periods 1961-1964 and 1979-1989, this period exhibits civilian pressure on the Army to respond to the challenge of low intensity conflict. The changes wrought by civilians in the 1990s have to be associated with the general continuity of ideas, and often of personnel, in the Reagan and Bush administrations. As in the 1980s, the pressure for change after 1990 came from both executive branch and legislative civilians.

Of the key civilians involved in pushing for reform in the 1980s, only Rep. Dan Daniel was gone. However, co-sponsors of his bill to create a National Special Operations Agency included Les Aspin and Ronald V. Dellums, among others, who remained powerful members of the House Armed Services Committee in the 1990s.[84] In the Senate, both Sam Nunn and William Cohen, co-authors of the 1986 legislation that created U.S. Special Operations Command and the position of Assistant Secretary of Defense for Special Operations and Low Intensity Conflict (ASD SO/LIC), remained powerful members of the Senate Armed Services Committee, which Nunn had chaired since 1987. Senators Edward Kennedy and John Glenn also maintained an interest in seeing the Nunn-Cohen Amendment fully implemented.[85] Thus, most of the chief legislative advocates for change in the 1980s remained to continue their activities in the 1990s.[86]

Additionally, one of the key legislative staff members behind the Nunn-Cohen Amendment, James Locher, was appointed by the Bush administration to be the Assistant Secretary of Defense for Special Operations and Low Intensity Conflict. Locher served for the entire Bush presidency and remained as a holdover in the Clinton administration until June 1993, adding farther continuity to civilian efforts.

Perhaps the most important civilian in the early 1990s with respect to low intensity conflict was Les Aspin. As chairman of the House Armed Services Committee, Aspin was a persistent critic of the Bush administration's slowness to recognize the importance of the changed security environment. In a series of House Armed Services Committee hearings, held from December 1991 through April 1992, Aspin criticized the Bush administration for not proposing deeper cuts in the armed forces.[87] His contention was that the Bush administration Base Force Plan was based on the world as of August 1990, and not on a world without the Soviet Union as existed by late 1991.[88] In an attempt to answer criticism that his proposals, which had become caught up with the Democratic presidential campaign by September 1992, would diminish U.S. defense capabilities, Aspin sought to provide a basis for the use of U.S. forces not only in regional conflicts of the Gulf War variety, but also in non-traditional arenas such as peacekeeping and humanitarian interventions.[89]

As the Posen model would predict, the military did resist many of these efforts, particularly in 1990-1991. After the fall of the Berlin Wall, according to one high ranking Department of Defense official, military leaders shifted their focus to other conventional threats - called "major regional contingencies," such as "blowing Iran and Iraq out of the water." James Locher, then serving as Assistant Secretary of Defense for Special Operations and Low Intensity Conflict, noted that resistance to the notion of low intensity conflict actually grew as services moved to protect their "core interests," which had been focused on the Soviet threat.[90] Consequently, the Army, along with the other services, initially kept its focus on a possibly resurgent Soviet Union.[91]

Even military leaders who agreed that a response to the changing strategic environment was necessary often disagreed over the appropriate means. This was particularly true for General Colin Powell, the Chairman of the Joint Chiefs of Staff, but also for some of his contemporaries in the Army, who differed sharply with Aspin, both in his position as chairman of the House Armed Services Committee and in his later post as Secretary of Defense, over the appropriate response to the problem areas of the post-Cold War world, such as Somalia and Bosnia. According to one civilian official, "Powell and his ilk" were much more cautious than the civilians about interventions abroad, but committed to the massive use of force once a decision to intervene was reached.[92] Aspin, on the other hand, was much more willing to attempt the judicious use of force.

Consequently, in the Bush administration, when Powell's influence was at its zenith, force was used on a large scale - Desert Shield, Desert Storm, and the humanitarian interventions, each numbering in the tens of thousands of troops, in northern Iraq and Somalia. When Aspin became Secretary of Defense, and Powell's influence was weakened, the Somali intervention was scaled back to less than 5,000 Army troops, but they engaged in protracted combat. Additionally, three hundred Army troops were sent to the Yugoslav-Macedonian border, and threats of "surgical" airstrikes were made against Bosnian Serbs.

On balance, this period tends to confirm the basic thrust of Posen's model - militaries change due to civilian pressure. However, this period also indicates weaknesses in the Posen approach. This approach cannot adequately explain why change proceeded slowly, 1990-1991, and much more rapidly 1992-1993. Part of the reason why change moved slowly in the first two years was due to military resistance, which Posen leads us to expect. The other reason is because much of the external impetus for reform was mitigated by disagreements among the civilians - a possibility not explored in the Posen model. Aspin and Cheney disagreed over the scope and pace of changes during the Bush administration. Within the executive branch in both the Bush and Clinton administrations, civilian officials also engaged in wasteful battles concerning authority over low intensity issues. These disagreements were particularly intense in the Bush administration.

As one officer serving on the Army staff at the time described it, James Locher was a "Nunn man" who tried to "break all the rice bowls." According to this critic, Locher tried to get the Department of Defense to make ASD SO/LIC the office ultimately responsible for low intensity conflict policy, a responsibility that then fell under the Assistant Secretaries for International Security Affairs (ISA) and International Security Policy (ISP). When Locher failed, he "tried to go over the heads of [Under Secretary of Defense for Policy] Wolfowitz and [Secretary of Defense] Cheney to his friends in Congress."[93]

Being a "Nunn man" also proved troublesome for Locher in the first months of the Clinton administration. Aspin, the former legislative critic, now ran the Department of Defense. He initially proposed eliminating ASD SO/LIC but found its Senate backing too strong. He then proposed bypassing ASD SO/LIC through the creation of a new Assistant Secretary for Democracy, Human Rights, and Peacekeeping. This new position was to have responsibilities which overlapped those of the legislatively-imposed ASD SO/LIC. This move was designed to further emphasize missions such as security assistance and peacekeeping.[94] In essence, ASD SO/LIC would have been left with only the oversight over programs concerning Special Operations Forces. Despite his credentials within the Democrat Party, Locher left the Department of Defense in June 1993.

Civilian turf fights weakened the reform efforts and certainly contributed to the Army leadership's efforts to protect its core interests by allowing the Army, and the other services, to play the competing officials against one another, particularly in 1990-1991. Posen's model does not speak to the problem of civilian reformers working at cross purposes to one another. In the model, civilians overcome military resistance through concerted pressure and generally by the use of a military maverick. As in the other periods studied in this book, there is no maverick. In the state of flux that characterized the military in the early 1990s, civilian advocates for meeting the low intensity challenge should have found it easy to cultivate and promote military mavericks of like mind. Yet nothing suggests that they did or were any more likely to do so than in the past.

Despite the turf battle over ASD SO/LIC civilian pressure became more effective in 1992 with Aspin's hearings in the House. After the inauguration of President Clinton, legislative and executive pressures dovetailed. However, the changes in Army behavior in 1992-1993 were not only due to more effective civilian pressure, but also because there was a more receptive leadership in the military. As in each of the earlier cases, the Army officers taking the lead were not mavericks, but successful mainstream officers. It is in understanding these dynamics internal to the Army that Rosen's model continues to be useful.

EXPLANATION II: INTRAORGANIZATIONAL INTERGROUP CONFLICT

As in chapter 5, for this period to confirm the Rosen model, the evidence would have to show that the Army would have changed its behavior with respect to low intensity conflict even in the absence of civilian pressure. Although there is evidence of group conflict over the future of the Army, the events of this period do not indicate that the Army would have changed itself to the degree that it did. Despite its inability to fully explain changes in Army behavior in this period, Rosen's model can still be used to offset the weaknesses in Posen's model.

In Posen's view of organizations, those in charge of an organization will resist externally imposed changes to their established patterns of behavior. The Army's standard pattern of behavior had been to focus most of its efforts on defending two borders - the DMZ on the Korean peninsula and the InterGerman border in Central Europe, with the latter being by far the most important. Given the civilian impetus to change in the early 1990s, this case should exhibit Army leaders fighting that change, unless, as is generally accepted in traditional organizational literature, three conditions obtain: budgetary feast, prolonged budgetary famine, or a crisis brought on by massive organizational failure.[95] Even under these conditions, organizational leaders can be expected to favor only incremental change, or at best, undertake change grudgingly.

Given that Army leaders in the early 1990s seem to have embraced change without prolonged "famine," and in the wake, not of failure, but of success suggests that some other force for change was at work.[96] Rosen's focus on intergroup conflict within the organization offers additional illumination of the on-going process not available in Posen's model. Rosen's approach requires the identification of the contending groups and the description of their major activities.

The transition between dominant traditionalist groups began in the 1980s as noted in the last chapter. The impact of Desert Storm gave strength to the inheritors of the heavy armored warfare tradition which had its roots in the Army's drive across Europe in World War II. However, this new group of traditionalists was weakened in the 1990s by the revolution in world politics brought on by the demise of the Soviet Union.

The traditionalists did not relent without a fight, though. They made their case on the basis of doctrine, training, and force structure that performed magnificently in Desert Storm to protect vital strategic interests in the Persian Gulf. Their suggestion was that the worst case scenarios of the future would be regional crises of the type provoked by Saddam Hussein. Much was made of the proliferation of armor, aircraft, and ballistic missiles to rogue Third World countries.[97] The fact that the JRTC fielded an armored opposing force unit (OPFOR) may suggest the kind of joint contingencies the Army originally envisioned.

To the small extent that the traditionalists cared about low intensity conflict, it was in the realm of combat operations, such as counterinsurgency or short-term operations such as the invasions of Grenada and Panama, which represented easy incremental changes from the established routines, and which, in fact, were the only combat experiences available to the bulk of Army officers until Desert Storm. As an example of this thinking, the Center for Low Intensity Conflict records that during a 1990 visit by the TRADOC Deputy Chief of Staff for Training, Brigadier General Craig A. Hagan, the general expressed his disdain for the Center's concern with the full range of low intensity missions. He felt that they should concentrate on becoming experts on "insurgency hotspots" around the world, because insurgency could be the "'big umbrella' mission for the future."[98] Given the Army experience in the 1960s, a reasonable assumption is that "counterinsurgency" really meant "guerrilla hunting" to those who advocated it as a future mission.

To the traditionalists, deployments for any other low intensity mission represented mere training opportunities which would support the "real" mission of the units involved. As one Army colonel put it, "We must never lose sight of our true purpose. On the other hand, peacetime engagement provides the opportunity to enhance our training."[99] This view is consonant with the expression in the 1993 edition of FM 100-5 that "Winning wars is the primary purpose of the doctrine in this manual."[100] Note also that this reflected the misconception that once war fighting is taken care of, other missions come easily - low intensity conflict as the lesser included case.

Perhaps most illuminating about the views of the traditionalists was the attitude of General Vuono, the Army Chief of Staff until June 1991. In January 1990, Vuono argued that "our present force structure does not meet the current needs of all U.S. commands worldwide."[101] Moreover, Vuono maintained that the successes of containment and flexible response "should not cause us to discard the basic elements that have made this strategy work."[102] Rather, only adaptations to those basic strategies were needed and NATO had to remain strongly oriented to Soviet actions. Vuono also noted the growing regional threat coming from the dozen Third World nations which possessed more than a thousand main battle tanks each.[103] This concern dovetailed with Vuono's emphasis on maintaining deployability to respond to combat contingency operations.

In his tenure as Chief, Vuono spoke to more than a hundred sizable groups of officers - the Pre-Command Courses for new battalion and brigade commanders, Army War College Classes, Command and General Staff College Classes, and Combined Arms and Services Staff School classes. His stock speech, developed in his first six months as chief, always addressed the strategic environment in which the officers would command. Normally he noted the threat of the Soviet Union and, after 1989, the proliferation of nuclear, biological, and chemical technology, and advanced conventional weapons throughout the

Third World. However, he only addressed low intensity conflict as an afterthought, if at all. Here is an example of his remarks on low intensity conflict in a speech that would have taken more than an hour: "And then finally, the international environment contains the low intensity threat, which is significant and growing. And we are going to continue to operate in low intensity areas...."[104]

At the end of Vuono's tenure, when it was clear that the Army would face a sizeable reduction and a reorientation to new missions, an officer in one of these briefings asked Vuono about the Army of the future and what bit of advice he would leave to his successor. Vuono replied,

> "I'll tell you the purpose of the Army is to win the wars of the nation. That's what the purpose of the Army is. Don't let anybody give you nonsense about peripheral issues or peripheral missions. Well it would be nice if the Army did so and so. That may be good for a cup of coffee down the hall here, to talk about. But don't spend more time than that on it. I sure as hell wouldn't."[105]

As for the bit of advice, Vuono added,

> "The first one is beware of the good idea guys....You see, there's a lot of good idea fellows running around. . . .Who have a great program that they just think we got to institute in the Army. And watch the peripheral missions. Okay? They don't contribute to a trained and ready Army."[106]

When Vuono spoke of fighting wars, he apparently

included short-term actions like the interventions in Grenada and Panama.[107] That the traditionalists still remained disdainful, however, of other low intensity missions in this period is clear. This was particularly true of politically ambiguous missions such as "nation-building," humanitarian intervention, peacekeeping, and even counterinsurgency (despite General Hagan's views to the contrary). As one civilian official described the dominant view: "Senior military leaders don't want another 'dirty little war' where the President gets them into a conflict and then leaves them there."[108]

Such disdain can explain the hostility to the very notion of low intensity conflict and existing low intensity doctrine that the CLIC officers encountered in the writing of the new FM 100-5 *Operations*, the resulting incongruities in the new manual, and such decisions as the use of an armored cavalry regiment as the opposition force at the low intensity-oriented JRTC. It also explains why no officer in the crucial Strategic Plans and Policy Division of the Army staff under Vuono had any oversight role for low intensity conflict.[109]

But what about the visionaries that we discovered in the 1980s? What were their effects on this process of change? The low intensity conflict advocates did not disappear.[110] However, uniformed advocates were not readily visible outside of a few in the SOF community and the newly created offices for peacekeeping in the Pentagon. Uniformed low intensity conflict specialists attended academic conferences and staffed the few centers of intellect that the Army devoted to the subject: the Center for Low Intensity Conflict, the JFK Special Warfare School, and a few faculty members at the Command and General Staff Colleges and the War Colleges. Yet, as one observer described the Army, there was a large undercurrent of believers in the importance of low intensity conflict.[111]

On the other hand, Colin Powell, an Army general serving

as Chairman of the Joint Chiefs of Staff, was instrumental in changing the U.S. strategic focus to encompass formerly non-mainstream missions, even though his views were not as expansive as those of Secretary of Defense Aspin. Additionally, Vuono's successor indeed embraced the peripheral missions contrary to his predecessor's advice. Sullivan did so knowing that he was breaking tradition: "Expanding the traditional understanding of the use of military force in war to 'operations other than war' makes both politicians and military leaders uneasy...."[112]

Consequently, one can argue that the visionaries were also active in this period, producing the 1990 edition of FM 100-20, changing the content of standard Army training courses and of the training at the CTCs, providing the crucial chapter on operations other than war for the new capstone FM 100-5, and in creating and manning the new offices on the Army staff to deal with low intensity missions, such as peacekeeping.[113] And, as Rosen predicted, their success came because a few leaders at the highest ranks, with impeccable mainstream credentials, led the way. The actions of the military visionaries were reinforced by the reform efforts of the civilians discussed in the section above.

In keeping with Rosen's model, the Army, under the influence of the visionaries, began to develop tasks to implement the new vision of Army operations in Army schools and training centers. What had not happened as of 1993, though, was the creation of a mainstream career pathway for low intensity specialists that would keep them competitive for higher positions of leadership, but also allow them to master the subjects of low intensity conflict. As noted in the last chapter, the only existing pathway was for members of the small special operations community who could at least aspire to command the unified Special Operations Command.

CONCLUSION

In the 1990s, a vision of warfare based on the Desert Shield and Desert Storm experience, as the armor traditionalists would have liked it, proved to be too politically unpopular with the civilian reformers in Congress and the executive branch, especially in the Clinton administration, which did not perceive such scenarios as credible. In such an administration, given a desire to promote democratic institutions abroad, the desire to use the Army for nation assistance, humanitarian relief, and low level military-to-military contacts came to be a major policy thrust.[114]

What we observe in this case in terms of the Army's behavior - as detailed in the dependent variables above - is change in progress. It was still too early to determine the outcome in 1993. In neither Rosen nor Posen does one get a good picture of what change might look like as it is happening. The cases of military innovation chosen by these scholars had already happened. The U.S. Army had now been formally dealing with low intensity conflict since 1961. The young officers who first entered the Army in the counterinsurgency era were, by 1993, at the uppermost echelons of the service. Some of those officers felt that the counterinsurgency efforts in Vietnam were a waste of resources. Others regretted the onset of the conventional war in 1965, and felt that if counterinsurgency had received the appropriate support, the outcome of the war would have been different. Consequently, much effort was expended studying the phenomenon with the purpose of expanding the Army's role in low intensity conflict, or reducing it.

In the early 1990s, the balance of power among the two groups shifted. In 1990-1991, the traditionalists had the upper hand, keeping the Army focused on the residual Soviet threat and looming Third World tank armies. By the end of 1991, under pressure from civilians, power shifted to the visionaries. Had the Army remained dominated by traditionalists, it would have found itself hard pressed to respond well to the missions it was given in an era of post-Cold War budgetary constraints. To meet the new missions, and avoid a disgraceful failure, the Army no longer had the luxury of dealing with such missions on the margin. It had to confront them directly.

Evidence was not yet available in 1993, but a reasonable assumption is that one of the reasons for the selection of General Sullivan as Vuono's replacement was Sullivan's willingness to embrace non-traditional missions. Moreover, the Clinton administration's choice for Powell's replacement was General John Shalikashvili, an officer with a background as an adviser in Vietnam, and who had participated in the large humanitarian intervention, Operation *Provide Comfort*, in northern Iraq. The Clinton administration's determination to use the military in non-traditional ways made officers who could think intellectually about the subject of low intensity conflict all the more important. Yet, these officers were not in any sense "mavericks."

As noted previously, Posen's model views military organizations as too rigid, and allows for only the odd maverick to take part in change. On the other hand, Rosen's model unnecessarily diminishes the possible impact of civilian reformers. The synthesis offered in the last chapter is still relevant here: civilian intervention into the operational doctrine of the Army can provoke change. However, the character of the change depends on whether the civilians act through "traditionalists" or through "visionaries." If the civilians work through the traditionalists, much of the impetus for reform will be thwarted, and any changes will be easily reversed peripheral changes. If the civilians work through visionaries, fundamental organizational change is possible over time.

In this case, civilian reformers in the Bush administration, and even more so in the Clinton administration, pushed non-traditional missions onto the Army. Initially, this external force for change encountered traditionalists, like General Vuono, who argued for maintaining a war fighting focus on the residual threat from the Soviet Union and from the "vast tank armies" of the Third World. And, he strenuously argued against taking on "peripheral missions." Had another traditionalist replaced Vuono, we would have expected the Army, under pressure, to change at the margins, accepting peripheral missions grudgingly and incrementally - those missions closest to the traditional focus such as counterinsurgency and raids. As one officer described his work in this period, "LIC ha[d] become a growth industry,...but just because you put it into mission statements and OPLANs doesn't make it so."[115] Real change, in this officer's view, required change in force structure and training.

General Sullivan was more of a visionary. Some force structure, in an era of force reductions, was maintained and enhanced because of low intensity conflict. Sullivan had the doctrine rewritten to bring such operations into greater focus, curbing the impulse to make Desert Storm the paradigm for the future. Finally, under Sullivan, Army training began to incorporate the tasks necessary to successfully implement low intensity missions.[116] To the extent that Sullivan, or a like-minded officer, remained as Chief of Staff, and to the extent that the civilian officials in the Pentagon continued to require the Army to respond to low intensity missions, then fundamental change would become possible over time.

That fundamental change would become concrete when the Army devised lists of tasks for each of the various missions within the concept of low intensity conflict, required units to train on those tasks at all levels from individual to higher level "war games," and when, as the officer just quoted above put it, "the Army sends its best people to LIC missions." Most important of all, those people who served in low intensity missions, developing special expertise, would then have to be promoted to the highest ranks for the changes to endure. By 1993 the Army had begun to move in these directions, but was not yet there. Hence, this was change still in progress with an as yet undefined outcome that set the stage for the use of the Army in many non-traditional missions in the rest of the 1990s and in the first decade of the new millennium.

Chapter 6 Endnotes

[1] Paul F. Gorman, et al, *Supporting U.S. Strategy for Third World Conflict: Report by the Regional Conflict Working Group Submitted to the Commission on Integrated Long-Term Strategy* (Washington, D.C.: Department of Defense, June 1988) 22.

[2] General Gordon R. Sullivan, Chief of Staff, United States Army, *Statement before the Committee on Armed Services, United States House of Representatives, 1st Session, 103d Congress, on the Fiscal Year 1994 Budget Proposals and the Posture of the United States Army*, 31 March 1993 (Washington, D.C.: USGPO, 1993) 6.

[3] Don M. Snider, *Strategy, Forces and Budgets: Dominant Influences in Executive Decision Making, Post-Cold War, 1989-91* (Carlisle, PA: Strategic Studies Institute, U.S. Army War College, 1993) 8-9. See also Harry E. Rothmann, *Forging A New National Military Strategy in a Post-Cold War World: A Perspective from the Joint Staff* (Carlisle, PA: Strategic Studies Institute, U.S. Army War College, 1992) 7. Both Snider and Rothmann were Army colonels working on the production of strategy statements in this period.

[4] Dick Cheney, *Annual Report to the President and the Congress* (Washington, D.C.: USGPO January 1990) 1. See also Dick Cheney, *1990 Joint Military Net Assessment* (Washington, D.C: Department of Defense, January 1990) III-3 for the "enduring problems of debt, terrorism, insurgencies, and drug trafficking...."

[5] Cheney, 1990, opening remarks.

[6] Cheney, 1990, 51-54.

[7] Dick Cheney, *Annual Report to the President and the Congress* (Washington, D.C.: USGPO, January 1991).

[8] Cheney, 1991, v. Bush had used this term in a speech at Aspen, CO, on 2 August 1992, the day that Iraq invaded Kuwait. The administration saw the Aspen speech as the debut of its new national military strategy.

[9] In the Aspen speech, Bush spoke of "renegade regimes" and of 20 countries with chemical warfare capabilities, and another 15 that would soon possess ballistic missile technologies. See the reprint of the speech in Cheney, 1991, 131-134.

[10] Snider 13. In fact the service chiefs asked for 2% real growth in the defense budget for several years.

[11] Vuono was successful in the early meetings with Powell, pegging the Army size to a total U.S. force in Europe of 150,000. See Snider 15. See also statements by Secretary of the Army Michael P. W. Stone and Chief of Staff of the Army General Carl E. Vuono, 29 March 1990 in U.S. Senate, *Department of Defense Appropriations, Fiscal Year 1991, Hearings before the Committee on Appropriations*, 101st cong., 2d sess., pt. 3 (Washington, D.C.: USGPO,

1990) 3, 17-18.
[12] Snider 25-28.
[13] See Aspin's statement, 25 February 1992, in U.S. House of Representatives, *National Defense Funding and the Fiscal Year 1993 Budget, Hearings before the Committee on the Budget* (Washington, D.C.: USGPO, 1992) 11. Also Snider 29.
[14] Snider 39. See also the comments by Senator Joseph Biden Jr., a member of the Senate Foreign Relations Committee, in Patrick E. Tyler, "Lone Superpower Plan: Ammunition for Critics," *The New York Times*, 10 March 1992 A12. Biden felt that the Pentagon's vision of the future "revert[ed] to an old notion of the United States as the world's policeman- a notion that, not incidentally, will preserve a large defense budget."
[15] See "Aspin: Post-Cold War Debate Over Use of Military Underway: 'The Use and Usefulness of Military Forces in the Post-Cold War, Post-Soviet World,'" News Release, House Armed Services Committee, 21 September 1992. Also William Mathews, "Post-Cold War Reality vs. Pre-Cold War Sensibility," *Army Times*, 12 October 1992, 26.
[16] General Colin Powell, *National Military Strategy, 1992* (Washington, D.C.: Department of Defense, 1992). The quotes come from Powell's opening statements.
[17] Powell 4, 11.
[18] Powell 7, and Dick Cheney, *Annual Report to the President and the Congress* (Washington, D.C.: USGPO, January 1992) 6- 10, 25, 40-41.
[19] Michael R. Gordon, "Aspin Overhauls Pentagon to Bolster Policy Role." *The New York Times*, 28 January 1993, A17.
[20] See Sean O'Keefe, Admiral Frank Kelso, General C.E. Mundy, *From the Sea: Preparing the Naval Service for the 21st Century* (Washington, D.C.: Department of the Navy, September 1992). The authors were, respectively, Secretary of the Navy, Chief of Naval Operations, and Commandant of the Marine Corps.
[21] General Gordon R. Sullivan and Lieutenant Colonel James N. Dubik, *Land Warfare in the 21st Century* (Carlisle Barracks, PA: Strategic Studies Institute, 1993) 8.
[22] I will continue to use the phrase "low intensity conflict" except when referring directly to official Army publications using the new phrase, "operations other than war."
[23] Sullivan and Dubik 8.
[24] Sullivan and Dubik 5. The Assistant Secretary of Defense for Reserve Affairs, Deborah Roche Lee, spoke of "utilizing military forces, and reserves in particular, to try to add value and give back and meet needs in America that are otherwise going unmet." See William Mathews, "New Chief Sees Increased Role for Reserves," *Army Times*, 21 June 1993, 20.
[25] Sullivan 3. Army end strength was slated to reach 545,000 by end of Fiscal Year 1995 in September 1994.

[26] Powell, 19, 22, 23. The light divisions included one airborne, one air assault, and two light infantry divisions.

[27] See also John W. Shannon and Gordon R. Sullivan, *United States Army Posture Statement, FY94: Change and Continuity* (Washington, D.C.: Department of the Army, March 1993) 60- 64.

[28] James R. Locher III and General Carl Stiner, *United States Special Operations Forces: Posture Statement* (Washington, D.C: Department of Defense, June 1992) C-l - C-3.

[29] Interview with Colonel Mack Dorsey, Assistant Commandant, John F. Kennedy Special Warfare Center and School, 10 February 1992. Dorsey was relatively new in the job. His understanding of low intensity doctrine was not deep as evidenced by his separating of low intensity conflict and peacetime contingency operations. His views also did not coincide with those of some of the principal staff officers at the school. See the interview with Lieutenant Colonel William Council below.

[30] This was the view of Lieutenant Colonel William Council, Chief of Doctrinal Development, John F. Kennedy Special Warfare Center and School since August 1989. Council's views were much more informative than Colonel Dorsey's due to the almost three years that Council had spent working on doctrinal and force structure issues. Note that Dorsey's views represent a traditional mindset about the purpose of SOF. Interview with Lieutenant Colonel Council, 10 February 1992, Ft. Bragg, NC.

[31] Lieutenant Colonel (retired) John B. Hunt, "Emerging Doctrine for LIC," *Military Review*, June 1991, 60. Hunt worked for the Army Proponent Office for Low-intensity Conflict at Ft. Leavenworth.

[32] See FM 100-20 *Military Operations in Low Intensity Conflict* (Washington, DC: Headquarters, Department of the Army, March 1990) 1-2 - 1-4, 1-8 - 1-9, and Appendix B "The Law and Low Intensity Conflict."

[33] FM 100-20 1-6.

[34] FM 100-20 2-17.

[35] FM 100-20 2-17.

[36] In reflection of the experience of the 1980s, the manual specifically distinguished between supporting insurgency and supporting counterinsurgency, while still disproportionately emphasizing the latter. The bulk of the second chapter addressed the general political environment of insurgency. Three of the six appendices were devoted to counterinsurgency. See FM 100-20, Chapter 2, and Appendices A, D, E. U.S. support for insurgency is covered on 2-17 and 2-18. U.S. support to counterinsurgency is covered on 2-18 through 2-25.

[37] Council Interview.

[38] Interview with Colonel McDonough, West Point, NY, 17 June 1992.

[39] McDonough Interview. Also interview with Major Rick Brennan, Office of the Deputy Chief of Staff of the Army for Operations and Plans, Strategic Plans and Policy Division, May 1992.

[40] James R. McDonough, "Building the New FM 100-5: Process and Product," *Military Review*, October 1991, 12.

[41] McDonough 8. See also General John W. Foss, "Advent of the Nonlinear Battlefield: AirLand Battle-Future," *Army*, February 1991, 22, 24. Foss was the commander of TRADOC, the organization responsible for writing Army doctrine. Foss made the same point about including low intensity conflict in the capstone manual.

[42] Interview with Lieutenant Colonel William McGrew, Center for Low Intensity Conflict (CLIC), 18 March 1993, Langley Air Force Base, VA. McGrew cautioned that while the closing of the separate Army office for Low Intensity Conflict apparently signaled an upgrading of the importance of the topic, it might very well mean that no office wanted to deal with the problem.

[43] Cheney, Annual Report, 1991, 6. See also Thomas W. Crouch, *Historical Report of the Army-Air Force Center for Low intensity Conflict (A-AF CLIC), 1 January 1991-30 June 1991* (Langley Air Force Base, VA: CLIC Reference Collection) 43-44. Hereafter cited as "A-AF CLIC" followed by the end date of the report.

[44] See Snider 4.

[45] Office of the Assistant Secretary of Defense for Special Operations and Low Intensity Conflict, "Peacetime Engagement," working paper, draft 4.0, 5 November 1991, 4.

[46] Thomas W. Crouch, *Historical Report of the Army-Air Force Center for Low intensity Conflict (A-AF CLIC), 1 July 1991-31 December 1991* (Langley Air Force Base, VA: CLIC Reference Collection) 34.

[47] A-AF CLIC, 31 December 1991, 34. See Supporting Document 83 for the trip report within which these observations were recorded.

[48] Lieutenant Colonel Clifton J. Everton and Lieutenant Colonel Arba Williamson, "Trip Report," 24 December 1991, 2. This is Supporting Document 83 to A-AF CLIC, 31 December 1991.

[49] Telephone interview with General (retired) John W. Foss, 5 August 1993.

[50] FM 100-5 *Operations* (Washington, D.C.: Department of the Army, June 1993) iv.

[51] FM 100-5 v.

[52] FM 100-5 v.

[53] FM 100-5 2-0.

[54] FM 100-5 2-0. Emphasis original.

[55] Foss interview.

[56] Sullivan and Dubik 8.

[57] FM 100-5 2-0.

[58] McGrew interview.

[59] For the differences in these two categories of conflict, refer to chapter 2 above.

[60] Remarks not made for attribution.

[61] In March 1993, the Center for Low Intensity Conflict was preparing a draft manual on "Military Support to Civil Authorities." The manual's topics included use of military forces in riot situations, natural disasters, combating the importation of illicit narcotics, re-building the national infrastructure, and using military personnel to provide medical care and education services to American inner cities. McGrew interview.

[62] FM 100-5 13-0.

[63] FM 100-5 13-2.

[64] FM 100-5 13-1.

[65] FM 100-5 13-2.

[66] FM 100-5 13-0. When soldiers are used merely for their technical capabilities, absent any potential for combat, such as vaccinations or filling potholes, it is undoubtedly true that their technical training and their existing organizational structures suffice. However, introduce the potential for combat and the question rapidly arises, "how are the soldiers trained to respond?" Training soldiers to respond to airborne or armored assaults is different than training them to respond to snipers, ambushes, or assaults by irregulars.

[67] Hunt 60.

[68] Interview with Major Rick Brennan, Office of the Assistant Secretary of Defense for Democracy, Human Rights, and Peacekeeping, 14 July 1993. Brennan had moved on 12 July from the Office of the Deputy Chief of Staff of the Army for Operations and Plans, Strategic Plans and Policy Division where he was responsible for Army policy on peacekeeping and peace enforcement.

[69] FM 100-5 v.

[70] Brian J. Ohlinger, *Peacetime Engagement: A Search for Relevance?* (Carlisle, PA: Strategic Studies Institute, 1992)

[71] Dorsey believed this. Dorsey interview. See also the quotation from page 13-0 of FM 100-5, 1993, used above. One of the Army's highest ranking generals, in remarks not made for attribution, also stated recently in response to a question on the impact of peacekeeping and humanitarian missions that "We train for war...[and] we can do these other things."

[72] This story is related in "Warriors or Angels," *Army Times*, 5 July 1993 8. The report also noted that "Soldiers were asked to be warriors one moment, angels of mercy the next."

[73] The story of the artillery officers comes from a telephonic interview with Lieutenant Colonel Bob Wood, Division Chief, Office of the Deputy Chief of Staff of the Army for Operations and Plans, Strategic Plans and Policy Division, 15 July 1992. Wood had just completed a study of Army training for peacekeeping with a special focus on the 10th Division's deployment to Somalia. He went to Somalia itself to research the effect of the training.

[74] James R. Brannon and Vernon Lowrey, "Lessons Learned: Somalia and Operation Restore Hope," *Engineer*, April 1993,23.

[75] Wood interview.

[76] "U.S. Macedonia Force Will Undergo Training; UN Orders Strict Rules of

Engagement," *Washington Post On-Line Service*, 10 July 1993.
[77] Brennan interview, 14 July 1993.
[78] Brennan interview, 14 July 1993.
[79] Interview with Major General Daniel Christman, 3 February 1993, West Point, NY.
[80] General Gordon R. Sullivan, "A Report from the Chief: Flexibility Sets the Pace at Combat Training Centers," *Army*, July 1993, 31. The other data in this paragraph comes from pp. 30-31.
[81] Sullivan, "A Report," 31-32. For the manner of training which incorporates the lighter, early deploying forces with later deploying armored forces, see Colonel Kenneth C. Scull, "Heavy and Light Force Integration at the National Training Center," *Military Review*, May 1993, 41-52.
[82] Sullivan, "A Report," 33. See also Steve Vogel, "'Stomachs Tighten' in Germany as V Corps Awaits Word to Deploy," *Army Times*, 17 May 1993, 4.
[83] Council interview. Council found the stationing of the armored force at the JRTC humorous. At the time of the stationing decision, with no identifiable adversary, the scenarios became entirely fictional, according to Council, in order not to offend politically any particular country or region of the world. Council called them the "unguerrillas."
[84] Daniel's bill was House Resolution 5109, introduced in the House Armed Services Committee, 26 June 1986.
[85] Telephone interview with James Bodner, Legislative Assistant to Senator William Cohen, 4 August 1993.
[86] For example, see the congressional inquiry into strained relationships between USSOCOM and the services, and into promotion rates for SOF personnel, in U.S. Senate, *Department of Defense Appropriations, Fiscal Year 1991, Hearings before the Committee on Appropriations*, 101st cong., 2d sess., pt. 2 (Washington, D.C.: USGPO, 1990) 272- 3. According to Bodner, Sen. Glenn, who sat on the Appropriations Committee, remained one of the "cadre" of Senators who watched over the 1986 legislation.
[87] See U.S. House of Representatives, *Potential Threats to American Security in the Post-Cold War Era, Hearings before the Defense Policy Panel of the House Armed Services Committee*, 102d cong., 1st sess. (Washington, D.C.: USGPO, 1992) for the December hearings, and U.S. House of Representatives, *Regional Threats and Defense Options for the 1990s, Hearings before the Defense Policy Panel and the Department of Energy Defense Nuclear Facilities Panel of the House Armed Services Committee*, 102d cong., 2d sess. (Washington, D.C.: USGPO, 1992) for the March-April hearings.
[88] See Aspin's 25 February 1992 testimony in U.S. House of Representatives, *National Defense Funding and the Fiscal Year 1993 Budget, Hearings before the Committee on the Budget*, 102d cong., 2d sess. (Washington, D.C.: USGPO, 1992) 2-62, but particularly 3-5, 11.
[89] "Aspin: Post-Cold War Debate Over Use of Military Underway: 'The Use and Usefulness of Military Forces in the Post-Cold War, Post-Soviet World,'"

News Release, House Armed Services Committee, 21 September 1992, and Mathews, "Post-Cold War Reality," 26.

[90] Telephone interview with James Locher, 30 August 1993.

[91] See Cheney, *Net Assessment*, 1990, VI-9, VI-10. See also Michael P. W. Stone and Carl E. Vuono, *Trained and Ready in an Era of Change: The Posture of the United States Army, Fiscal Year 1991* (Washington, D.C.: Department of the Army, undated) iii, 1-2, 1-3. This is the glossy publication of the Army's statement to the House and Senate Armed Services Committees.

[92] Remarks not made for attribution. Two of Powell's retired contemporaries supported this view of his actions.

[93] Remarks not made for attribution.

[94] See Michael R. Gordon, "Aspin Overhauls Pentagon to Bolster Policy Role," *The New York Times*, 28 January 1993, A17. Additional information came from interviews with Bodner, Brennan, and Mellon.

[95] For a summary of these three causes, see Graham Allison, *Essence of Decision: Explaining the Cuban Missile Crisis* (Boston: Little, Brown, 1971) 85.

[96] Prolonged famine may have begun by late 1991, relative to the Cold War budget "feast" but its full effects were not yet clear by 1993.

[97] The Army concern for the conventional capabilities of Third World nations began soon after the initiation of changes in Eastern Europe. See General Carl Vuono, Chief of Staff of the Army, "Speech to ISSP Conference on the Army," Fletcher School, Tufts University, 3 November 1989, Speeches and Remarks, 24 Oct-15 November 1989, Vuono Papers, U.S. Army Military History Institute, Carlisle Barracks, PA. In this speech Vuono states "We can no longer consider the Third World to be militarily insignificant." The next day, the Berlin Wall was opened. In Vuono's stock speeches until Desert Storm, a favorite reference was to the sophistication of the Iran-Iraq War and the "vast armies" of main battle tanks in the Third World. See for example, any of his speeches to Pre-Command Courses at Ft. Leavenworth, July 1989-August 1990. For other examples, see *National Security Strategy of the United States* (Washington, D.C.: USGPO, August 1991) 14-16, and Cheney, *Annual Report*, 1992, vi, 4-6.

[98] Thomas M. Crouch, *Historical Report of the Army-Air Force Center for Low intensity Conflict (A-AF CLIC), 1 January 1990-30 June 1990* (Langley Air Force Base, VA: CLIC Reference Collection) 25. See also Ohlinger 11: "Low intensity conflict operations should be limited to primarily combat-type operations - e.g., counterinsurgency."

[99] Ohlinger 10. Ohlinger was a colonel in the Army engineers. This view of low intensity missions was also expressed by Dorsey in my interview with him.

[100] FM 100-5 v.

[101] General Carl E. Vuono, Chief of Staff of the Army, *A Strategic Force for the 1990s and Beyond* (Washington, D.C.: Department of the Army, January 1990) 3.

[102] Vuono 5.

[103] Vuono 6.

[104] Speech to Army War College Class of 1990. 31 Oct 1989, Vuono Papers, Speeches and Remarks, 24 Oct-15 November 1989. See also Vuono 9-10. Low intensity subjects were clearly last in priority. They were addressed last, and occupied less than one of eighteen pages. Or, see Stone and Vuono, where low intensity missions get only several paragraphs on pp. 1-14, 1-15, and IV-2.

[105] Address to Pre-Command Course 91-9, 20 May 1991, Vuono Papers, Speeches and Remarks, 5 May 1991-11 June 1991.

[106] Address to Pre-Command Course 91-9, 20 May 1991, Vuono Papers, Speeches and Remarks, 9 May 1991-11 June 1991.

[107] Telephone interview with General (retired) Carl E. Vuono, 16 August 1993.

[108] Locher interview.

[109] Interview with Lieutenant Colonel Jim Reed, 16 June 1992, West Point, NY. Reed served in this Division under Vuono 1987-1989. Reed said that most of the work done on low intensity conflict in this period was done by Andrew Krepinevich, but Reed was not sure whether Krepinevich did it as a professional responsibility, or out of personal interest. This assessment of the Strategic Plans and Policy Division was corroborated by Lieutenant Colonel Andrew Krepinevich in an interview, 3 December 1992, West Point, NY. Krepinevich served in the Division through 1986 before moving into the office of the Secretary of Defense. His view of the Division in this entire period of time was that "Nobody gave a shit" about low intensity conflict.

[110] One retired general remembered heated arguments over the future of the Army in the periodic meetings of Army four-stars. Some generals, whom he did not name, agitated for accepting non-traditional missions of all sorts. Others argued for retaining a focus on more conventional missions. Foss interview.

[111] Reed interview. Reed noted that it was these believers who agitated successfully to make Special Forces a new combat branch for officer personnel management in the 1980s. This was a change that was done internal to the Army without significant outside pressure. Before this change, officers served tours in Special Forces, but were not expected to make it a career, nor could they if they hoped to be competitive for promotion.

[112] Sullivan and Dubik 12.

[113] Major Brennan filled that job before transferring to a similar job on the staff of the Office of the Secretary of Defense.

[114] The Bush administration had already emphasized these as "Forward Presence Operations."

[115] Council interview.

[116] However, the U.S. Army activities in Somalia in the search for the warlord Mohammad Farah Aideed, suggested that the Army still had a ways to go. The units still used firepower too generously in the eyes of some critics.

CHAPTER 7
CONCLUSION

History shows that the bill payers of failed policy and short-sighted national security planning are the military forces of the nation.

> — Rear Admiral Phillip R. Olson, speaking to a conference on low intensity conflict.[1]

According to Stephen Peter Rosen, "No good explanation of bureaucratic innovation exists."[2] This may result from the fact that innovation in bureaucracies is so rare. The problem is that, in the case of public organizations such as the military, it is necessary that they change to meet the needs for which they were created. To be truly effective, militaries have to be integrated with the strategic needs of the country. Therefore, it is necessary to understand why militaries change and the process of that change. However, the focus of most studies is on sweeping military change of the kind which is most noticeable after it has occurred. Another phenomenon which ought to elicit interest is peripheral change.

This is so because the nature of the peripheral change can tell us much about the future of the organization.

During the Cold War, given the threat of the Soviet military poised in eastern Europe, the Army had to be able to wage armored warfare.[3] The fear of low intensity conflict throughout the Cold War was the fear of bleeding to death from small bites. In this vein low intensity conflict was equivalent to an economy-of-force operation where our adversaries struck at us in our most vulnerable areas - terrorism, subversion, and insurgency. But, the challenge of low intensity conflict transcended the Cold War. The Soviets are gone, but the style of conflict remains: the security environment of the future may look more like the urban hell of Beirut, Sarajevo, or Baghdad where hand-held missiles and crude homemade bombs threaten air and ground movement, and more like the jungles of Vietnam or the mountains of Afghanistan, where the physical and human terrain negates or reduces the effectiveness of heavy weapons and high technology devices.

The question for the Army during the Cold War was whether it could simultaneously develop adequate capabilities to wage armored and low intensity conflicts. It could not be simply a "heavy" or simply a "light" army. Given the primacy of the European mission, the only change that was possible was a peripheral change.

This has been a study mostly of change on the periphery of the Army. While the study of sweeping reorganizations of militaries is a flashier topic, one cannot just dismiss peripheral change. Rather one should seek to understand its nature because that establishes its importance. The peripheral change may be incremental - what James Q. Wilson calls an "add-on" change.[4] This is the expected behavior of organizations. Or, the peripheral change could signal that more fundamental change is in the works. Finally, such change could indicate that, under pressure, the military organization is adapting defensively to unwanted pressure. Dismissing "add-on" change is too easy because understanding the latter two types of peripheral change is important for both scholars and policy makers. Recognizing the differences between types of peripheral changes allows for more complex studies of organizations, and the calibration of their behavior.

The aim of this project was to explain the Army's response to a set of non-traditional missions known as low intensity conflict in a defined period of time. Despite a large number of works that dealt with some aspect of low intensity conflict, no study had focused exclusively on the evolution of the Army's response to this security challenge. Understanding this evolution is important because the problems of terrorism, insurgency, peacekeeping, and contingency operations - the categories of low intensity conflict - took on new relevance in a world without the Soviet Union.

The great bipolar confrontation had, for 45 years, submerged many of the world's ethnic, religious, and economic passions. The end of the Cold War gave these passions a new, violent and bloody freedom. Although interstate conflict remains a threat, many of the aforementioned passions give rise to internal conflicts which require the use of force in non-traditional ways. The Army did not respond well to the challenge in the past, costing thousands of American lives and setting up the only strategic defeat that the United States has suffered. By the early 1990s, the United States government once again determined that it wanted the capability to respond to these challenges.

The changes in the early 1990s to the national strategy and the subordinate military strategy placed far greater emphasis on low intensity missions for the Army than had been the case since the early 1960s. Much of the post-Cold War Army would be based in the continental United States, and organized for rapid deployability in response to regional crises. Thus, the greater focus on conflict at the lower end of the spectrum colored the Army's, as well as the nation's, foreign policy abilities in the rest of the decade. Understanding the process of organizational change in the military, then, is necessary to the appropriate management of the Army's mission. If the Army does not prepare well to enact changed national strategy, the costs, as Admiral Olson's quotation above points out, are quite high in human terms. And, as the defeat in Vietnam demonstrates, the political costs to the nation are quite high, too. We have now engaged in a decade of war after the 9-11 attacks, mostly of the low intensity variety. This study sets the stage for understanding the process the Army went through before it entered that decade, and can help us understand how the Army changed during the war (see below).

FINDINGS

In looking at how the Army responded to non-traditional challenges since President Kennedy issued his first orders to create such a capability up to the point where it was clear that the USSR was definitively gone (1993), this study found that the Army reacted in three main ways. In each of these it was never simply civilian pressure and never simply intergroup conflict that determined Army behavior. It was, rather, the nexus of civilian pressure and intergroup conflict. The Army changed most when civilian officials applied pressure. However, the pressure was most successful when civilians chose to act through uniformed leaders with impeccable, mainstream, traditional credentials, but who agreed with the visionary goals of the civilians. First, in the periods 1961-1964 and 1980-1989, under pressure from civilian officials, the Army responded vigorously, but grudgingly, to low intensity conflict. Second, from 1965 until 1979, absent civilian pressure, the Army placed its counterinsurgency programs of the previous period into a decidedly secondary category as it moved to wage the Vietnam war in a traditional fashion. With the U.S. failure in Vietnam, the Army, still absent civilian pressure to the contrary, then moved to purge the counterinsurgency experience by ignoring the challenge of low intensity conflict and concentrating on its preferred mission of defending Central Europe, and secondarily the Korean DMZ. Third, in the 1990s, still under civilian pressure and without the Soviet Union as a central focus, the Army elevated low intensity conflict to near-equal status with traditional missions.

This study also documented some enduring misconceptions about low intensity conflict that made it easy for the Army to ignore or downplay the challenge, or to squeeze it into preferred concepts. Among the most salient was, first, the misconception that any soldier trained to handle missions associated with mid- or high intensity armored warfare was versatile enough to handle a low intensity mission. Second, if conventional soldiers were not quite good enough for the low intensity challenge, then true elite soldiers of the special operations community were all that was necessary. Third, if the Army had to perform low intensity missions at all, then the only ones that mattered were, first, counterinsurgency (preferably simply counterguerrilla operations complementing "real war"), and second, combat-oriented contingency operations such as in Panama in 1989. These two mission categories represented the easiest incremental choices for the Army. These misconceptions cut across the entire time period, complicating the tasks of both civilian and uniformed reformers.

In attempting to explain the actions of the Army, this study contrasted two opposing models for military change. The first model derived from structural theories of the creation, maintenance, and growth of organizations.[5] The second model derived from the point of view that organizations are essentially a collection of self-motivated groups which contend for power within the organization. Both models shared one key point: the concern for the security environment external to the military organization. The first model placed more emphasis on international factors in that environment while the second model added domestic societal and governmental factors. For both models, the security environment functioned as a set of permissive causes, which in themselves, were not sufficient to drive change in military organizations.

With respect to the first model, Barry Posen suggested that military organizations, like all organizations, are resistant to change, only more so given the high cost of errant change in terms of lives and national security. Moreover, military organizations tend to favor those doctrines that reinforce military autonomy, prestige, and power. In the case of the U.S. Army, the focus on defending Central Europe served this purpose. This focus is what Andrew Krepinevich called the "Army Concept," and what Carl H. Builder called the Army's "mask of war." As Builder described it, "Something happened to the Army in its passage through World War II that it liked; and it has not been able to free itself from the sweet memories of the Army that liberated France and swept victoriously into Germany."[6]

What did the European focus do for the Army under this school of thought? Prior to the stationing of a large body of troops in Europe, the Army was much smaller and poorly equipped. With the mission of defending Europe, the Army could remain large after the formation of NATO. It could contest with the Navy and Air Force for high technology weaponry. By operating along a trip-wire border several thousand miles from home, the operational autonomy of the Army was vastly increased as was its strategic and political importance.[7]

Posen's view of organizations is the traditional, structural view that originated with the writings of Max Weber. Organizations are created - structured – to accomplish some function. Within this view, James Q. Wilson tells us that:

> "[W]e ought not to be surprised that organizations resist innovation. The reason an organization is created is in large part to replace the uncertain expectations and haphazard activities of voluntary

endeavors with the stability and routine of organized relationships."[8]

Yet, routine behavior, however efficient and comfortable, might not match the needs of a changing organizational environment. When this is the case, efficiency, comfort, and familiarity work against the uncertainty inherent in change. No different from any other private or public organization, militaries develop expertise by endless practice on a set of specific tasks that derive from the vision of expected warfare - the "Army Concept" in this case.

How does a government, convinced of the need for change, get a military to change its routine, given that the routine is ingrained in that organization's daily existence? Posen maintains that militaries are unlikely to reform themselves to focus on new missions. Rather, civilian reformers outside of the military must force the change over the resistance of military leaders. That resistance can be lessened and the civilians strengthened, Posen further suggests, if the civilians utilize uniformed "mavericks" to institute and manage the process of change.[9] The civilian case for change is also strengthened if the military organization faces some crisis, such as defeat or budgetary famine, which loosens the control of organizational leaders.

The second model uses a human resources view of organizational behavior. Stephen Peter Rosen used this model to challenge directly Posen's claims that organizations were so hidebound that change had to be imposed by external reformers. Rosen also attacked Posen's notion of the effectiveness of mavericks.[10] In Rosen's model, fundamental military change is the result of a change in the organization's vision of future warfare. In the Army's case for the period of this study, this would amount to a change in the Army's vision of a tank-dominated conflict in Central Europe.

However, this change in vision comes about only as the result of a change in dominant groups within the military. These groups, according to Rosen, function as communities of belief which contend with each other for control of the organization. The point of contention between the groups is the vision of future warfare, and the requisite forces, equipment, doctrine, and training derived from the competing visions. Fundamental change results when high-ranking military leaders with mainstream credentials become converts to a new vision, and then use their influence to create new pathways for the promotion of like-minded junior officers. The new pathways must be based on the tasks necessary to cope with the new vision of warfare. This change process, according to Rosen, means that military organizations are capable of sweeping peacetime change completely in the absence of crisis and without the help of internal mavericks or external civilian reformers.

COMPARISON

Neither of the offered models produces an entirely coherent explanation of the Army's peacetime changes in the 33 years covered in this study. Rarely do such studies produce clear, unambiguous results. Rather, as Graham Allison once observed about the results of organizational studies, "these loosely formulated propositions amount simply to tendencies.... In particular instances, tendencies hold - more or less."[11] Therefore the question is which of the two approaches holds more often, and what are the strengths and weaknesses of the approach in this instance?

Posen's view of change being forced on a recalcitrant military explains some of the changes produced in 1961-4. Without the outside pressure provided by civilian officials of the legislative and executive branches, it is unlikely that the Army would have changed as much as it did. Was the Army better able to wage counterinsurgency in 1964 than it had been in 1961? The answer is undoubtedly yes.

Yet, what was the nature of change that the external reformers produced? The change was primarily structural. In direct keeping with the structural model of organizations, when faced with a new task to be done, new types of units were added to the force structure, new sections and agencies were added to headquarters and staffs. The prime example is President Kennedy personally selecting the Army Special Forces, units originally designed to carry out raids and support partisans behind enemy lines in conventional warfare, to be refashioned and expanded into his tool for handling counterinsurgency. The other changes in training and doctrine, though numerous, were mostly cosmetic.

Posen's structural approach also leads one to search for the use of a military maverick by the civilian reformers. While some such officers were available, like Brigadier General William P. Yarborough, the civilians chose not to use these men as agents of change. Rather, the case shows the reformers within the Kennedy administration working through mainstream traditionalists like General Maxwell Taylor. However, these traditionalists did not agree with all the visionary changes sought by the civilians.

While civilian initiatives set change into motion in this period, Army leaders continued to resist these changes, thereby lessening their effect. The structural view of organizations would lead one to expect this reaction. However, that view does not explain well how concerted presidential leadership fails, unless one places supreme emphasis on the Kennedy administration's failure to use a military maverick. On the other hand, Rosen's human resources approach allows us to explore more fully the process of change in this period.

The change that civilians initiated in this era was channeled or stymied by the visions of the dominant group in the Army - those who believed that armored warfare was the defining paradigm and the defense of Europe was the primary mission. This dominant group watered down important initiatives and delayed others. The Army gladly accepted those parts of President Kennedy's flexible response doctrine that reinforced the Army's primary mission of defending Central Europe, while viewing counterinsurgency as a nagging peripheral mission.

Consequently, the potential of the helicopter was exploited not for the mobility it provided to counterinsurgency forces, but for the mobility it could restore to the dispersed, potentially nuclear battlefields of Europe. The new counterinsurgency courses and manuals were often poorly done, emphasizing the hunting of guerrillas and the use of heavy firepower far more than the greater host of politico-military tasks inherent in counterinsurgency. Counterinsurgency training often consisted of tasks common to soldiering which would be as useful on the European battlefield as in counterinsurgency. Although the Army deployed more than 20,000 advisers to Vietnam by the end of this period in 1964, it did not deploy a single, complete Special Forces Group, even though these groups supposedly had been reorganized for just this mission.[12]

Counterpoised to this dominant group was a group of officers who took the president seriously. Most of the members were young and involved with waging counterinsurgency in Vietnam. Some were members of the Special Forces who were less wedded to the unconventional warfare heritage of these elite units. Because of their youth, this group had little power to affect the hold of the dominant group.

While the human resources approach helps us to understand the way the Army behaved in this period, it unnecessarily depreciates the role of civilian reformers. The Army did respond to civilian pressure, but not in the manner the civilians would have desired. Both models fail to offer a complete explanation.

The period 1965-1979 provides illumination about how the Army behaves without significant civilian pressure to change. Superficially, the Army behaved as the structural view would predict. It did as it pleased, following the mission most likely to give it greater resources, prestige, and autonomy. Therefore, this case merely confirms the traditional view of organizations. However, this traditional view does not offer a rich description of the Army's preferred rejection of all low intensity missions.

In the early part of the period, 1965 to 1972, the Army was engaged in mid-intensity war. After the large-scale introduction of conventional ground units by both North Vietnam and the United States, the conflict in Vietnam was no longer a low intensity conflict. What happened to the counterinsurgency capabilities in this period is, nevertheless, illustrative and provides insight into the path the Army took after 1972.

Most of the Army was given over to hunting and destroying Viet Cong guerrilla units or North Vietnamese units which used the stealthy tactics of guerrillas. The politico-military tasks of counterinsurgency, known as "pacification," ultimately became the responsibility of a new structure - the civilian-headed Civil Operations and Revolutionary Development Support (CORDS) office for pacification at the Headquarters of the Military Assistance Command for Vietnam. This office controlled between five and six thousand Army soldiers, the majority of whom were not officers. While this new structure allowed the pacification effort to reach new levels of efficiency and effectiveness, it never threatened control of the war effort by the Army leaders who fought the war with tactics incrementally modified from those they had conceived for the European battlefield.

Even the Special Forces began to expend more of their resources on the more glamorous missions derived from unconventional warfare. Projects Sigma, Delta, and Omega had more to do with partisan warfare than with counterinsurgency. In the training and use of indigenous tribesmen as airborne soldiers, the Special Forces reached the furthest possible point from the original intentions for their counterinsurgency role in the Kennedy administration.

The structural view of organizations would have predicted this reversion to type during the conventional war. It would also have predicted the minor change that did occur in military structures to accommodate CORDS. Yet, the structural view does not provide enough illumination about the inner workings of the Army. Absent any civilian initiatives, the pendulum not only swung away from pure counterinsurgency, but did so violently. To get the full flavor of this era, the human resources view is necessary.

The Army's dominant group enshrined an armored, firepower intensive, Eurocentric view of warfare in the period 1972-1979. After 1972, the Army quickly and adamantly focused itself on re-tooling for the European mission. It went so far as to plan the mechanization of all its infantry divisions, making them much less useful for any future low intensity mission, almost all of which require readily deployable, more lightly armed units. These plans elicited little comment from civilian officials. In word and deed the Army made quite clear that the conflict it envisioned itself waging was one of heavy tanks clashing on a firepower-dominated battlefield. The leaders of the Army in this era were the last of the soldiers who had been bred on the European battlefields of World War II. To them, Vietnam was an aberration.

The group of officers who had believed in

counterinsurgency, or at least believed that the Army needed some capability to wage such wars, had always been few in number. They were further tainted by the defeat in Vietnam, as the dominant group saw counterinsurgency, and those associated with it, as a diversion of needed resources from the war that they had sought to wage. There is scant documentary evidence that this group continued to exist, but on occasion, as the case showed, some officers did note that the Army was unduly constraining itself for the most probable future operations in its zeal for defending Central Europe.

This case demonstrates that the two approaches to organizational change do not conflict over the power of the dominant group.[13] However, only the human resources view offers insight into the machinations within the Army, such as they were, given the relative weakness of the counterinsurgent group.

In the 1980s as in the early 1960s, civilian reformers again sought to get the Army to face the challenge of low intensity conflict. This time the challenge was more varied than simply counterinsurgency. The challenge also included supporting insurgency, conducting combat-oriented contingency operations such as the one in Grenada, countering terrorism, and peacekeeping. Was the Army better able to accomplish the major low intensity missions in 1990 than it had keen in 1979? The answer is once again clearly affirmative. However, were the changes of the quality sought by the civilian reformers? Did the changes lead to an adequate capability to meet the challenge of low intensity conflict? No.

Posen's structural approach proves relevant again to the extent that it predicts that the Army would respond to the concerted efforts of the civilians in the executive and legislative branches in instances such as the Nunn-Cohen Amendment to the Goldwater-Nichols Act. This act created a new structure designed to handle low intensity conflict - the Army-dominated Special Operations Command. Once again, the civilian reformers did not act through military mavericks, preferring instead to use mainstream officers.

Both the strengths and the weaknesses of the structural approach are similar to those exhibited in the early 1960s. While this approach can explain the impetus for change, it cannot explain the ultimate direction of change. Once again, the civilian efforts were filtered through the lens of the Army's intergroup politics. The human resources model sheds light on this process.

According to Rosen, a new vision of war requires that mainstream military leaders become its champion. These leaders must provide an intellectual basis for the vision, translate the vision into new combat tasks, and then provide pathways of promotion for their younger adherents. From 1979 until 1987 the Army was led by Chiefs of Staff who became converts to the need for a response to low intensity conflict: Generals Meyer and Wickham. Meyer had been aware of the problem before assuming the top position and before the crucial international events of in the last months of 1979 occurred. Because of the problems in Iran and Afghanistan, Meyer focused mostly on building a capability for short-term crisis operations. By the time General Wickham became the Chief of Staff in June 1983, the missions had grown to include nation-building in Central America and peacekeeping in the Sinai.

Consequently, Wickham launched several doctrinal and force structure initiatives designed to address the various categories of low intensity conflict. Other Army leaders who were crucial in providing intellectual support in this phase included Generals Wallace Nutting, Paul Gorman, and John Galvin, all of whom commanded the U.S. Southern Command with responsibility for the nation-building and other counterinsurgency support programs in Latin America. Civilian pressure, therefore, met a more willing audience in the 1980s than it did in the early 1960s.

But what of the dominant group whose focus was armored warfare in Central Europe? They continued their resistance to any change in the focus on Europe. While Meyer was trying to create contingency forces, the commander of Training and Doctrine Command, General Donn Starry, was working to ensure that any units created would be fully capable of fighting alongside armored units in Europe. The commander of Forces Command in the mid-1980s, General Richard Cavazos, who was responsible for providing trained and ready soldiers from the continental United States to joint commands, resisted the use of Ranger and aviation assets in low intensity missions because such use detracted from their readiness for European missions. Finally, the Chief of Staff who succeeded Wickham in 1987, General Carl Vuono, shifted the emphasis on the use of light forces from utility for low intensity conflict to interoperability with heavy armored forces.

As in the early 1960s, the traditionalists functioned to deflect the full impact of reform with the ultimate aim of protecting what they saw as the primary mission. The Army may have been more capable to confront the range of low intensity missions in 1990 than it was in 1979, but the decade ended with the traditionalists firmly in power. The change that civilian and uniformed reformers had put into motion in the first seven years of the decade was successfully shifted or stymied. However, the contending group, whom I called "counterinsurgents" in the previous cases, should be properly described now as "visionaries."

They were greatly strengthened by the support they received from the actions of Meyer, Wickham, Gorman, and Galvin. What of the post-Cold War period? The traditional view of organizations holds that organizations resist change unless

Rick Waddell

there is a crisis. In his study of military cultures, Carl Builder postulated the crucial question for the Army in 1989, just before the unforeseeable tumbling of the Berlin Wall that ended the Cold War:

> "Would the Army, as an institution, be happy if our NATO allies really stepped up to the challenge of defending Western Europe and said, 'America, thank you very much, now you can take your troops back home again if you like'?"[14]

While this did not happen, the collapse of the Soviet Union and the reunification of Germany did, which posed the same problem. Thus, for the Army, the post-Cold War drawdown represented an institutional crisis that required it to reorganize.

Moreover, many of the legislative civilian reformers of the 1980s remained in power. The Army thus faced a crisis over its primary mission coupled with continued civilian pressure to provide a capability for low intensity missions. The Posen model would lead us to expect that the Army would change in the direction of the pressure, perhaps dramatically so given the crisis caused by the disappearance of the Army's preferred mission. The Army did change. It produced new doctrine which elevated low intensity conflict to near-equal status with conventional missions. The Army changed training in order to devote more attention to the restraint of firepower, and even to missions involving little chance of combat such as humanitarian assistance. However, there was some indication that the changes did not go as far as some reformers, such as Secretary of Defense Les Aspin, desired. There was also no maverick present in the evidence.

If the Posen model, with its focus on the nexus of crisis

300

and external pressure, works well in this final period, what can the human resources model add? The previous cases indicated that even when civilian pressure induced change, as in the early 1960s and in the 1980s, the human resources model is useful to explain how that external impetus was deflected within the Army from its original aims. In the early 1990s, there was less deflection, and the human resources approach does help explain why. Rosen argued that fundamental military change could in fact occur without crisis as a stimulus. However, Rosen implied in his examples that crises have the potential to weaken significantly the dominant group, creating latitude for alternative visions of warfare.[15] For example, the crisis created in the Navy by Pearl Harbor allowed carrier advocates to advance their cause. From this point of view, the organizational crisis in the Army, brought on by the demise of the Soviet Union, seriously weakened the Eurocentric traditionalists and enhanced the multi-role visionaries.

Consequently, traditionalists such as Vuono could, and did, argue for budget increases and a very cautious approach to the break-up of the Soviet Union. Or, when the rapid pace of change invalidated those views, the traditionalists could argue for a vision of warfare that was a very close second - armored warfare against vast Third World tank armies which would allow the Army to use the same doctrine and even the same deployment skills developed for the European scenario. This is the essence of incrementalism. These moves turned out to be no more than a holding action which enabled the traditionalists to delay reform for only a short period of time in the wake of the euphoria over Desert Storm. Vuono's replacement, General Sullivan, was one of the visionaries. He began working with other visionaries and Aspin to refashion the Army.

In summary, the evidence shows civilian pressure in three periods: 1961-1964, 1979-1989, and 1990-1993. In the first two periods, the Army changed peripherally. In the last period, the civilian pressure, coupled with a crisis in the Army's primary mission, may have instigated a process leading to fundamental organizational change. These results indicate substantial support for the traditional approach to organizational change.

On the other hand, the evidence also demonstrates that, once civilians initiate change in the Army, that change often proceeds differently than was originally intended. While organizational resistance is expected, Posen's structural approach does not account well for the application of civilian pressure which results in incomplete change. Posen indicated that civilian pressure could be applied directly or through the use of a maverick. In none of these cases do we find a maverick. Hence, the point of investigation has to shift to the relationship between civilian reformers and mainstream officers who lead the Army - the direct application of civilian pressure.

It is in the study of that relationship that we find the utility of Rosen's human resources approach. Rosen's focus on intergroup conflict within the military helps to explain the ways in which the dominant group resisted, delayed, or deflected the civilian reforms observed in this study. This approach also helps us to understand the zeal with which the European mission was pursued in the 1970s. Another important conclusion, although seemingly obvious, is that with either model, change takes time. Most studies of organizational change in military organizations have necessarily been done looking back on completed change. However, the study of the Army's response to low intensity conflict since 1961 suggests that it was change that was still in progress as late as 1993 when the bulk of this study was written, and indeed, is a process still underway. The current situation may be analogous to observing the transformation of the Navy or Marines in the 1930s as they were developing their new organizational visions – this is some of the richness that using a "process-tracing" methodology can illuminate. The results of this comparison indicate that a synthesis of the two models is necessary for an adequate representation of the cause and the process of the Army response to low intensity conflict.

SYNTHESIS

The evidence of these Army cases and logical extension of the theories investigated suggest that peacetime military change can proceed along five pathways. Two of the pathways depend on the willingness of civilians to intervene, and on their willingness to work through the non-dominant group, which we can continue to call "visionaries."[16] These two pathways compose one possible line of causality. The three remaining pathways lie along another line of causality derived from the human resources model.

The first civilian intervention pathway is a distinct variation on Posen's civilian-maverick axis: if civilians work through the visionaries, then fundamental military change is possible, particularly if a crisis weakens the dominant group.[17] This fundamental change will direct military efforts to new missions and shift the dominant view of future warfare. Along this pathway, military efforts should be integrated with civilian perceptions of strategic needs. This pathway explains the change process in the years 1979-1987, and 1992-1993.

Along the second civilian intervention pathway, if the civilians work through the dominant group, then peripheral change is likely - but this is defensive peripheral change aimed at protecting the enshrined vision of warfare. Consequently, military efforts may not meet the strategic needs of the country. This pathway can explain the Army changes in 1961-1964, 1987-1989, and 1990-1991.

The alternative line of causality contains three branches which follow more closely Rosen's model - neither civilians nor crises are necessary conditions for change. The only necessary condition is that at least two different groups internal to a military organization are in conflict over the security demands of the international system. This line subdivides into three possible pathways.

The first human resources pathway is simply the Rosen model. If the visionaries win the intraorganizational conflict, fundamental change takes place over the space of a generation as Rosen maintains. The visionaries enshrine a new vision of future warfare complete with derivative combat tasks and paths for promotion for adherents of the new vision. This pathway explained none of the cases in this study, but it remains a logical possibility given Rosen's findings.

The second human resources pathway represents some compromise solution between the two competing groups. The compromise results in a peripheral change, an accommodation that the dominant group allows its competitors. It is a change of the variety that may signal future fundamental change if the intergroup conflict is renewed. This could explain the manner in which the Army marginalized counterinsurgency efforts – through accommodation of some aspects of counterinsurgency missions as an adjunct to the main fighting - after the onset of the main force war in Vietnam, 1965-1972. This pathway might also prove useful to study other peripheral changes, such as the adoption and expansion of Army aviation.

The last human resources pathway occurs when the dominant group wins and the organizational status quo is maintained. The problem with this outcome is that the military organization that emerges may not be adequate to meet the coming security challenges of the international environment.[18] However, the group that loses does not necessarily give up the fight. This path explains Army actions in the period 1973-1979. [See Table 7]

What of the military mavericks that Posen emphasized? Rosen effectively demolished the case for military mavericks as agents of externally-driven change.[19] This study has found nothing to weaken Rosen's conclusion. Hence, a pathway containing a maverick was not included in the final possibilities.

TABLE 7

Periods		Independent		Observed Results
	Rosen	Posen	Proposed Synthesis	
1961-1964	Visionaries Active	Civilian Intervention	Civilian-Traditionalist Interface	Defensive Peripheral change
1965-1972	Traditionalists Dominate	Intervention Diminishes	Intergroup Compromise	Inconclusive Peripheral Change
1973-1979	Traditionalists Dominate	No Intervention	Traditionalists Dominate	Traditional Vision Strengthened
1979-1987	Visionaries Active	Civilian Intervention	Civilian-Visionaries Interface	Fundamental Change Possible
1987-1991	Visionaries Active	Civilian Intervention	Civilian-Traditionalists Interface	Defensive Peripheral Change
1992-1993	Visionaries Active	Civilian Intervention	Civilian-Visionaries Interface	Fundamental Change Possible

IMPLICATIONS

Future research might use this synthesis to explore the behavior of other U.S. services. For a direct comparison in the Kennedy counterinsurgency era, a good case might be the Air Force acceptance of the FB-111 in the 1960s. The new plane was championed by Secretary of Defense McNamara, but it did not fit the desires of the bomber generals who then dominated the Air Force. Nonetheless, they eventually accepted a few of the planes, but did so with the clear intention of marginalizing it and continuing their push for a new strategic bomber.[20] From more recently, as low intensity conflicts have come to predominate in the post-Cold War era, the results of this study could be used to analyze how the Air Force, Navy, and Marines adapted to this new security environment.

Another avenue for research could be an application of the synthesis to the services of other countries, particularly those which have faced similar low intensity challenges, such as Britain or France. One study has used a similar approach to explain the rise of the German Navy in the period 1888-1940, which suggests that such a synthesis is suitable for testing and refinement against foreign situations in general.[21]

Further research should also test the model against the evidence as the Army changed to face the new missions of the 1990s in Haiti, Bosnia, and Kosovo. Perhaps more relevant, though, would be an application to the Surge in Iraq, 2006-2008. On 11 September 2001, when the threat of asymmetrical warfare became a bloody reality, the Army and the rest of the U.S. armed services, but principally the Army, were asked to wage mid-intensity regime-change warfare in Iraq and Afghanistan, and then counterinsurgencies thereafter, while also undertaking raids and support to foreign internal defense (the old IDAD mission) in the Horn of Africa, Yemen, and the Philippines. How did the Army respond, given the findings above, after it had had eight more years of practice in much smaller "peace operations" in Haiti, Bosnia, and Kosovo? These peace operations led to political repercussions in the 2000 presidential campaign, with the winning candidate running against the notion of nation-building as a military vocation. Ironically, the Army had to undertake similar nation-building missions as a fundamental part of the war after 9-11, not as a preferred strategic option as was the case in the 1990s, but as an operational necessity.

The form of low intensity conflict that cuts through all

periods of this study, and provides the main fear of "another Vietnam" – counterinsurgency - is now the main type of operation that has occupied the military in the decade since 9-11 in both Iraq and Afghanistan. Arguably, the counterinsurgency phases in Iraq and Afghanistan are not truly low intensity conflicts since both campaigns had direct congressional authorizations to overthrow sitting governments in sovereign countries. Iraq and Afghanistan, though, are the reverse of the sequence in Vietnam, which began as a counterinsurgency effort in support of the Government of South Vietnam, and progressed to a war between the main forces of sovereign states after the Gulf of Tonkin Resolution. In Iraq and Afghanistan, the counterinsurgency phase only began after the overthrow of the Baathist and Taliban regimes. Thus, consistent with the definitions established at the beginning of the book, the subsequent counterinsurgency campaigns have been waged against non-state actors in support of the sovereign governments of both states.

The 9-11 attacks significantly changed the security environment of the United States, and the civilian leaders demanded a military response. Since the attacks had been mounted by a non-state terrorist group, albeit sheltered in and supported by a sovereign state, perhaps inevitably this response would become of the low intensity variety. Although the primary sources are not yet available to conduct a thorough analysis – a process tracing – of cause and effect, we can speculatively apply the model from Table 7 particularly to the Surge in Iraq.

The leaders of the Army at the time of the Surge in Iraq seemed more comfortable with the main force armored war that toppled the Saddamist regime in only a few weeks in 2003. In the aftermath of the stunning victory, those leaders, both in Washington and in the field, were forced by tactical circumstances to use units such as armor and artillery in essentially light infantry roles to combat Sunni and Shia insurgents and Al Qaeda terrorists. These converted units were equipped with vehicles – the High Mobility Multipurpose Wheeled Vehicles (HMMWVs) – never designed as a primary battle platform. The early goal after the main force battle concluded was to establish as rapidly as possible a new Iraqi army and police force, turn the security mission over to them, and exit the country. The civilian leadership in Washington was split between "transition as an exit strategy," consistent with the opposition by some in the Bush administration to nation-building expressed during the 2000 campaign, and other politico-military strategies that would require leaving behind a stabilized Iraqi government at least minimally capable of basic governance in conjunction with an improving Iraqi security environment.

The early years of the Iraqi counterinsurgency resemble the "civilian-traditionalist" pathway described above that resulted in defensive peripheral change. As such, the Army grudgingly adapted to the counterinsurgency mission without embracing it as a necessity in the hopes that a quick exit could allow it to return to preferred missions. Change occurred when the President himself decided to undertake a different strategic approach with the goal of stabilizing and improving the Iraqi political and security situations. President Bush replaced his Secretary of Defense and chose a new commander for Iraq – General Petraeus – who had just led the first revision in twenty years of the Army's counterinsurgency doctrine. That strategic decision required new operational and tactical approaches to protecting the Iraqi population centers while training and operating alongside the new Iraqi Security Forces – re-learning in fact the hard lessons of successful counterinsurgencies in the past. To ensure that adherents to the new approach and doctrine were advanced, the new civilian leadership in the Pentagon appointed General Petraeus to head the board selecting new brigadier generals during his first year in command in Iraq. This pathway to change resembles the "civilian-visionary" pathway in Table 7 that could lead to fundamental organizational change in the Army.

As this book goes to print, the Surge in Iraq proved to be a success despite the many military, academic, journalistic, and political critics that pre-judged it to be a failure, and such a colossal failure that it would likely worsen the situation in Iraq. Contrary to these expectations the Iraqi Surge was so successful that the new Obama administration – filled with former critics of the Surge – decided to implement essentially the same approach in Afghanistan, and placed General Petraeus in charge of executing the first critical year of the Afghan Surge.

As stated previously, the primary sources are not available to determine whether the process described above is entirely accurate. The synthesis model derived from the cases studied in this book should be tested against the full range of experiences in the later 1990s and against the even more wrenching changes of the 2000s. Preliminary analysis suggests that the model does indeed have explanatory power at least for the most recent controversial events surrounding the Surges.

Samuel P. Huntington once described the Army's unique background:

> "The Army participated in a diversity of tasks - Southern reconstruction, Indian fighting, labor disorders, the Spanish War, Cuban occupation, Philippine pacification, construction and operation of the [Panama] Canal, the Mexican punitive expedition. Accordingly, the Army developed an image of itself as the

> government's obedient handyman
> performing without question or hesitation
> the jobs assigned to it..."[22]

The Army left this well-worn path when it was given the long-term mission of defending Central Europe during the Cold War. In the early 1990s, with the new world order looking ever more like the old, uncertain, fractious pre-Cold War world order, the Army once again got ample opportunity to practice the handicrafts of the distant past even as it tried to remain ready for modern war of higher intensities. In the first decade of the new millennium, the Army faced both mid-intensity and low-intensity warfare, putting a premium on what General Sullivan in 1993 presciently called the ability "to rescue societies caught in the pre-industrial revolution, while still able to fight 21st century wars."[23] The "government's obedient handyman" is still on duty. Understanding how the Army changes to meet the shifting security environment is as important as ever.

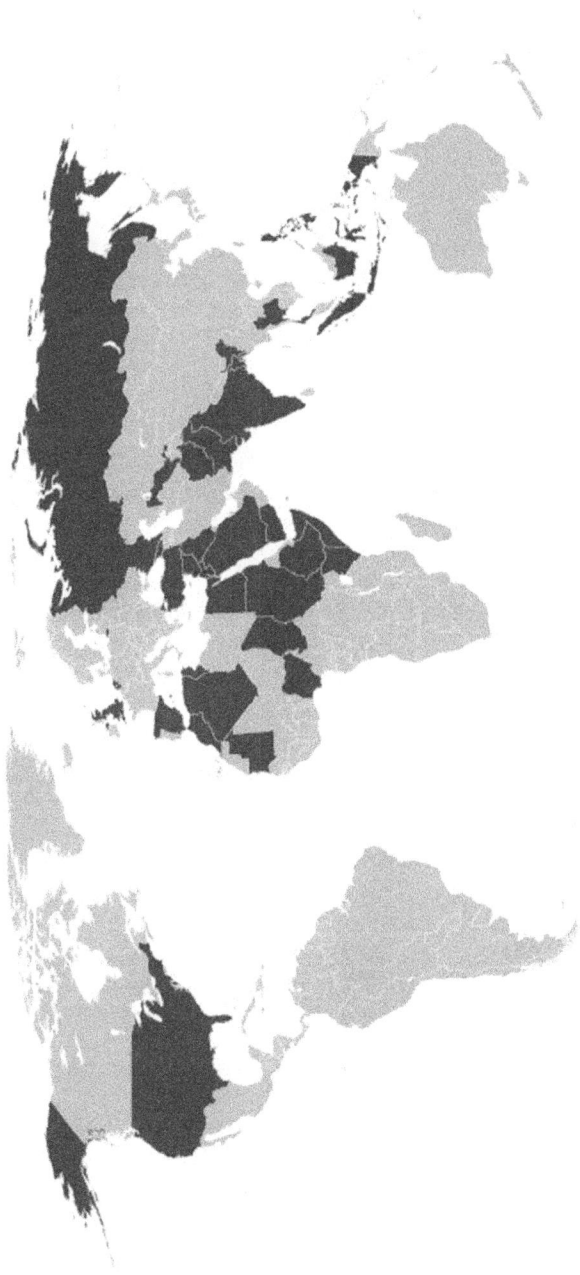

COUNTRIES ATTACKED BY ISLAMIC TERRORISTS ON OR AFTER SEPTEMBER 11, 2001

Chapter 7 Endnotes

[1] Rear Admiral Phillip R. Olson, "Low Intensity Conflict: Myths and Trends," *Key LIC Speeches, 1984-1989*, ed. William F. Furr and Ronald L. Zelms (Langley Air Force Base, VA: Center for Low Intensity Conflict, 1989) 85.

[2] Stephen Peter Rosen, *Winning the Next War: Innovation and the Modern Military* (Ithaca, NY: Cornell, 1991) 4.

[3] Indeed, the major revisions in Army doctrine and organization to confront the Army's primary mission in Europe have been treated already at length in other scholarly studies. For historical treatments of these revisions, see Paul H. Herbert, *Deciding What Has to Be Done: General William E. DePuy and the 1976 Edition of FM 100-5, Operations* (Ft. Leavenworth, KS: U.S. Army Command and General Staff College, 1988); John L. Romjue, *From the Active Defense to Air Land Battle: The Development of Army Doctrine from 1973-1982* (Fort Monroe, VA: U.S. Army Training and Doctrine Command, June 1984). For analytical explanations of these changes see Jeffrey M. Long, "The Evolution of U.S. Army Doctrine: From Active Defense to AirLand Battle and Beyond," Master of Military Art and Science thesis, U.S. Army Command and General Staff College, Ft. Leavenworth, KS, 1991; Kevin Patrick Sheehan, "Preparing for an Imaginary War? Examining Peacetime Functions and Changes of Army Doctrine", Ph.D. dissertation, Harvard, 1986.

[4] "Government agencies change all the time, but the most common changes are add-ons: a new program is added on to existing tasks without changing the core tasks or altering the organizational culture." James Q. Wilson, *Bureaucracy* (New York: Basic Books, 1989) 225.

[5] See the discussion in chapter 1 above. I borrowed the classification of organizational theories from Jay M. Shafritz and J. Steven Ott, ed., *Classics of Organizational Theory*, 3d ed. (Pacific Grove, CA: Brooks/Cole, 1992).

[6] Andrew Krepinevich, *The Army and Vietnam* (Baltimore: Johns Hopkins, 1986) 29; Carl H. Builder, *The Masks of War: American Military Styles in Strategy and Analysis* (Baltimore: Johns Hopkins, 1989) 38. See also chapter 6 "Culture" in Wilson. See also Morton H. Halperin and Arnold Kanter, "The Bureaucratic Perspective," in *International Policies: Anarchy, Force, Political Economy, and Decision Making*, 2d ed., Robert J. Art and Robert Jervis, ed. (Boston: Scott, Foresman, 1985) 444.

[7] For a fuller treatment of the European focus, see Builder, chapter 12, "The Service Concepts."

[8] Wilson 221.

[9] Barry Posen, *The Sources of Military Doctrine* (Ithaca: Cornell, 1984) Chapter 2. For an example of the role of mavericks, see Posen 173-175.

[10] See Rosen 21.

[11] Graham T. Allison, "Conceptual Models and the Cuban Missile Crisis," *Understanding International Relations: The Value of Alternative Lenses*, ed. Asa A Clark IV, Thomas F. Lynch III, and Rick Waddell (New York: McGraw-Hill, 1993) 403.

[12] The Special Forces soldiers originally worked for the Central Intelligence Agency. Later, the Army formed a provisional command. It was only after the counterinsurgency era ended, and the main force war was beginning in 1965, that the Army sent the headquarters of the 5th Special Forces Group to Vietnam.

[13] In a very lucid explanation of what organizational theorists mean, Builder goes so far as to say that military organizations have a personality that is as well developed and noticeable as any individual's personality. See Builder 7. The human resources school would only differ to the extent that it would argue that the organization's personality is the personality of the dominant group.

[14] Builder 181.

[15] I infer this from Rosen's discussion of the development of carrier aviation in the Navy and amphibious doctrine in the Marine Corps. Before the advent of World War II engendered a crisis for the dominant groups in these services, the carriers were second in importance to battleships. Before the conquests of the Japanese forces in the Pacific, the Marine Corps, despite having developed a doctrine and desired force structure for amphibious warfare, was still too small and still too committed to its pre-war constabulary missions.

[16] My concept of visionaries is similar to Rosabeth Moss Kanter's "change masters" who "have an intellectual, a conceptual, and a cultural aspect. Change masters deal in symbols and visions and shared understandings as well as the techniques and trappings of their own specialties." Rosabeth Moss Kanter, "The Architecture of Culture and Strategy Change," *Classic Readings in Organizational Behavior*, ed. J. Steven Ott (Pacific Grove, CA: Brooks/Cole, 1989) 535. See also chapter 1 above.

[17] Rosen does mention a similar pathway. Civilians could contribute to military innovation, but only by supporting the actions of visionaries, which makes the civilian reformers purely auxiliaries to the process. See Rosen 22. I am suggesting that the civilians are primary factors in this path, but that they will not be successful unless they find visionaries willing to help them.

[18] Posen terms this failure of military capabilities to meet security needs "disintegration." See Posen 51-53.

[19] See Rosen 10-21.

[20] See Builder's discussion of the Air Force's motives, 15-16.

[21] See Carl-Axel Gemzell, *Organization, Conflict, and Innovation: A Study of German Naval Strategic Planning, 1888-1940* (Stockholm: Esselte Studium, 1973) Gemzell contrasts the explanatory power of "structural functional" views of organizations with social "conflict" theories. While similar in the contrasting of the two views of organizations, the study went further to assess the impact of conflicts internal to the German Navy on the German government and on international relations. See Gemzell 415-417.

[22] Samuel P. Huntington, *The Soldier and The State: The Theory and Politics of Civil-Military Relations* (Cambridge, MA: Harvard, 1957) 261.

[23] General Gordon R. Sullivan, Chief of Staff, United States Army, *Statement before the Committee on Armed Services, United States House of Representatives, 1st Session, 103d Congress, on the Fiscal Year 1994 Budget Proposals and the Posture of the United States Army*, 31 March 1993 (Washington, D.C.: USGPO, 1993) 6.

www.ingramcontent.com/pod-product-compliance
Lightning Source LLC
Chambersburg PA
CBHW031125090426
42738CB00008B/977